Martina

**MARTINA NAVRATILOVA
with George Vecsey**

FAWCETT CREST · NEW YORK

A Fawcett Crest Book
Published by Ballantine Books
Copyright © 1985 by Martina Enterprises, Inc.

Library of Congress Catalog Card Number: 84-48894

ISBN 0-449-20982-2

This edition published by arrangement with Alfred A. Knopf, Inc.

Manufactured in the United States of America

First Ballantine Books Edition: July 1986
Seventh Printing: May 1992

Cover Photograph by Carol L. Newsom

*To my mother, father, sister, and grandma,
all of whom suffered more than they will ever let me
know, and whom I love more than they will ever know...*

Acknowledgments

Thanks to Peter Johnson and I.M.G.; all the companies that have stuck with me through thick and thin, namely, Yonex, Puma, Porsche, Computerland, and Vuarnet; George Vecsey, who is not only a wonderful writer and a great human being but now, due to this collaboration, a real friend. And mainly thanks to all my old and new friends on the tour and off the tour who shall remain nameless because they know who they are. And lest I should forget my babies—K.D., Tets, Ruby, Yoni, and Puma—who don't even bother asking if I won or lost and kiss my face anyway.

Martina Navratilova

Many people helped in many ways to put this book together. In no particular order, and with gratefulness to all, I would like to thank:

The Navratil family, Mirek, Jana and Jana, for the home-cooked meals and the warm welcome in Revnice. Zdenek Navratil, for the guided tour of Karlstejn and the English version of Svejk. Martin Navratil, for insisting I read Skvorecky.

Aja Zanova and George and Jarmila Parma, for showing

me the friendship they have felt for Martina. Sandra Haynie, for finding the time on a busy day. Dr. Renee Richards and Melissa Hope Vinson, for enlivening many a day at the tournaments.

Lee Jackson, Peggy Gossett, Marcia Robbins, and Chris Evert Lloyd for helping me know more about Martina on the tour over the years, and Mary Carillo, for doing such a good job with Martina in "Tennis My Way." Mike Estep and Barbara Hunter, a good doubles team at any party. Judy Nelson, for her suggestions about the book.

Dr. Gary Wadler and Nancy Wadler, co-authors of *How to Cope,* for his medical expertise and her literary instincts. Nancy Lieberman, from one Queens kid to another, for the friendship that endures. Renee Lieberman, for caring. Pam Derderian, for the long chats at poolside and courtside.

The music of Smetana and Dvořak and the writing of Skvorecky, Kundera, and Hasek, for putting me in the mood. Jan Kodes, for many favors in recalling the old days at Sparta. George and Stella Repper, for helping me feel just a little bit Czech. Jan Krejci, for being an expert taxi driver and instant friend.

Journalist friends like Neil Amdur, Jane Leavy, Susan Adams, Frank Deford, Ira Berkow, Peter Bodo, Jane Gross, Steve Jacobson, and Roy Johnson, for writing and talking about Martina with great insight. Walter Schwartz, for handling my business matters so well. Ed and Karen Mase, my relatives in Big D, for the room and the car and the good company. Tina Oliver Christian, for always getting the messages right.

Peter Johnson, Bev Norwood, and Laura Nixon of the International Management Group of Cleveland and New York, for originating the project and always being there to help me carry it through.

Vicky Wilson, our editor at Knopf, for wanting the book

so much, and Cindy Miller and Kathy Hourigan, for their logistical and personal support.

My family, for keeping life stable around me, and particularly my father, George Stephen Vecsey, 1909–1984, who would have liked this book.

George Vecsey

Prologue

My father took me to a shoe store when I was twelve.

I was used to people mistaking me for a boy.

I was the last girl in my class to get her period, and as for a figure, forget it.

"Scout," an old lady once called me.

"Scout, could you help me across the street?"

This time I saw myself in a full-length mirror and started crying.

Big calves. Big ears. Big feet.

"I'm always going to look like a boy," I cried.

My father had to hustle me out of the store.

"Don't worry," he told me. "You're a late bloomer. I can tell you're going to be pretty when you grow up."

My father also told me about tennis.

Told me to play aggressively.

Like a boy.

I already did.

Rush the net.

Put it past them.

Take a chance. Invent shots.

He told me I would win Wimbledon some day.

I believed that part.

Apple Trees

I was three years old when my mother and father divorced. We left the ski lodge in the Krkonose Mountains and moved into a single room in my mother's childhood home, the room overlooking the tennis court.

That court was the last vestige of my mother's family estate, where she had lived when she was young, with a nanny to take care of her. They once had thirty acres, stretching from lush fruit arbors on the hillside to rich farmland along the Berounka River. After the Communists took over Czechoslovakia in 1948, my mother's family lost almost everything except the red-clay tennis court and the cement family home, which they now shared with other people.

From our bedroom window, I could see the tennis court falling into disrepair, later used mainly for our soccer games. And from that same window, I could see a grove of fruit trees that had once belonged to my family.

I have never told this to anybody before, but I used to sneak across the street and take apples from the grove. I would eat as many as I wanted and share the rest with my friends. I felt the apples were part of my heritage. Almost all Czechs and Slovaks felt we had suffered a loss from the takeover in 1948, and my mother's family had lost more than most. The least I could do was recover some of the family apples.

Sometimes when I was little, I'd see my mother looking off into space with a sad look on her face and I would guess she was daydreaming about the time when she was little, before the war. I think my mother and my grandmother carried a sense of *litost,* a Czech word for sadness, that I picked up, a feeling of loss at the core of their souls.

All the time I was growing up, I had a sense of things not being quite right, like staring out my window at a grove of trees that used to belong to my family, knowing they had been given to somebody else. That violated my sense of justice. Somehow I had the sense of things being out of focus, out of place, the sense that I should be somewhere else.

My second father—I never called him my stepfather—always reassured me that my time was coming, but sometimes I felt I was a misfit, particularly after I started playing tennis.

By the time I was ten, I was so committed to tennis, played it every day, that I had a totally different identity from everybody around me. But even before tennis, I played soccer and ice hockey with the boys. I was as good as them, I figured, so why not?

I didn't feel I belonged anywhere, until I came to America for the first time when I was sixteen. I'm not a mystic about many things—I tend to be pretty pragmatic about life —but I honestly believe I was born to be American. With all due respect to my homeland, things never really felt right until the day I got off the plane in Florida to play in my first tournament in 1973. For the first time in my life, I was able to see America without the filter of a Communist education, Communist propaganda. And it felt right.

I am not referring to my well-known past love affair with the fast-food emporiums of the New World, when I gained twenty pounds during my first month in the States. The way it's been written, I came here with a mission to eat as many Big Macs as I could find, like the Flip Wilson joke about Christopher Columbus going to America to find Ray Charles. Martina was not going to America to discover Ronald McDonald.

This country was waiting for me. It would give me the friends and the space and the freedom and the courts and the sneakers and the weight machines and the right food to let me become a tennis champion, to play the best tennis any woman ever played, which I think I have done in the past few years.

Excuse me if that sounds like bragging, but being blunt with your feelings is very American. In this big country, I can be as brash as New York, as hedonistic as Los Angeles, as sensuous as San Francisco, as brainy as Boston, as proper as Philadelphia, as brawny as Chicago, as warm as Palm Springs, as friendly as my adopted home town of Dallas–Fort Worth, and as peaceful as the inland waterway that rubs up against my former home in Virginia Beach.

A lot of people think I'm a champion and a tough competitor, while others still think of me as a "choker" because of a few big matches I lost, for various reasons, years ago. Some people think I'm a good sport, some call me a complainer. Some people think I'm hard as nails, yet others who know me will swear I sniffle through dopey television commercials with cute little animals in them: the family secret is that I'm a softy.

I speak with a slight accent. I come from behind the Iron Curtain. There are Americans who hate communism but somehow think I should have stayed in my homeland under a system they personally don't like. I came to live in a country I love; some people label me a defector. I have loved men and women in my life; I've been labeled "the bisexual defector" in print. Want to know another secret?

3

I'm even ambidextrous. I don't like labels. Just call me Martina.

The nice thing is, I can be all these things, can be myself, in America. It's a free country. It said so right in the brochure I studied for my citizenship exam. When I came here, it was like going home again, to a world somebody had taken from me. I had the family freedom back.

After I came to America, I was able to help my parents purchase a new home in our village of Revnice. They tell me they have over forty apple trees on their property, and that in the fall they make gallons of fresh, sweet cider. I may never be able to taste that cider because I have not been allowed to visit my homeland. But this much I know: my family has apple trees again.

My Real Father

I am not the first tennis player in my family. My mother's mother, Agnes Semanska, once beat the mother of Vera Sukova in the Czech national tournament, and this became part of our family legend, particularly after Vera became a Wimbledon finalist in 1962, the best a Czech woman had ever done up to that point. We were glad to have this bit of reflected glory for my grandmother, who had lost her family home and been told to work in a factory when she was forty or else she would not be eligible for a pension in her old age. She worked until she was seventy.

My mother, Jana, never became as good a tennis player as my grandmother. She did not like the pressure her father put on her to play tennis. She is a big, strong, supple woman. You take one look at her in a tennis outfit or a bathing suit and you can see where I got my athletic ability. It's in the genes.

My mother did not like being browbeaten by her father, Jan Semansky, a nasty little old man, as I recall him. They say he mellowed in the last few years of his life, after I left, but it would be hard to prove it by me. I just remember nearly having a fistfight with him when I was around ten. Although I didn't know it at the time, he and my grandmother had been divorced years earlier, but they ended up living together anyway—maybe because living space was so hard to come by in Czechoslovakia. I found out more about him later, how his parents had died, and his uncle had raised him, apparently pushing him around pretty well. It's showing up now that most cases of child abuse involve people who were abused as kids.

My grandfather had wanted to make my mother into this great tennis player. He would torture her, not let her drink any water if she played badly, or else he'd sprinkle cold water on her in the morning to wake her up. He was so nasty that she finally just quit. Wouldn't play.

Her brother, Josef, the only other lefty in the family, played more but he wasn't as smart as my mother, and you really have to be smart to be a good tennis player. You think about it: Chris Evert, Jimmy Connors, John McEnroe— they all have native intelligence. Yes, and Björn Borg, too. He's led a pretty sheltered life, but he's smarter than the average person. He'd have gotten more education if he hadn't played tennis—and so would I.

My grandfather ruined any chance of my mother being

5

a good tennis player. He pushed her and slapped her, hit her head against the wall, which I'm sure is the reason she has migraines now. Even though her life has been really good since she met my second father, she's still nervous today; she gets all upset when she watches me practice. I think getting pushed around by my grandfather had just as much to do with my mother's and grandmother's sadness as losing the family land.

My mother's sport was skiing—I guess because of the freedom it offered. The old man couldn't follow her down the slopes and smack her around if she didn't turn her skis the right way. Czechoslovakia has several mountain ranges with snow half the year, and skiing is something you can do easily near your house, not a big expensive deal like in the States. My mother skied in the Krkonose Mountains on the northern border as a young woman, and she was working as a ski instructor at a lodge when she met my father—my real father—Miroslav (Kamil) Subert, pronounced *Shubert*.

His real job was managing restaurants in Prague, but after he and my mother were married, they lived near the village of Spindleruv Mlyn, in a ski lodge named Martinovka, which means "Martin's Place," or something to that effect. For two and a half years they lived 1,200 meters high in the Krkonose Mountains, with no ski lifts or transportation. They had to walk up higher to the other lodge, where my father worked and was head of the ski patrol.

Late in the summer of 1956, my mother returned to Prague, where she gave birth to me on October 18, during the same autumn when Russian tanks rolled into Hungary, and only twelve years before they would roll into my country, too —an event that marked, and you might even say scarred, my life, as well as the lives of all other Czechs and Slovaks.

They named me Martina, the feminine form of the mountain lodge where I was conceived. Although I have a cousin named Martin, it was not a common name for a man in

Czechoslovakia, and Martina was pretty exotic, too. Now, I am told, Martina is a much more popular name than it used to be.

In the Czech language, every girl takes the feminine ending "ova" after her father's family name, and later she takes the same ending after her husband's. So for the first ten years of my life I was Martina Subertova.

Five weeks after I was born, my mother moved back to Martinovka with me. The ski season was coming and she was needed to give lessons. Two years later she was giving lessons to me. Can you really recall something that happened when you were two years old? I feel I can remember whizzing down a hill for the first time, the hard-packed snow under my skis, the sun in my eyes, a big smile on my face. Or maybe I've looked at the pictures of me so many times that I only think I remember. I was a happy little kid, just out of diapers, really, zipping down the big slopes of the Krkonose Mountains. Although I guess they really weren't very big slopes, not at two.

Shortly after I learned how to ski, my parents split up and my mother returned to her home, just outside Prague. Because I was born in the city, and often talk about the train ride into Prague to take tennis lessons, I make it sound as if I grew up there, but the fact is I am a country girl. After we moved back from the Krkonose Mountains, the next part of my childhood was spent gathering mushrooms and blueberries on Brdy Mountain above my village of Revnice.

The Czech language is not the easiest to learn, but to know me you've almost got to know a bit of it. My home town of Revnice has a little upside-down circumflex over the R, turning it into a *zh* sound. So I'm not really from Prague. I'm from *Zhev-NEE-tzeh*.

My father lived in Prague then, and every couple of months he would come out and see me. He was not exactly into creative child custody.

I don't remember my real father too well, but people say that my wild mood swings, the gush of tears after a loss, the giddy exuberance when I was on a roll during the early years of my tennis career, were like my father. It's impossible for me to say. I have very few memories of him, and my mother doesn't have any pictures. She doesn't like to talk about him. After I left Czechoslovakia, I once wrote to my father's sister for more information about my real father, but I didn't get much.

I do remember spending a week with him at a ski lodge when I was around four. I remember him carrying me in a poncho wrapped around both of us. Sitting by the fire at night, he would tell me stories about the giant, Krakanosh, who lived up there. I don't know how it is now, but when I was a kid, all the little kids in Czechoslovakia knew about Krakanosh, who was twenty feet tall, had a beard, and wore a green hat. He was even on television in children's stories when I was little. My father told me that Krakanosh would get me if I wasn't good, and I believed him. It wasn't hard to believe stories like that up in those mountains, where every sensation is magnified: the light is bright, the night is pitch black, and giants seem very plausible.

I also remember there were about ten collies at the ski lodge where my father stayed, and I think that's where I got my love for animals. I've got three dogs at the moment and take them almost everywhere I go.

That week with my father was the longest time I ever spent with him. After my mother remarried, my father would come around a couple of times a year and take me to the Prague zoo or something like that. I seem to recall that he wasn't very healthy, or maybe people just told me that to cover up the dark secret about my father.

When I was eight, my father stopped coming altogether. I didn't really think much about it because I had a new father living in the house with me, taking me places, teaching me tennis, giving me all the love and discipline that a father should give.

I learned of my real father's death in a roundabout way. In Czechoslovakia, when someone dies we have a custom of sending a funeral announcement, called a *parte*, with a black border around it. When I was around ten or eleven years old, we got a *parte* in the mail announcing my Grandfather Subert's death. I wasn't that close to my grandfather, so I started asking my mother some questions about him and also about my father.

"Oh, your father died a few years ago," my mother told me. "He had a stomach operation and he died."

I don't recall crying at the news of my real father's death. It explained why he hadn't come to see me lately, but I did think it was strange that my mother hadn't told me.

I didn't learn the real story until I was twenty-three and my parents moved to the States for a few months. It was the shock of learning of my relationship with Rita Mae Brown that caused them to tell me how my real father died. They decided I had a major character flaw and predicted a bad end for me.

We were in my new house in Charlottesville, Virginia, having a good old-fashioned family conversation, just like lots of other families.

"You're sick," my father told me.

"You're so emotional, you're going to end up just like your father," my mother said.

"What's that supposed to mean?" I asked.

They looked at each other for a moment, and then the words came tumbling out. They said my real father had been a very mercurial person who would open up to people, become their best friend after five minutes, trust them and do things for them, and if anything went wrong, he would be hurt. He suffered from excessive highs and lows, just like me, they said, and that's why he'd committed suicide.

It was the first I had heard about this. My real father had always been a shadowy figure to me, a man who disappeared into the mists like some of our legendary snow apparitions in the Krkonose Mountains. Now, in the middle of a raging argument, at the age of twenty-three, I found out he had remarried, divorced, had a stomach operation, and, when the woman he was in love with came to the hospital to tell him she was leaving him for another man, he committed suicide in the hospital. Now they were convinced I would do the same.

"Well, it's not in my plans," I told them.

I guess I've inherited some of my real father's vulnerability in trusting people. I'm getting tougher but I don't want to get cynical, either. I've been hurt but I've also kept most of my friends—and I certainly don't intend to commit suicide over the few low points in my life.

I intend to die at a very old age. And by that time I expect to have a college degree, a lot more championships, maybe a child, and a few careers after tennis. It's like my father told me: I'm a late bloomer.

My Mother and Father

Shortly after my mother and I moved back to her family's house in Revnice, she joined the municipal tennis club up on the hill. The courts were made of crushed red clay, like most courts in Europe, and people in the town spent their free time playing the slow, friendly, almost ceremonial European game: plunk-plunk-plunk.

In the springtime, after the snow had thawed on the mountain, everybody had to work on the maintenance of the courts. This was a way for new members to work off the initiation fees, since very few people had extra cash. Money was always scarce in our economy, where people had to work two hours to afford a pack of American cigarets and three hours for a whole chicken.

I was a regular court rat, following my mother around, chasing balls, making a pest of myself. One spring day when I was about three and a half years old, I was tagging along behind some men carrying fresh clay to the courts. One man, a very hard worker, would make little jokes with me, and after he had dumped the clay and was pushing the empty wheelbarrow, I plopped myself down in it and said: "Give me a ride"—just like that. I was a fresh little kid.

He didn't seem to mind. He came from a few towns away and was known as a pretty gregarious bachelor. His first name was the same as my real father's, Miroslav, and people called him Mirek. His last name was Navratil, which is a fairly common name in Czechoslovakia.

The next time he came to the courts, he brought me a piece of Kofila, a Czech chocolate that you can't get in the States. I started looking forward to him bringing me the Kofila every weekend and the one time he forgot it, I was so upset that he felt worse than I did.

It never crossed my mind to get Mirek Navratil together with my mother, but one day I ran over to the courts and saw them talking together on a bench. They had discovered each other without any help from me, but when he realized I was her daughter, he was pleased.

Before long he started coming to visit my mother. He was very handy around the house. I remember a window in our

II

bedroom door had been broken and my mother didn't have enough money to have a new pane of glass put in, so she stretched a potato sack over the hole. Mirek came by one Saturday and put in a new pane of glass. Other times he'd bring food, and after a while he was helping with the household bills.

Mirek Navratil brought a feeling of joy into my mother's life, did away with some of the sadness that I sensed from her earlier life. At this point my mother was still married to my real father. In fact, my real father and Mirek Navratil had known each other before any of this happened. Now that Mirek was courting my mother, the two Miroslavs would run into each other, an awkward situation, so my mother finally got a divorce.

She and Mirek were married on July 1, 1961, in the city hall at Marienbad, the spa near the German border. I was happy for both of them—and for me, too, because he was already my friend. When they came back from their honeymoon, he moved in and I called him Mirek, the same as always, but after a while I started calling him Tato or Tatinku, two variations of Daddy. My mother I always called Mami.

One nice thing about the marriage was that now instead of two sets of families, I had three. My new father's older brother, Zdenek, a lawyer and teacher from Prague, likes to recall how I sang the same song over and over again on my first visit to the Navratil family. Life was bustling; I even had a new cousin named Martin, a few years older than me.

After my father and mother were married, the three of us lived in an upstairs room in my grandparents' house, with my grandparents on the same floor. On June 20, 1963, my sister, Jana, was born and the four of us lived there together for a year or two longer. I can still see the room, in the southeast corner, facing the sun, with plenty of light in the morning. We stayed in that room till I was about nine.

My mother was forever getting up in the middle of the night because the baby was crying, but after Jana got over that, she was a sunny, bright little sister, young enough for me to fuss over, with no jealousies either way. Later, when the people downstairs moved away, my grandparents moved down and my parents had a room, and I shared the room with Jana. We even had a piano and some green Formica furniture my father had made. My mom had the kitchen to herself, which is where I spent most of my time.

I think my father was happy to have an instant daughter who could keep up with him. He'd take me up to Brdy Mountain above the town to go mushroom-picking, or berry-picking, or cross-country skiing in the winter. He had a motorcycle, and when it snowed he would pull me on skis all around the town. When the heavy snows came, our family would go to the Krkonose Mountains to ski. In the summer we'd swim in the lakes and rivers around us, and just before Christmas we would go up on Brdy Mountain and cut down a fir tree for the house. My sister, Jana, said "it is not allowed" for us to ever buy a Christmas tree. The ritual was that my father must cut it down.

My father liked being busy. One year he was out of work after a foot operation, but he still managed to work on the red-clay tennis court that was one of the last things remaining from my mother's estate. He got it into great shape, and we all played a lot of tennis there that summer. I remember Jana falling from the top of the umpire's chair when she was around three, just tumbling down and landing on her back, getting a slight concussion.

When we went mushroom-hunting, we would eat some of them fresh and the others we would dry and cure in the attic. What a great smell! I loved to stand at the door to the attic and breathe in the aroma of drying mushrooms, but I was petrified to go in there because we had only one tiny light bulb in there.

I was convinced there were monsters in the attic. I wasn't afraid of a thing in broad daylight—not even the Noon Witch, who was supposed to come out at midday and punish all the bad little kids. I could handle the Noon Witch, but whatever was up in that attic I wanted no part of. If I needed something, I'd just reach in one step, I was so scared. I always imagined how I would fight the monsters.

My parents kept their zest for living, for cooking and gardening and taking care of themselves, even as the Czech economy continued to crumble because of the "assistance" of our friends from Moscow. We often had shortages of one kind or another. My father worked as an economist in a factory, and my mother also went to work. Both of them refused to join the Communist party, which was the only way to really get ahead, so it was hard to be comfortable, even with two salaries. We never had a car when I was growing up. Until I was about twelve, we didn't even have hot running water and had to heat water on the coals to take a bath. Still, we had a good life compared to the way most people lived. We had our own house, my father had a good job, he didn't have to do any physical work, we took our vacation every year, we went skiing.

My mother went back to work as soon as we returned from Martinovka, but she never stopped caring for me, and later for Jana, in every detail. I look back to my early years and I think of her as very sweet, very giving, very maternal. The care she gave to me is exactly the kind I want to give to a child if I decide to have one in a few years—which I think I will.

I remember her singing to me, taking me around on this

little two-wheel cart with handlebars, like they have in the circus, when I was around three or four. And I always remember her in the kitchen, where Czech people—like most other people, I guess—spend much of their time. I can remember suppertime, with the sun going down outside, the warmth in the kitchen, with a fire in the stove, and everybody bustling around, crowded, happy.

I still get flashes of that now, when my mother and my sister visit me in the States. I love to see my mom bustling around and cooking a special training meal for me and another meal for herself and Jana and anybody else who happens to drop by.

"Do you want some soup?" she'll ask.

The only thing my parents argued about was the budget. My father would get paid once a month and give my mother the money, but every so often she'd run short and ask for more. Somehow he would always produce more money, although I don't know how or where he got it.

One time she lost her wallet with about 300 crowns in it. That was a lot of money in those days, maybe $40 or $50 on the official scale. She was so upset that my father went out and bought her a present.

My father was the disciplinarian in the household. If I did something wrong, he'd say, "Okay, you can't do this or that." One time I couldn't use my bike because of something I had done, so I was kicking the soccer ball against the garage and I broke a window. I was just petrified. But when I went to tell him, he said: "Because you busted your window, you can ride the bike."

If I deserved it, though, he would really punish me. My mother would go along with whatever he said, but sometimes when he wasn't around she would say: "All right, but don't tell your father." If only my mother was home, I knew it would be all right if I came home late. She would just say:

"You're supposed to be home . . ." But if my father was there, I might get a tap on the behind.

I always heard these horror stories of kids in my class whose fathers would smack them around, but mine never did that. Sometimes he used a wooden ruler if I was really bad, put me over his knee and spanked me, but he was always fair.

One time I was supposed to be home from kindergarten at five o'clock, but I decided to go home with another girl whose mother later was my Russian teacher in school. Of course we didn't have telephones the way everybody does now in Czechoslovakia or the States, so I couldn't call my parents. I stayed at my friend's until six or seven o'clock and by that time it was dark and my parents were really worried something had happened to me. They never thought of looking for me there because it was about a mile walk right through town. When I finally got home, my father spanked me hard.

Another time—I still don't know what got into me—I called the woman who lived downstairs a cow. In Czech, that's very bad—much worse than in English. I still don't know what possessed me. Those were my two good spankings. Sometimes my mother would get mad at me and try to smack me, but her hand would hurt more than my butt.

She was delighted to have a man around to take care of being a father. And he was very much a family man. He'd do anything for me and my sister. He never regarded me as extraneous, never once gave me the feeling that he just put up with me because I was my mother's kid. He and I were very close. I mean, I knew him before she did.

They were really lucky to find each other. They both love sports and are pretty much on the same level intellectually. They both like classical music and the theater, although my mother reads a lot more than my father does. Even before

I began playing tennis and casting my eyes to the West, she would be reading an Agatha Christie mystery in English, just to learn another language, or she'd be reading a book about the American Civil War. She was a proud Czech and she still is, but she wanted to know more about the world. I know I get my language ability as well as my athletic ability from her.

For a while, my mother worked in Mokropsy, the third town toward Prague on the railroad line. In the morning, she'd fix breakfast and wake me up just before she left, and then I'd wake Jana and walk her to kindergarten before going to my school. In the afternoon, my mother would take the train and get home at three-thirty. When I was around twelve years old, she started working in Revnice, and that was much better for everybody because she didn't have to leave so early. I laugh now when I read about "latchkey kids" in America. In Czechoslovakia, where everybody works, all the children are latchkey kids and they manage to survive.

The only bad thing about my mother and father and grandmother working was being home alone with my grandfather. He was still upset about losing his thirty acres of family land. After my mother went to work in Revnice, he developed a phobia about locking doors. Everything had to be locked: fence, back door, every room. He produced these huge keys you had to carry, like church keys. He would lock his own door and insist you do the same. Nobody was around. It wasn't exactly like having a ground-floor apartment in Manhattan, where the piranhas will pick you clean in thirty seconds. This was Revnice, Czechoslovakia.

Sometimes I'd run into the garden and try to get back in the house minutes later and find he had locked the door. Then he started calling Jana names like "spoiled brat." I almost got into a fistfight with him a couple of times, but he backed off. He was really short, and he knew I would whip him.

Jana and I would go through stages where we wouldn't talk to him for months. My grandmother didn't take that well because she was in the middle. She had already divorced him, but they were still living together. I felt bad because I thought grandfathers were all supposed to be sweet old men. My other grandfathers were fine, but this old man was just plain nasty. I thought of him as Old Scrooge —yes, we used to be very big on Dickens.

Sometimes he would be really nice, teach me how to play chess or something, but the next time he'd be nasty again. Looking back, I guess maybe he was schizoid, had a split personality. I heard he calmed down after I left, and died a sweet old man, after all.

Having my new father around helped give me the strength to stand up to my grandfather. I could see how my mother had lost her zest for tennis when she was a kid. Who could compete with somebody like that browbeating you? I see some of the younger women on the tour with bullies for fathers, and I see what my grandfather could have been like. No wonder some of these kids have the problems they have.

My mother did fine in her own life. She loved so many other sports and was still in love with tennis, too. She just never became a national player. She would play volleyball and gymnastics and tennis with friends and at some of the sporting clubs we have in Czechoslovakia. She was always a full-time athlete, full-time worker, full-time mother. And she made it all work. I learned my lesson from my mother at an early age: sports are good for young women. It's good to compete, good to run, good to sweat, good to get dirty, good to feel tired and healthy and refreshed. We had no idea of tomboys—there's no word for it in the Czech language.

Women played sports and had families and jobs. That simple. My mother was my role model.

I've grown up a lot like my mother. She's very smart, is always reading, tries to keep up on world news as well as possible, something I try to do even in the cocoon of the tennis tour, where little outside information filters in.

Sometimes my mother has problems communicating. She didn't want to give me bad news when I was a little kid because she's a procrastinator who hates to deal with problems, particularly emotional ones. I'm the same way. I'm terrible. When it comes to conflict, I try to avoid it at all costs. I just let things build up and get worse.

One of the reasons my career started to go down the tubes in the late seventies was because I let other people make decisions for me, and I couldn't say no. I wanted to please everybody, but I was the only one out there on center court getting beat love and love by Chris Evert. After I met Nancy Lieberman, she would say: "Tini, just do it!" And now I'm a little better at confronting things.

My mother had a hard time telling me the facts of life. When I was about fourteen, I needed a medical exam in order to be allowed to play against senior players. I didn't know what a gynecologist was—but I certainly found out when I was in the office. Scared me out of my wits.

Not only was I shocked at the gynecological examination, but a few days later I came down with my first period. I actually thought the doctor had caused me to get it. That's how unknowledgeable I was. I knew how children were made but that was about it.

My father was annoyed at my mother because she hadn't told me what was ahead of me. When I asked her how children were made, she sent me to him and he told me. He was always very natural about talking about sex, but she was uptight.

I didn't find out I had a half-brother until I was twenty-three. I was living in Dallas then and went to a psychic who told me: "You have a sister," and "You were close to your grandmother," and "You have a brother, too, don't you?"

I said, "No, I don't," but he insisted I did so I finally said, "Well, my mother had a miscarriage, it could have been that."

I lost my faith in the psychic when he kept insisting I had a brother, but when my family came over for a visit in 1979, I said, "Mami, you won't believe what some psychic said. He said I have a brother."

My mother looked a little uncomfortable and said: "You mean you don't know?"

"Know what?"

"That your father had a son before we were married."

Then my mother told me that my real father had never married the woman who had his child, so I have no way of knowing whether my brother has his father's name or his mother's name. All I know is that he would be a few years older than I am. God knows, I might have met him and not even known who he was.

My brother could have been one of those pale-faced young men in soldiers' uniforms that used to crowd into the trams in Prague, or he could have been a student swarming out of Charles University, or a young farmer staring at my train as it went past. I think about my brother occasionally, even though I doubt I'll ever meet him. So far, nobody's tried to say he was my brother, and if anybody ever does, he'd better have a lot of proof because I'd be very suspicious at this stage.

It's hard to miss somebody you never knew. Besides, I had Jana from the time I was nearly seven. I was thrilled to have a sister. You look in all the pictures, and I've got a big smile on my face, usually hugging Jana and mugging for the camera. She says I used to let her go places with me

—*if* she did my share of the dishes first, but I can't imagine myself doing something like that.

I gave her my old tricycle when she was big enough to use it, and we'd ride our bikes on the road in front of the house. Or sometimes I'd put her up on my bicycle and drive her around town. She says I used to drive "very quickly," which is possible.

My father was always joking with us, calling us all kinds of names. When Jana was a few years old, he nicknamed her Chickenshit because she was timid about skiing or going fast on my bicycle. The name sounds harsh in English, but he would turn the Czech word into a Russian-style diminutive: Posera, Poserovitch, Poserovitchenko, which is very affectionate to the Czech ear.

I called her Janka or Jani or Janitchko, she called me Martinka, and my mom called me Marti or Martino. My father called me Pluto, like the Walt Disney character. I claim this evolved from him calling me Prut, which means "branch," because I was so skinny, but my family thinks it was also because I was always chasing after a ball. My father also called me Little Rascal, for obvious reasons.

In addition to my apple expeditions across the road from the house, Jana and I used to slip into other people's gardens and sample their nuts and cherries. One time when I was around twelve and Jana was five, a lady caught us in the garden and we had to give back the nuts we had picked.

One of the big holidays in Czechoslovakia is December 6, St. Nicholas's Day. That's the day you are visited by the Angel, the Devil, and St. Nicholas, all at the same time. They'd actually come into your house and argue about whether you had been good that year.

"I hear you've been bad this year," the Devil would say in a rough voice.

"No, she's been a good girl this year," the Angel would say.

And St. Nicholas would be standing there, wondering whether he should leave you any presents.

Usually, the Angel won out, and St. Nicholas would leave you baskets of oranges, grapes, and bananas, which were always a big treat back home.

Jana used to gobble her fruits down, just devour them, but I liked to savor mine, so I'd take little bites and always have some left after she was finished. Then she would stare at me with "dog's eyes"—did you ever have a dog stare at you while you were eating?—until I'd give her a piece of mine. I always gave her some, except one time when I ate my banana so fast because I didn't want to give her any.

We all used to go swimming in the Berounka River, right near the house, and on windy days we'd go out to the fields to fly a paper dragon kite my father had made. Once in a while the winds would tear the string right out of our hands and we'd never find it again, but my father would just go to work and make a new one.

I was so happy to have a father, but I felt sorry for him because some people who knew me as Martina Subertova thought his last name was Subert. When I was ten, I changed my name to Navratilova.

My new name was pronounced with the accent on both the *a*'s—*Nav-RAH-tee-low-VAH*—although you'd never know it by the way it's pronounced in the West. People began saying *NAV-rah-ti-LOW-vah*, making me sound like an Italian countess. Now it's too late to get it right. I'll settle for the Italian pronunciation rather than the way they used to botch it at Wimbledon, where they'd be calling everybody else Miss This and Mrs. That and I'd be "Ummm . . . Martina." At least until I'd won it a few times, but they still mess it up sometimes.

I'm proud that Mirek Navratil's family name is embossed

on the trophies from Wimbledon and the other tournaments I have won. He was a father to me in every sense of the word, and it was his energy, his enthusiasm, that gave me my chance in tennis.

The Two-Handed Kid

As soon as the weather turned good each spring, my parents spent almost every nice day at the little tennis club in Revnice, playing soft, friendly doubles games or chatting on benches or in the clubhouse.

I inherited one of my grandmother's old-fashioned wooden racquets, a little crooked at the head, no tape for a grip. It wasn't sawed off or anything, it was regulation size, so I held it in both hands to hit a ball against the cement wall: four-and-a-half-year-old Martina Subertova, queen of the two-handed backhand.

While my parents were playing club matches, I'd practice for hours, just hitting the wall. Sometimes they'd drag me away for a while to do something else, but as soon as they weren't looking, I'd run back and start all over again. My relationship with the wall became love-hate because you could never beat it. You'd hit a ball and it would come back harder than you'd hit it.

I remember the first time I played tennis on a real court. I'd been playing against the wall, right near the last court at the club, and my father took me out on the court and tried to teach me how to hit a forehand. He was at the net and I was between the service line and the baseline.

The moment I stepped onto that crunchy red clay, felt the grit under my sneakers, felt the joy of smacking a ball over the net, I knew I was in the right place. I was probably about six years old when that happened, but I can remember it as if it was yesterday. I could have hit with him all day. I had all the energy and all the patience in the world.

I was tiny, not an ounce of fat on me—nothing but muscle and bone—just sheer energy. In school I was kind of embarrassed about being so small, but on the tennis court it didn't really matter that much, as long as you could get to the ball and hit it. My reflexes were always faster than other kids'. I never could understand why I could catch a ball and they couldn't. I'd think to myself, If only they would try . . . But they probably were trying. It was just a gift I had, a skill.

I played as soon as the snow had melted in the spring until it returned in the fall. One year I left my racquet at the court overnight and it snowed, and we didn't recover the racquet until springtime. We still have it in the garage somewhere.

I was the school jock. When the teacher needed somebody to run an errand in a hurry, she'd send me. I loved to run. I'd run around my garden and pretend it was a track. In the summer the kids in Revnice would go to this schoolyard, all grass, and we'd have track meets. There was one boy who was as fast as I was—he wound up playing for a good soccer team—but the other girls weren't even close.

The girls started to fill out in the sixth or seventh grade, but I didn't wear a brassiere until I was fourteen—and God knows I didn't need one then. I was more than a little upset about developing so late, but it was a blessing when playing soccer and ice hockey and skiing.

From the time I started school, tennis was my sport. From first grade to fifth grade, my school was down in the village square, a few blocks from our house; but from the sixth to the ninth grade, I went to a bigger school up on the hill, across the street from the tennis courts.

From my class windows I could see the courts and dream about being on them. I couldn't wait for cooking class to be over, so I could run over there. The kids knew I loved tennis and they'd ask: "Martina, what are you doing with all the tennis?" and I'd think to myself, Ah, one day you'll know.

I already had an image of myself as a tennis player. It was formed the night my father took me to the Sparta sports center in Prague, an arena where ten thousand people can watch a hockey game or tennis match. The big attraction that night was Rod Laver, the redheaded left-hander from Australia, the Rocket. God, what power and agility he had, what drive! I saw him rocketing around the court and I thought, That's it, that's me, that's the player I want to be. Women didn't play like him, not then, and not now, really, but if ever there was a player I wanted to copy, it was Laver.

Years later when I was playing for the Boston Lobsters in World Team Tennis, Emmo—Roy Emerson, our coach —would go out for beers with Laver whenever we played his San Diego team. I must have been out half a dozen times with those guys—just a bunch of mates and sheilas, having a great old time—and I never could bring myself to tell Laver he was my greatest sports idol.

After seeing Laver play, I knew what world-level tennis was like. I began having dreams about winning on Centre Court at Wimbledon or winning the Federation Cup for Czechoslovakia. They were the two greatest things a woman could do. Wimbledon was the mecca for every European tennis fan. All the other tournaments were just prelims. It didn't matter that England was part of the Western world. Even the Czech officials had great respect for the tradition of Wimbledon. It was one dream you were allowed to have.

My father helped put that dream in my head because he believed I could be a great player. He would hit the ball to me for hours, telling me I could be a champion. He would tell my mother and she would nod her head and say, "Of course, of course." She always encouraged me to be the best I could, but she had been pushed into tennis by her father, and she had mixed feelings about competition.

She would play with me, but she didn't know the technical aspects of tennis as well as my father did. While he was working me out, she would sit alongside the court, smoking a cigaret, and if I missed a shot, she'd say, "How could you miss that?" and I'd say, "You're a player, you've missed it before." Meantime, my father would be saying, "Here's what you did wrong."

He was a pretty tough instructor but nothing like some of the tennis fathers on the tour now, and not just those from the States but from parts of Europe, too. They seem to be living their lives through their daughters. You wonder whether some of these guys would actually push their daughters around for playing badly.

I look at some of the kids coming along today and their lives are all tennis. Some of these young kids are really slow. They don't say anything. They're just too young. They quit school in their middle teens and come right into the cocoon world of the tour. That's why I respect Tracy Austin, Andrea Jaeger, and Pam Shriver so much for finishing high school while they were out on the tour. God knows they could have quit.

I never finished high school after I defected at the age of eighteen, but up to that point I was going to a regular school in Prague, living a normal life, taking a full load of courses. At that stage of my life, tennis wasn't much different from the piano lessons or German classes I took. On Monday and

Thursday afternoons, I took gymnastics in the town gym, and later I also took German lessons until I switched to French. In school, nobody was about to make an exception for me, so I got a heavy dose of languages, science, and grammar. I wanted to know everything. I knew I couldn't play tennis forever. What if I broke a leg?

A woman I know visited one of the sports academies where kids live year-round and she kept hearing the parents say: "We've got our kid in the program, and she's going to be Number One," as if nothing else mattered. If their kids couldn't be Number 1, they would consider them failures, little realizing there were twenty other parents with the same goal. My friend was in total shock seeing the parents live their lives through their children.

The boys seem worse off than the girls. There is a degree of socialization on the women's tour—not as much as in the past, but we still play cards or gossip or have a meal together once in a while. Most of the men seem like little boys, very childlike, living in a shell, not caring about growing up or finding out if there's life beyond the fuzzy balls. They start making so much money, so fast.

My father was intense and demanding but only in a verbal way, as a teacher. We had no idea, when I was just starting, that you could make money at tennis. He was always positive because he knew I was having fun. He'd say: "Make believe you're at Wimbledon." That was the biggest thing you could win. Stand at Centre Court, hold up your trophy. My father planted those dreams in me, but he had a receptive audience. I could dream on my own.

I could see myself on television, doing it. Even though Billie Jean King, Margaret Court, and Nancy Richey were already way up there, I didn't realize how good they were. I thought I could be up there, too.

After I'd been playing tennis a while, we ran into my real father at the tennis court, and my second father told him

27

that I was going to be a tennis champion someday. I don't think my real father believed that—what was I, seven?—but Mirek was convinced.

He was so sure I was going to be a great tennis player that he took a rather daring step when I was nine years old. He brought me into Prague to try to get me into the city's best coaching program. One of the best tennis players in Czechoslovakia then was George Parma, who used to play on the Davis Cup team and in some of the European tournaments.

A bad back and Czech tennis politics had taken George out of the tournament circuit, and now he was about twenty-nine years old and giving lessons at Klamovka Park on the western edge of Prague. It was the only indoor facility in that part of Czechoslovakia. Given the Czech weather, if you didn't play for George Parma at Klamovka, you didn't become much of a tennis player. Only one person could decide whether or not you played indoors, and that was George Parma.

When I turned nine in the fall of 1965, my father took me on the train to Prague and then we got on a red streetcar that stopped at the bottom of the hill. These days when I talk about Klamovka, I make it sound rather grand, but in truth it was just a dinky little Quonset hut that looked more like a 1930s gas station than one of these new American tennis emporiums. It had only three indoor courts at right angles to each other. The best one was heated, but the others were sometimes so cold you'd play in hat and gloves and still feel icicles on you.

There was a little locker and shower area, run by Madame Kozelska, who lived in a tiny apartment over the office. She had a house in Revnice and had helped us get court time at Klamovka a few times in the past. I thought she had been whispering in George Parma's ear about me, but he seemed a little vague at first.

"How old is he?" George asked.

He saw my short hair and wiry build and thought I was a boy. I was getting used to it, but that didn't mean I liked it.

George told my father that he was very busy with lessons, that he only had a few hours open for new players, and that he couldn't promise anything. He'd hit with me for a little while, and if I wasn't good enough, he'd have to tell us right away.

"Don't worry, she's good enough," my father said.

I'm sure my father wondered how this coach could spot talent in a few minutes of hitting, but it really isn't all that mysterious. I can spot it right away today. A kid might not have decent strokes but I can see if she's a good athlete, if she moves her feet well. I guess George Parma was confident he could hit me a few balls and then advise us to get back on the streetcar and return to Revnice.

I was wearing a little burgundy warm-up suit and carrying the secondhand wooden racquet my father had given me. This tall, handsome man took me out on the court and started hitting balls at me. I was still using the two-handed backhand, and he kept hitting the ball down the sideline, trying to see how far I could go for it. I would dig out a few shots and get them back over the net. I knew this was no friendly little hit. Looking back, this man was giving me a test that might be more important than any test I'd ever take in school. But at the time, it was just a chance to show off and hit some tennis balls. I was loose and confident and having a good time.

The tryout lasted for half an hour, much longer than we'd expected. When George Parma stopped hitting to me, he walked over to my father. I rushed up to hear what he would say.

"I think we can do something with her," George Parma said.

The Commuter

I was pretty full of myself when George Parma accepted me into his program. Once a week I would hurry from school to catch the commuter train to Prague, usually rushing across the platform with my tennis racquet sticking out, gym bag at another angle, school bag hanging down to my ankles. I always tell people that I developed my strength and my speed running for trains when I was nine and ten years old.

I felt very proud, very mysterious, to be this little pipsqueak of a girl with all the equipment going into Prague to play tennis. You didn't see kids running around Czechoslovakia with tennis gear the way you do in the States, and I would imagine people asking themselves, Who is she? and I would be thinking to myself: Some day you'll know.

I can still recall those slow train rides along the Berounka Valley, through sleepy little villages: Dobrichovice; Vsenory; Mokropsy, where my mother worked in a factory; Cernosice, where my mother's grandmother used to have a farm; Radotin, where my mother's brother, Josef, lived near the station, and sometimes I could see him from the train, working in the garden; Chuchle, where my grandfather lived.

After thirty minutes or so, we'd pull into Smichov, a drab commuter station across the Vltava River from the historic portion of Prague. From Smichov, I'd take the red streetcar to the Klamovka section and walk up the hill to the courts and George Parma. After a few lessons, I would have walked through fire for this tall, handsome man with blond wavy hair. He was like a god to me—cool, intelligent, well educated. He had traveled outside Czechoslovakia many times and knew five languages. He always looked immaculate, as if he were going out to play for the Davis Cup again.

He was the most patient coach a kid could have. He would never shout or downgrade me in any way. All he'd have to say was, "Come on, Martina," and I'd chase down every shot. I'd follow every word he said, and if I thought he was going to tell me something, I'd rush right up to the net and stare into his light blue eyes.

If you ever saw a girl get a crush on her teacher, this was it. I used to think to myself that if only I was older, I could have married him. It didn't matter one iota that he already was married, that his wife, Jarmila, was a beautiful and very nice person. I believed George Parma would have been the perfect husband, but that's the way it goes when you're ten.

Once in a while George would come to Revnice to work outdoors with me. It was such a big occasion to have him visit our town that I would wear a white tennis skirt to practice with him. Here was a former Czech Davis Cup player, all decked out in Fred Perry gear, giving lessons to me on the town court. I was so excited to work with him that I'd chase balls until I ran out of breath.

The first thing George did was change my backhand. My father had let me use a two-handed backhand at five and six years old because I'd been too weak to get much on the ball with one hand. But later George could see that all I wanted to do was come to the net and volley, so I was going to need all the reach I could get. So he took my right hand off the racquet and that let me extend my reach a few more inches. If he hadn't, can't you just see Chris and me having the battle of the two-handed backhands?

If I were teaching children now, I would teach a two-handed drive backhand, a one-handed slice, and a one-handed approach and a one-handed volley, to give variety. I wouldn't mind having a two-handed blast for some shots, but I'm not about to retool my game at this point—and also I'm blessed with plenty of power with just the one hand. Kids have more control with two hands, but you're also vulnerable approaching with two hands. Learning both variations is almost like learning an extra stroke, but it's definitely the perfect way to play tennis. Mats Wilander is the best with two-handed or one-handed backhands that I've seen.

George Parma knew what he was doing at the time. His job was to develop good tennis players. Czech women are pretty sturdy and they handle some heavy jobs in factories and shops. He didn't mind working me hard, since there was no sense of tennis being a social outing or a recreation. He had a skill to teach me, and he went at it.

George wanted to refine my game, which made sense. He told me to learn to play the baseline more but still be aggressive. He told me I was like a cat, like a tiger, but that sometimes even a tiger has to be conservative.

I didn't believe in playing conservatively then, and really I still don't. Some of the worst tennis I've played has come when I was too tentative, when I waited for my opponent to make the mistakes—like the time I let myself get talked into sitting back on Kathy Horvath and got zapped right out of the 1983 French Open. But sometimes when I was younger, I wanted to be too perfect, to hit the perfect winner on the first exchange. I'd try some fancy drop shot and George would raise his eyebrows or say, "Just hit it back, Martina," and I'd get in the groove and hit a few forehands.

But if I saw an opening, I'd rush the net again, and he'd have to remind me that I was taking a lesson, not playing for the Czech championship.

"Ordinary shots are what make a player," he would say.

George began to give me tips on how to behave in matches, what to do if people tried to cheat me, how to vary my strokes. I could tell he thought I was developing.

He would talk about the international circuit from his own experience. He once told me how it had been impossible for him to get good training growing up during World War II and right afterward. He undoubtedly could have been a better player if he'd had better coaching, and he thought things would be better for me. By my time, Czechoslovakia was much more open about producing good tennis players to compete on an international basis.

In the mid-sixties, the Communists could see the value of sports as a way of making people proud and keeping their minds off the less pleasant aspects of life. They approached sports the same way they approached the economy: with a plan. You would hear jokes about how the Russians expected Czechoslovakia to produce a certain tonnage of screws every year, so the only way you could achieve your goal would be to produce huge ones that nobody could use. Or if your quota was elevators, you'd produce the proper number—even if they couldn't be serviced.

Sports were easier to plan. The Communists more or less emphasized a different sport in each country: weight-lifting in the Soviet Union, track and field in East Germany, gymnastics in Rumania, tennis in Czechoslovakia.

In my country, sports were one way to show national pride, one of the few safe ways. You could cheer for a Czech hockey team or soccer team, even against the Soviet Union. It was a tradition going back to the nineteenth century when people formed sports clubs like Sokol, to compete in gymnastics. It was the only way you could say to the Hapsburgs, "Look, we're still Czechs, even if we now belong to the Austro-Hungarian Empire."

Right after World War II, the Soviet soccer team came to Czechoslovakia and lost three straight matches—they didn't even show up for the fourth. This embarrassed the Russians so much that when the Communists took over the country in 1948, they closed down the sports program as a way of curbing nationalism. But by the time I came along, sports were safe again and the government was pouring money into them.

George was a government employee, so he had to follow a certain schedule. Some afternoons he gave lessons and other afternoons he trained a junior team for the government, but he could also make separate deals with people for private lessons, all aboveboard.

Czechoslovakia had been a Middle European capitalist country until 1948; people were still used to working hard to earn some extra money, and some people still had money to pay for lessons for themselves or more court time for their kids. But George Parma never asked a penny for my lessons and my father never paid him a penny. George saw my talent, and he worked with it.

I also had Madame Kozelska on my side. That little old lady was all over the courts, cleaning out the lockers, dragging the clay, keeping an eye on everybody from her little apartment. She was a regular scuttlebug, and she knew who were the good kids and who were the bad ones. She had taken a liking to me, and she kept telling George to give me more court time. After I had been there a few months, he told me I could have an extra hour for the junior program because I was already at the top of my age group. So I began coming in a second day.

"Work hard, Martina," he would tell me. "Compete wherever you have the chance. Get to see the world. Sports is one way you'll be able to travel."

George never complained about the system, but you could pick up a sense of sadness in him, just like in my mother and other people of that generation. They had been raised by parents who were hopeful for Czechoslovakia's future after World War I, but first the Germans and then the Russians had squashed that hope. George had gone through the dreary Communist game of having his passport withheld or being inexplicably left off a Davis Cup trip he deserved. He would never say anything political, but when he talked about travel, about tennis being one way of seeing the world, you could tell he was thinking about more than just playing a game. He was thinking about being in touch with the world outside our borders, a world to which we belonged, by tradition and by temperament.

He would tell me to set my sights on becoming a good European player—maybe, just maybe, in the top ten in the world. Meantime, my father was telling people I was going to be a Wimbledon champion someday and I wasn't about to disagree with him.

When I was a skinny little girl with the tennis racquets on the train, I'd dreamed of going back on the streetcar to Klamovka and having people recognize me as Wimbledon champion. But I never got the chance, and the Czech government isn't going to let the people know much about me now.

People in Czechoslovakia don't read about most of my tournaments, and my matches are never on Czech television; although you can pick up the West German stations in western Czechoslovakian towns like Pilsen, you're not supposed to watch West German television. I hear that *Rude Pravo,* the party newspaper in Czechoslovakia, is loosening up a little bit and actually printing the results when I win Wimbledon and the U.S. Open. For a long time after I left, I was a non-person in their sports pages.

Even in the souvenir shops of Czechoslovakia you can

find a poster of the latest junior hotshots, but you won't see any of Ivan Lendl or Hana Mandlikova, who are still citizens but live mostly in the West. And even if they could make money selling Martina mementoes, they wouldn't do it.

At the Revnice tennis club, where I spent hundreds of hours learning the game with my father and mother, there are only four posters of players taped to the wall: Jimmy Connors, Adriano Panatta, Björn Borg, and Czechoslovakia's sweetheart, Christine Marie Evert. The skinny little runt with the racquets flopping all over on the commuter train? Not a trace.

Grandma

As the little red streetcar snaked its way into the Klamovka section of Prague, I'd be peering out the window at all the old ladies in their black or gray dresses, looking for Grandma Andela Subertova. Sometimes she'd be waiting at the tram stop with a container of carrot salad in her hands.

"Eat it; it's good for your eyes," Grandma would say, just like the grandmothers in the States who like to ply you with chicken soup or pasta.

While my parents and my coach were encouraging me to be the best tennis player possible, I was getting a different kind of attention from my real father's mother, who touched another part of my nature in a way nobody else has ever done.

I loved Grandma Subertova so much that she almost did not get into this book. Every time I started to talk about her, I would break into tears, and feel weak and tired deep inside.

I still have recurring dreams about Grandma. I see her going into the Metro, the subway, and I call after her, but I can't run fast enough to catch up with her and she can't come back. Or sometimes in my dreams Grandma's across the street and I call to her but she can't wave back. She's in my dreams more than anybody else, and is the main reason why I think there might be a hereafter. Or let me put it another way: she's the main reason I hope there is one.

Grandma was the most generous person I have known. If somebody had thrown rocks at her, she would have offered him a loaf of bread in return. I wanted to be like her when I was young. I once told Stephanie Salter of *Inside Sports:* "When I was a little kid in school, if I brought an orange for lunch—and they were not easy to come by in Czechoslovakia—I'd always give the bigger half to a friend." I got that part of me from Grandma.

This part of me may not show these days, while I'm out on the court smashing a volley into the seats and taking home the cold hard cash, but there is a giving side to my nature that has gotten me into trouble over the years. I'm not as open as I used to be, since some reporters and other people I considered friends violated what I thought were confidences, but I have always given presents and made loans and befriended all kinds of strays, both two- and four-legged.

Everybody should be so lucky to have a Grandma Subertova. She was the voice of approval that I always heard in the back of my mind, the person who loved me whether or

37

not I had a good day at the tennis courts or finished my homework or cleaned my room.

That's the nice thing about grandparents, that they can love you wholeheartedly without the discipline and the conflicts that you have with your own parents. People say grandparents are going out of style in the United States because everybody wants to act young and live in Leisure Villages and go to discos or play tennis or whatever. I had the real thing: a little old Czech grandmother who loved me and whose memory keeps me going today.

Grandma wore mostly black and gray dresses. She used to be really thin when she was younger, but she was getting heavier when I started to visit her. She used to joke that she was growing into the ground—getting shorter and wider. She had a big nose, just like mine, and her hair had been dark but was getting pretty gray.

I don't think she ever held a factory job, but she did work on a farm when she was young. After my Grandfather Subert died when I was around nine or ten, she moved into a small apartment in the Klamovka section, only a few blocks from the tennis courts.

Sometimes Grandma would walk up the hill with me and watch my practice, but she'd never say a word. She was not one of these tennis annies whom you see in posh tennis clubs in the United States now, where parents, grandparents, aunts, and uncles all stand around shouting encouragement to the kids. Tennis was not a big thing to Grandma, although she was proud to see me out there taking lessons from such a well-known coach as George Parma. By the way, Grandma also had a crush on George.

After my midweek lesson she'd walk me down to the streetcar and make sure I was on the car. But when I had a lesson on Friday, I'd stay at her apartment so I wouldn't have to come all the way back again the next morning.

Her apartment was small, just one bedroom and a kitchen–living room area, where she'd fix up a couch into a bed for me. She'd make dinner with lunch meat or chicken and the ever-present carrot salad with apple syrup poured over it. The apple syrup was one of our few staples; we'd mix it with water to make our version of a soft drink. Then we'd sit around and talk all evening, me calling her Babička and she calling me Martinka or Martinečka.

Sometimes she'd call me Zlata Holčička—"Golden Little Girl."

Having been born under the rule of the Hapsburgs and endured the Nazi occupation during the war, Grandma spoke fluent German. I was studying the language in school, so I'd try to impress her with what I had learned that week.

Sometimes Grandma would talk about the big adventure in her life, a trip she had taken to Holland a few years earlier. The thing she remembered most was the steward-esses on KLM, how nice they were, how she could understand their Dutch because of her German. She was proud that as a little old *babička* she could visit a foreign country and speak the language. Grandma could have been a linguist, or a schoolteacher perhaps, but growing up on the farm at the turn of the century she never had a chance for an education beyond grammar school.

She loved figure skating, one of the great traditions in my country. She knew the names of all the Czech champions, like Aja Zanova, who later became a close friend of mine in New York, and she even had a scrapbook with pictures of skaters like Sonja Henie.

Grandma didn't have a television set, but we'd listen to music and news on the radio or we'd do crossword puzzles. She was pretty good at them. Ninety-nine percent of them she could do, but every so often she would find something she couldn't fill in—sporting trivia or the names of cities or something to do with geography. She'd save them for me

39

and we'd finish them together. I didn't realize until years later that Grandma probably saved those items because she knew darn well I could fill in the answers and she wanted to make me feel like a big cheese. I could cry just thinking about the way she made me feel so special.

Some days Grandma didn't meet me at the tram stop or the tennis courts but would wait for me by the window of her apartment. I would wave to her before racing up the three flights of stairs to try to beat her to the door. Sometimes I'd get there faster than she expected and she'd say: "How fast you are." When we came home together, she always had to rest on the landing after each floor, even though I was helping her along the way.

Sometimes in the evening, we'd sit around and tell jokes, mostly about the Russians, the way other people tell other ethnic jokes.

Grandma never asked me much about tennis as a career. It was too far removed from what she knew. When I started to play in tournaments and travel around the world, she was proud of me, but I never got much time to really explain to her what life was like in the States.

When I left Czechoslovakia in 1975, I didn't dare say good-bye to Grandma or anybody else. I just packed and went to play the tour and never came back. I thought I'd never see her again, but in 1979 they let her visit me in the States. They hadn't allowed any others in my family out but they were glad to let older people out, hoping they might stay and the state wouldn't have to pay their pension anymore. People under sixty-five still had value in the eyes of the state, so it was much harder for them to get out.

At the age of eighty-three or eighty-four, she flew all the way from Prague to Dallas, with a few stops in between. I'll never forget how much energy she had getting off the plane after nearly twenty-four hours. She was ready to go. I was so happy to see her; of course I was crying, like I am now, just thinking about her.

Grandma was overwhelmed by Texas. Everything there was on a bigger scale than what you see in Czechoslovakia. I had bought an average middle-class house in Dallas, the first house I ever owned, about 3,500 square feet, and it just knocked her out. Carpeting, furniture, three TVs, the remote control for the TV, she couldn't comprehend it all. And the microwave oven! Put something in and two minutes later it's hot. I don't understand the concept myself, but I can use it. She'd just stare at the thing and shake her head.

She had no idea how much money you could earn in tennis, or any other occupation in the States, but Grandma was a realist and she knew enough to be amazed by all the American gadgets. Sometimes she'd look around the house and say: "And you did this all by yourself."

I was sharing a house with Sandra Haynie, the golfer, a close friend who was my manager at the time, and the two of them became fast friends. Haynie had this shocking-pink warm-up suit that she used to wear around the house. On her last day in Dallas, Grandma told me how much she liked the suit, and when I told Haynie, she went into her room and took it off and gave it to my grandmother to bring home to Czechoslovakia.

A couple of times we took Grandma for rides around Dallas, which must have seemed like outer space to her. She was happy just to be with us, but she also got to see me play in a tournament in Dallas and then in the Avon championships at Madison Square Garden in New York. When I beat Tracy Austin in the finals there, Grandma could finally see the payoff for all those years of practice at Klamovka.

Seeing me win was nice, but Grandma was more impressed by some of the celebrities she met in New York. I took her to The Czech Pavilion, the restaurant that Aja Zanova and her husband, Paul Steindler, were managing. Aja had been a star in the Ice Follies for years after leaving Czechoslovakia, and Grandma was thrilled to see a former Czech world champion figure skater.

Another thrill for Grandma was meeting Lee Majors, the Six Million Dollar Man. She had never seen the show at home, but she'd been watching television in Dallas and she liked it. I saw him in the lobby of the hotel where we were staying in New York and introduced him to Grandma. She couldn't get over meeting somebody she had seen on television.

But the biggest thrill of all was meeting Grandma's favorite tennis player. My grandmother talked about her all the time, how perfect she was, so when we were playing in Dallas, I brought Grandma into the locker room.

"You're *the* Chris Evert?" Grandma asked in Czech.

Chris was great. She gave Grandma a big hug and a kiss whenever she saw her in Dallas and New York. Chris was a celebrity and a model tennis player to Grandma. I was still Zlata Holčička—Grandma's Golden Little Girl—and that was good enough for me.

Before Grandma left, she gave me her robe that she had worn for years. I still have it, and sometimes I go to the closet and press my face against it, feeling very close to Grandma.

When I put her on the plane, she had a smile on her face, I think because she had seen her Golden Little Girl again, when she might have thought she never would. I was sobbing because I knew I might never see her again.

About a year later, when I was living in Charlottesville, I picked up my mail and found a letter from my aunt in Revnice. Inside was one of those black-bordered funeral announcements, a *parte.* I saw a cross in the middle of the page and then I saw Grandma's name.

Sobbing, I placed a call to Prague and found out that my grandmother had come down with cancer shortly after the trip to the States and had died a few weeks before I got the letter. I asked my mother why she hadn't told me Grandma was ill, but she couldn't really answer me.

Later that year my parents came to live with me in Dallas for a while and I asked them again: "Why didn't you let me know?" They still didn't have an answer. It was probably just as well they hadn't told me she was sick because what could I have done? I wasn't an American citizen yet, so I couldn't have even dreamed of visiting Czechoslovakia.

Still, it was rough finding out that way. It was almost the same secondhand way I later learned about my real father's suicide. My parents just basically blurted it out, but by then it was too late to ask my grandmother about her son, or try to find out more about his suicide and how she felt about it. She never talked much about her life or her feelings, anyway.

Grandma always gave me the feeling I was one of the most important people in her life. She never showed feelings of sadness over some of the sad things in her life, like the loss of her son and husband. She just loved me and encouraged me to enjoy life. She came to Dallas, saw me with a nice house, some good friends, and a successful career, and she went home smiling. Nobody has ever loved me so completely, so acceptingly, as Grandma. I can only hope that some day somebody will.

School

Schoolwork for me was just like tennis. It came pretty easily to me and I never had any patience for people who couldn't pick it up quickly. I could sit in class and come up with the answers right out of my head, and I could never understand why somebody else had to think about it, or why somebody got it wrong.

I went to kindergarten when I was four and five, and then started first grade at the age of six. I remember my first day of school quite vividly: my mom made me put on a skirt with patent-leather shoes and white ankle socks, so I'd look like a little girl. I remember swinging on the swings in the yard the first day. There was this one boy in my class, who was a little crazy, who hit all the kids over the head with a wooden train. I was already pretty spunky, even on the first day of first grade, so naturally I got into a fight with him and got my clothes all dirty.

It really didn't make any sense to wear such pretty clothes to school—particularly since none of our clothing was wash-and-wear and none of our mothers had washers and dryers. One little altercation in the schoolyard could ruin your outfit.

The first elementary school I attended was in an old

building right near the town square with wooden floors and old wooden benches, with holes for ink. It was impossible to stay clean because of the wooden floors. There were slanted desks with a rack for your books underneath. The benches were wide enough for two or three people and you could slide back and forth when nobody was looking.

Most of the time you had to sit up straight, and the teachers made us keep our hands behind our backs on the theory that it would improve our posture. And that way we couldn't mess around with anything—we had to pay attention. At least that was the theory.

They were rigid about our posture and our conduct. We had to raise our hand when we had something to say, and we were supposed to raise only our index and middle fingers. Before long I was raising my whole hand and flapping it about. The better students sat in the last row and sometimes I would lean against the back wall and keep my hand up because I usually knew the answers. Naturally, the teachers wouldn't call on me all the time, so I'd just keep my arm up. Maybe that built up my muscles for my serve.

The teachers were not comfortable with my being left-handed, just like my mother. When I started school, I used to write with my left hand, which made the ink smudge during penmanship lessons. After a while, my teacher told me to write with my right hand, so I did—just like that. I didn't realize I could do it until I tried it.

One time, my athletic ability failed me in the first grade. We had a fat, nasty woman for physical education and she would tell us we had to do somersaults. I had a hard time keeping my head straight, so I was always rolling sideways. And I couldn't do the backward somersault at all.

The teacher wrote a note to my parents: "Martina cannot do a somersault."

My father wrote back: "Show her how to do it." He knew

she was too fat to do it, but he said any teacher should be able to demonstrate her skill, not just talk about it.

One teacher used to like to slap our hands if we misbehaved, but she didn't do it to me too often. In the third grade, my mother had me dressed up in a skirt and brand-new white tights. I can't remember what I did wrong, but the teacher made me kneel on the dirty wooden floor for punishment. I ruined the tights, which were not easy to get in Czechoslovakia. My parents thought there had to be a better way of disciplining kids than to ruin their clothing.

Other times the teachers would make us write a hundred times: "I will not chew gum" or "I will not talk in class." Same as anywhere else, I guess. Once I got in trouble for crawling around the classroom. I was trying to smuggle a note to a classmate and the kid next to me wouldn't pass it, so I started to crawl through all the aisles. I was clear across on the other side of the room when the teacher caught me.

I never did fit into the mold. I probably would have been considered outspoken in the States, too, but in Czechoslovakia I was really an outsider for asking questions, speaking my mind. I would get in trouble for it, in the classroom, at the tennis courts, or wherever. You weren't supposed to say things, whether it was mimicking the teachers behind their backs or asking questions. My outbursts were usually in good form, nothing nasty, but I would do anything for a laugh.

I had to curb myself from saying what was on my mind. In those days self-restraint was a serious concern for adults who wanted to avoid being thrown in jail. Now that I'm an American, I have to curb myself for a different reason: so people won't take me the wrong way, won't read my words in the newspaper and say, "God, how could she say that?" I may not have meant it that way, but people here are not

46

used to sharp remarks, particularly not from female athletes with foreign accents.

In school, kids had to keep quiet to avoid getting in trouble with the authorities. A couple of times I got caught trying to help my classmates who had trouble with all the little marks in the Czech language that completely change the sound of a word. By that time I guess I had accepted the fact that not all students were created equal, but I still didn't think it was very fair. So I'd try to help them out with the answers and sometimes get into trouble for it, but not very often.

My early days in school were probably much like those of children growing up in other parts of Europe or the States. Czech kids are just like kids anywhere else. You see them on the corner or in the streetcar and they're giggling and teasing and maybe the boys are pushing and shoving. There are the kids that always study and suck up to their teachers and spy on the other kids. Then there are the good rascals, and the bad kids—the ones you know will wind up in jail. I don't think most Czech children start noticing the limitations until they get older. Then they start developing a morose acceptance of what they can do and what they can't. I think I was a little different; I always had a sense that something was not quite right.

I was happy when I got into the sixth grade and moved to the modern school up by the tennis courts. It had long marble hallways and regular chairs, nicer blackboards. My favorite classroom was the chemistry lab, because it had all the goodies for the chemical experiments. But the instructor, one of the school's few male teachers, favored the boys and didn't think girls should be in chemistry class. If he was explaining something and saw you were talking or not paying attention, he'd throw the chalk at you. It was his way of getting our attention, and it worked.

My sixth-grade history and geography teacher was named Kovalova, and we called her The Nun because she looked so stern and proper and she wore glasses, but she was really neat. She introduced me to the ancient Romans, my favorite period in history, telling us about the emperor Caligula, his horses and his chariots.

I was fascinated by the gladiators in the arena. I think of them sometimes when I'm waiting to go into the great big bowl at the U.S. Open or the old green stadium at Wimbledon. It's the same idea: the two warriors, the fight to the death, the crowd rooting for its favorite. I always accepted that notion of winning and losing, of surviving on your wits and your courage and your skill.

Miss Kovalova would take us on field trips because she really loved nature, and if the kids seemed really interested, it would hit a soft spot in her and she would talk more and more about the subject. She dropped her nunlike qualities out in the woods, jumping over creeks, not minding getting dirty. We thought she was pretty old to be taking us for romps in the woods: she must have been in her late thirties or early forties.

My teachers seemed to feel strongly about me, one way or the other, and I reacted the same way to them. Fairness, that was always the main thing to me. I didn't care how good they were as long as they were fair. Strict but fair, like Miss Kovalova. My literature teacher was nice, too, even though she sent me out of the room because I blew my nose too loudly. I still remember that. Later, I went to high school in Prague and had a teacher in her sixties named Zemanova. She was so emotional about Czech literature that she'd start crying when she lectured. I wasn't doing very well in her class, but she knew I was bright and wasn't giving it all I had because I was traveling, so she'd try to help me catch up. She was fair.

My grammar teacher, named Smrzova, was nice, but my

gym teacher hated me because I was a smartass and always talked back to her; she had a chip on her shoulder toward me, and vice versa. I think she was jealous because I was a jock, already involved in tennis. Also, I had no interest in the calisthenics she was making us do. To me, you just went out and played your sport; you didn't need a tune-up. My home economics teacher didn't like me either. I basically had the same ideas of diet and conditioning until a few years ago when I got better advice. But maybe I was getting good advice then and wouldn't listen.

When I got to the upper school, I'd say I was the third or fourth best student. Two boys were smarter than I was, or maybe they just did more homework. I don't want to say they were smarter. I got good grades in Czech language, literature, and mathematics. Our grades ranged from one to five, with one being the best. I had mostly ones, a couple of twos for drawing and domestic skills.

Algebra, I approached like tennis. Serve-and-volley. Either I beat you or you beat me, right away. I'd zip through the equation, get right down to $35 = 7x$, and just scribble down the answer like trying to hit a backhand cross-court-volley winner. Wouldn't even prove it out. Just write down the answer as 5. I was always very quick at adding and dividing and solving logic problems, but I was never any good at double-checking, and I didn't like geology, where you had to memorize Latin names for rocks and flowers. As soon as the exam was over, you forgot it, anyway.

Another thing I didn't like about school was the visit by the dentist. My teeth looked nice and white, but they were soft and I always had cavities. The dentist came right to school and called you out, class by class, name by name. Because my name was Subertova for the first ten years, I would always be near the end, and of course, I'd be trembling by the time my turn came. They didn't use any painkiller or X-rays. The dentist would tap your teeth with a pointed metal tool and when he figured he found something wrong, he'd mark you down, and a few weeks later he'd call you in and start drilling. One time he was drilling on me and I bit him right on the hand. He threw me out but two days later he came back and called my name again.

Another time I had to have root-canal work done, where they pour a poison on the nerve to kill it. I vowed I'd never go back but I did. Later we went to a woman dentist in Pilsen, a friend of my family's, who actually used novocaine. What a blessing. My sister, Jana, who is studying dentistry, says the Czechs still don't use any painkillers or X-rays in some places.

Another part of school I didn't like was painting classes, probably because I wasn't very good at painting, or thought I wasn't. I also hated it when we had to dig up the schoolyard and make it neat and trim the bushes. I wanted a racquet in my hand, not a trowel.

I never learned much about cooking at home. My mother was a good cook and she still loves to fuss over me with soups and traditional Czech dishes, but she never had much time to teach me—or maybe she tried and I didn't want to learn. It's possible. Anyway, we got to the eighth grade and all the girls had to take home economics. To make things worse, the class was held in a room overlooking the tennis courts. And there I was, cooking—and resenting it like hell because I really wanted to be outside playing.

Wouldn't you know it, the first thing I had to cook was lentil soup—and I absolutely hated lentils. But if you didn't agree with the teacher, you kept it to yourself, because you definitely did not want to be on her bad side. So I made the lentil soup and of course I had to taste it, and I ended up liking it! Now lentil soup is one of the staples on the diet that has helped my tennis so much—and I can make it for myself.

My first friend was Eva Pekařková, who lived right across the street from me, but after the first and second grades we weren't as close. My best friend in later grades was Květa Vlášková, who lived over the butcher shop, right next to the little movie theater. She was pretty smart, right next to me, and a good athlete. We didn't play with dolls too much, although I remember having at least one doll and a couple of toy animals.

Mostly I liked little models of sports cars, the kind with the wheels you can roll on the floor. I also had small trucks and a train, but the sports cars were my favorites. I think I was preparing for having one car for every day in the week, which I did during my early years in the States.

In all those years, playing ice hockey and soccer with guys, I only really got hurt twice. One time I was practicing gymnastics and I slipped running for the trampoline as I tried to jump over a table and wound up hitting my head on the metal plate at the edge of the trampoline. Another time I was running down a hill near the volleyball court when I caught my face on some barbed wire covering a light bulb at the hockey rink at the bottom of the hill. The wire hooked me right on the right eye, and I felt this sharp pain and put my hand to my face. When my mother came running over, she thought I had put out my eye, but fortunately I'd just cut the lid. To this day, you can still see the scar.

We played a lot of hopscotch, but the game that was really popular was pitching pennies. Everybody would pitch pennies into the center of a rectangle. The person who came closest got to pick up the money, toss it in the air, and call heads or tails: all the coins that came up on your side, you got to keep. Then the second person would go, and so on, until the wealth was redistributed. I seem to recall coming out a bit ahead in those games.

Another game we loved was cowboys and Indians—just like kids play in the States, or used to play before video games. Sure, we had cowboys and Indians in Czechoslovakia. Somehow, the dinky little theater in our town rented a series of films about an Indian chief, Vinnetou, played by a French actor, Pierre something-or-other, and a cowboy, Old Shatterhand, played by Lex Barker. It seems the Apache had saved the life of the cowboy, and they became blood brothers by slitting each other's wrists and making a blood oath.

The movies must have been dubbed, because I can't remember hearing any English spoken that early in my life. I do remember how I loved playing the part of Old Shatterhand whenever we pretended to be cowboys and Indians. We had wooden guns and bows and arrows, very primitive because the arrows would only fly ten yards at the most.

Sometimes I would climb in the spruce trees next to our house and pretend I was Old Shatterhand spying on my mother. I'd call her name, and if she couldn't see me up in the trees, I would think to myself, I gotcha, just like in the westerns. Another one bites the dust, courtesy of the biggest, baddest dude ever to ride through the Berounka Valley —Martina Subertova/Navratilova/Old Shatterhand, the original Czech cowgirl.

Growing Up

I didn't think much of it at the time, but I formed some pretty strong attachments to a couple of my teachers when I was young. I certainly had a crush on George Parma. I thought he was the most attractive man I'd ever seen, and still do.

I never felt attracted to Kovalova, The Nun, even though I thought she was neat, and the best teacher I had. But I felt strongly about my math teacher; she was a friend of my mother's, married, a good athlete, and a really fair teacher. I would find myself staring at her, trailing after her, just finding any excuse to watch her play sports or listen to her talk.

If anybody noticed, they never brought it up. From what I understand, it's pretty normal for kids of eleven, twelve, and thirteen to have crushes on teachers of the same sex. I never considered myself unusual at that time and never felt any attachments to girls my own age, but I definitely had strong feelings for a few adult women, which were still there when I grew up.

I'm not very psychologically oriented and I have no idea how I was affected by my real father's abandonment, the secrets and the suicide, or my feeling about being a misfit, a skinny little tomboy with short hair. In Czechoslovakia, nobody ever put me down for running around with the boys, playing ice hockey and soccer. From what I've been told, people in the States used to think that if girls were good at sports their sexuality would be affected. Being feminine meant being a cheerleader, not being an athlete. The image of women is changing now. You don't have to be pretty for people to come and see you play. At the same time, if you're a good athlete, it doesn't mean you're not a woman.

Being a good athlete carried no stigma for me growing up, but I was always aware of not having a feminine body. I liked being able to do things with my body, though, and I'd gladly sacrifice the looks—what the feminine type looks like—to be able to do what I do.

My father always told me I'd be better looking the older

I got. Well, it's true. I'm still growing into my body, and learning how to dress. People don't get a chance to see you dressed up very often when you're an athlete. They see you sweating, and then they see you with makeup on and they blurt out, "Oh, you look so much better than on the court." Sometimes I ask: "Does that mean I'm ugly on the court?" just to watch their reaction.

It was hard to know how to dress and act when I was growing up. Even in a Communist state, there were images of glamour left over from our Middle European heritage. We saw beautiful actresses and singers and dancers at the theaters in Prague and on television. But there was also the image of the patriotic factory worker with her short hair and muscles.

I didn't know exactly who I wanted to look like, but I definitely wanted to look more feminine. I couldn't do much about it, though, couldn't just chop down my muscles. They were in the genes. My mother dressed for work in the office and she didn't use a lot of makeup. She put all her energies into balancing a job and two children and a husband and tennis and other sports.

I'm sure playing tennis made me more independent, more self-confident, because I could do some things better than other people—but affect my sexuality? I don't see it. Some things you're born with, for no known reason; that's how I see it. But I didn't feel different from the girls I grew up with. They were my friends.

After a while, the tennis separated me from the other kids in Revnice. It wasn't so much that it gave me a big head as it just put me in a different category. From the time I was ten, one or two days a week I would hustle out of school and catch the train into Prague. By the time I got home, I'd barely have time to do my homework before I fell asleep. This cut out a lot of the friendships that other kids had.

I was able to stay friendly with Květa even when I became a tennis player. I'd visit her whenever I was home from my trips and we would talk and fool around the same as ever.

Every once in a while I still get a card from her. She's married now and has a baby. I think I'm the last one left from my class who doesn't have a baby. I hear that one of us has three babies from three different men and finally married the third one. Yes, that goes on in Czechoslovakia, too, even though abortions are possible there. When I was still at home, a couple of girls got pregnant when they were fifteen, which seemed a little early. I had just gotten my first period then and was two years away from my first adventure with a man.

When I hear about Květa and my other friends having babies, it makes me wonder what my life might have been if I hadn't become a tennis player. I'd still like to have a baby before I'm too old. People raise their eyebrows when I say that, but it's important to me. I'm not sure how marriage fits into the picture, but I'd definitely want to choose the right father. He would have to be bright and sensitive and a good athlete—and good-looking, of course.

One of the nicest men I know, and one of the best looking, too, is Wayne Gretzky, the greatest scorer in the history of hockey. Can you imagine the genes Wayne and I could put together?

Free to Compete

One thing I've noticed since I came to the States is that fans do not like female athletes to be outspoken and aggressive. A great competitor like Chris Evert is accepted because she doesn't make waves on the court, but another great competitor—anybody you can name—is criticized because she opens her mouth. I'm convinced a lot of it has to do with sexual stereotyping by the public and the press, whether the players fill the female roles expected of them.

Case in point: I've got a reputation for fairness with the other players. I cannot stand sloppy officiating, whether it helps me or hurts me. I knew the officials were doing their best, but sometimes I would drive them wild when I first came up by complaining when a point was mistakenly called in my favor. Sometimes I'd deliberately double-fault if I got a blatant call in my favor.

One time I tried to turn back a call in my favor. The courts were very dusty, so it was easy to see the ball was inbounds on my side. I just pointed with my racquet and said, "It was in." The next day the papers said: "Navratilova Blasts Officials." You can't win, so I learned to keep quiet about most calls.

I discovered that people were turned off because I had

opinions, because I showed my emotions on the court. Americans are not as comfortable with strong personalities as they think they are—particularly strong female ones. I'm not exactly John McEnroe or Jimmy Connors out there, and in fact I play my worst matches when I do smile and kid around and start feeling companionship with my opponent.

The outspoken part of me, the competitor, turns some people off. Yet this is a part that was greatly encouraged when I was growing up. I learned my tennis never feeling any sexual barriers—because of the support from those two confident men, George Parma and my father. They rarely put restrictions on me, rarely told me what I couldn't or shouldn't do. And my mother, who loves tennis and skiing and working and thinking for herself, never tried to make me adhere to any stereotypes of what a woman should or shouldn't do.

I don't think playing sports had anything to do with my feeling attracted to both men and women at different points in my life. I had a crush on George Parma before I ever had a crush on one of my female teachers—and it was basically the same feeling: that person knows so much, that person is so confident, that person is so nice, that person is so attractive.

My game was rushing the net, playing aggressively, playing for fun, playing to win. My father encouraged it and so did my coach, and the freedom and intensity they endorsed led me to a lot of other choices in my life. I grew up hearing my parents and my coach tell me: "Go for it." And that's exactly what I've done.

I've always been grateful that my father never tried to stop me from rushing the net. I'm not exactly making that tactic into a simile for life, but there are times when I've played my life just like a tennis game. I got that directly from my father. He just wanted me to enjoy the game, to develop my attacking instincts. He had no stereotyped ideas of how little girls should play tennis, thank God. Playing with my father, there were no psychological hindrances, no subtle pressure to "be a good little girl" and not run around so much.

He was great. He never questioned. He was always there. He spent a lot of time going with me to tournaments and lessons and hitting with me. He was relentless. He never wavered. I never had to beg him to practice. That kind of support makes a difference with a young athlete, particularly a tennis player. I couldn't have done it without him.

It seemed that everything turned out right for me to have a career in sports. I had parents and a coach who had no qualms about a young girl being an athlete. There is nothing in the Czech culture that would prohibit me from being the best I could. I didn't have to affect an overly feminine walk or style of dress. Czech women are used to using their bodies at work and at home, building up their muscles and strength.

It wasn't so much a "fitness" mentality about diet and exercise for health's sake as it was an innate sense that sport was good. We grew up seeing spectacles of hundreds of Czech women performing gymnastics in public exhibitions and later on television. We saw women working in the fields and in factories. Sure, there was a tradition of glamour and style from the old days, before the Communists took over, but most Czech women had less time and money for makeup and clothing and hair styles than Western women. Now in my late twenties, I'm just learning the right amount of makeup, eye shadow, the best shampoos and conditioning for my hair. That wasn't a matter of sexuality; it was a matter of culture.

In fact, after I slimmed down in 1982, I was used in a *Time* magazine cover story about the new concept of femininity—the idea being that today's women are in shape, not just shapely, that having muscles is all right. There I was, forearms and all, right next to Olivia Newton John.

Coming from a strong Czech family with lots of intelligent and athletic women, I was well prepared for the feminist movement that was going on in the West when I first started to travel in 1973. I liked what I heard about the Equal Rights Amendment: equal pay for equal work, equal opportunity for all. That sounded pretty American to me.

As an athlete coming West, I found myself in the right place at the right time. Billie Jean King and Rosie Casals and some others had made pretty strong stands to give the next generation of women tennis players a better break. The money was just starting to come in.

Billie Jean gets upset because she thinks the younger players are not putting enough back into tennis, that everybody is just taking the money and not trying to improve things. I guess she's right about that, but some of the younger players are more aware.

Her match with Bobby Riggs didn't prove very much— what was the big deal in Number 1 woman of the day beating a fifty-five-year-old man? In 1984, Vitas Gerulaitis sneered at women's tennis by saying that I couldn't beat the one-hundredth-ranked player on the men's tour. I came back and said that I would be competitive with some male players, but no woman player in her right mind would say she could beat the best male players on the tour.

All you have to do is watch me practice with my coach, Mike Estep, a pretty good tour player, to know that men and women were not created equal in terms of power and speed. But Billie Jean showed something else that was just as important: the competitive side of women. She went out there and tried to beat this wiseguy. She was a crusader fighting a battle for all of us. She was carrying the flag: it was all right to be a jock, a competitor, to be tough, to question the officials. Chris did it her way, I did it mine, but

Billie Jean did it first. Suddenly women were displaying a proud new competitiveness, and a lot of men appreciated that, too.

I look around now and I don't see the same pride, the same strength, in some of the kids coming along. They're not part of anything. It's almost more like a way of making money and becoming famous—they're entertainers as much as they are jocks—and I think something has been lost.

A few years ago it was considered good to be intense. Sometimes I would get too intense or too emotional, but never because I didn't care. Part of that came from the mood generated by Billie Jean and her generation but part of it came from my origins, from my father and George Parma expecting me to be competitive.

I've run into lots of hang-ups on that score. I was supposed to endorse a certain health product a few years ago, but the company executives got nervous after seeing Rita Mae on television hustling her latest novel and making a few comments about me, like: "Some relationships are a marathon and some are a sprint. Ours was more like a sprint." After that, it didn't matter to them that I was the best tennis player in the world at the moment. I had a label on me—and they were afraid that label would hurt the sale of their products.

I know these companies are not inventing this anxiety, either. There really is an image problem. My friends who are honest with me say they sit in the stands and hear people rooting against me because of my sexuality. One friend said he heard a woman rooting for Chris at the U.S. Open finals in 1983. She was shouting: "Come on, Chris, I want a real woman to win." That's too bad, because there are so many good reasons to cheer for Chris on her own merits.

My image definitely hurts me at times. It was no accident

that I was never on the cover of *Sports Illustrated* until I won the 1983 U.S. Open. I had already won everything else in tennis, but the corporate big shots would rather have a model in a bathing suit on the cover than the best woman tennis player in the world because they sell their magazine to men, and they think they know what sells.

Or take *Sports Illustrated*'s Sportswoman or Sportsman of the Year honor. In 1983 I won three of the four events in the Grand Slam, losing only one match all year, but they gave the top award to Mary Decker, the track star. Nothing against Mary Decker, a fantastic athlete who had a great season, but I thought they could have given it to me just as well.

I'm not necessarily arguing with their choice, but I am arguing with their style. In the feature article on Mary, they made a big point about how badly she needs to be protected and loved and supported, how she had gone through the breakup of her marriage and met this gentle man, Richard Slaney, whom she later married. It was all very tender and nice and it featured a picture of this big guy with his arms wrapped around little Mary.

But when Nancy Lieberman helped me during a low time in my life, there were a lot of snide remarks about the so-called Team Navratilova. It's fine for a great runner and a great competitor like Mary Decker to find a new source of support, but a great tennis player like Martina Navratilova is treated like a curiosity item because she has a support system.

The same magazine ran an article about me having a masseuse and a dog-walker and wanted to know whether I was Muhammad Ali or somebody, with a cast of followers. Nancy came right out and said, "Look, just because a friend of ours comes to the U.S. Open, stays at the house, and walks the dogs while we're at the stadium doesn't make her a dog-walker." The friend who walked my dogs is Pam Derderian, who does a lot of work for me, my foundation, and my retail stores.

Everybody made fun of Team Navratilova. Mike Lupica wrote in the New York *Daily News:* "I like Martina Navratilova but I don't like Team Navratilova." The funny thing was that Team Navratilova was far from a cohesive unit: Nancy and Renee Richards were never that comfortable with each other and were often in direct opposition. Some team.

People made jokes because Nancy, Renee, Robert Haas, my dietician, and a few other friends sat together in one row when I played. Meanwhile, in the next row, there would be Chris's mom and her sister, with John Lloyd almost always present, along with some of Chris's loyal friends, and sometimes Dennis Ralston, her coach. And that's fine. Chris deserves to have her friends and family out front rooting for her. So do I. But the way the public sees it, she has friends and I have Team Navratilova.

Born American

The cowboy-and-Indian movies were my first exposure to American culture, but I am convinced I was born with some American genes in me. Even as a little girl, I was entranced by the names I heard in school: Florida, California, Las

Vegas, Miami Beach, New York, Chicago, Empire State Building. Even when they were teaching us bad things about America, it still sounded pretty good to me.

We didn't see much of American culture until the mid-sixties, when I was ten years old. The music on the radio was mostly classical, with some waltz and polka music thrown in, and we also heard some famous pop singers at times. One girl in school had a Beatles album around 1965 or 1966, which she played over and over, but until then you hardly ever heard a song in English on the radio.

From the time I was little, I thought of America as a magical place. When my parents played a record of *The New World Symphony* by Dvořák, the brooding American folk hymns made me feel the space and freedom of the New World.

I was also fascinated by Australia, because that was the mecca of tennis, with champions like Margaret Court and Rod Laver; and by Japan—I wanted to visit Tokyo, a city of thirteen million people in those days—but mostly I was fascinated by America.

I was about thirteen the first time I met anybody who had been to America. There was a girl at one of the tournaments whose family had actually lived in Philadelphia and then moved back. I loved talking to her about Philadelphia, just saying the name and writing it. I could even spell it correctly. To me, at that time, to live in Philadelphia would have been the greatest thing in the world.

After that first Apache movie series, we started to get more American films. When I was in high school, on weekends I'd go to the movies in Revnice or the theaters off Wenceslas Square in Prague and I'd sit in the dark and gape at Fred Astaire and Ginger Rogers, Katharine Hepburn and Spencer Tracy. They were so cool, so well-dressed, so elegant, and most of them were so *decent*. They formed my impression of America, which did not exactly mesh with what the Communists were telling us in school or in the newspapers.

I'd go to the movies and see all those sleek limousines, those ornate Cadillacs, and I'd think: So that's America . . .

Along with the American movies, we started to hear American pop music—"Your Cheatin' Heart," done by Czech singers instead of Hank Williams—but later we began to get the real stuff from Radio Luxembourg. We'd try to pick up the hit songs on the radio, but the technology was so bad that we couldn't get a good sound. Still, by the late sixties, we had an idea of what American music was like.

But Hepburn and Tracy, Rogers and Astaire, Hank Williams and Ray Charles were hardly the image of America that the Communists tried to implant in us at school. The official word, straight from Moscow, was always the down side of things. You'd read that the American imperialists were taking advantage of the poor, that the rich got richer and the poor got poorer. You'd hear how everybody was living in poverty and blacks were not allowed in restaurants.

I remember in 1964 how happy we were when the Czech gymnasts beat out the Russians and American track star Bob Hayes won the gold medal at the Olympics. They had always told us how American blacks were so oppressed, how poor they were, and yet here was a black athlete, obviously in terrific shape, winning a gold medal for his country. That told me something about the Communist propaganda was not quite right.

The Czech skepticism quotient was already pretty high, after centuries of propaganda from outside rulers. My part of the country, Bohemia, was once, briefly, the center of Middle Europe under Karel I, our imported king, who became Charles IV of the Holy Roman Empire—and don't think we've forgotten it. My home town of Revnice is only a few kilometers from Karlstejn, the mountaintop castle of Karel I. I used to go there with my boyfriend in high school and dream about the glory days—back in the fourteenth century. Karel I founded Charles University right in the center of Prague and he is immortalized by statues and the beautiful Charles Bridge over the Moldau River in Prague. For me, growing up under Communists, Karel I was a reminder of what Bohemia used to be, what it could have been.

After that we fell under the thumb of the Hapsburgs, the Prussians, and later the Russians. On October 30, 1918, the nation of Czechoslovakia was formed from Bohemia, Moravia, and Slovakia, putting several different ethnic groups under the same national heading. The differences may not seem important to the outsider, but they were important within Czechoslovakia—and they had something to do with my own personality.

My friend Ted Tinling, the tennis designer, once said of me in *World Tennis* magazine: "She is the greatest serve-and-volleyer women's tennis has ever seen. She has fantastic concept, unbelievable imagination." Then he added: "She has that dramatic Slav temperament that requires the stimulus of a crisis. She's always going to have the storm; she's always going to underassess her opponent and underassess her own ability to handle it when the storm hits. I've always said she goes from arrogance to panic with nothing in between."

He was right about my moods—at the time. But was he right about my ethnic temperament? My mother, my real father, and my father all came from the Bohemian sector of Czechoslovakia, which makes me a Czech and a Slav but not a Slovak. The Slovaks came from the east. There were no Slovaks in my little town of Revnice when I was growing up. We studied the Czech language and in the eastern part of the country they studied Slovak. The languages are somewhat different, although if you understand one you can understand the other.

There was no prejudice. You'd meet Slovaks and wouldn't treat them any differently, but everybody knew they weren't Czech. You'd think of the Slovaks as being less sophisticated—farm people. The Slovaks have never really stood on their own in history, they always belonged to somebody else, whereas the Czechs, for a while, had their own country.

When the Russians staged their takeover in 1948, the Slovaks took over many of the major posts in the country. They were much closer to the Russians geographically, as well as in language and customs, and they were more willing to be dictated to. In Prague, in the western part of Czechoslovakia, people had strong memories of capitalism, still knew how to help themselves, still had a sense of pride.

My father worked as an economist in a factory. We took our vacation every year and went skiing. Some people would even go to the ocean and we'd say, "Gee, how did they afford that?" But my parents lived all right, and they showed me an example of independence by refusing to join the Communist party. They would have nothing to do with it.

I must have picked up some of my attitudes from them, but I was worse than anybody. I was so stubborn, so independent, that I was more American than Czech, even as a little kid.

It might have been a good idea if I could have followed the example of The Good Soldier Svejk, the best-known character in Czech literature. My father calls him "our leader."

Everybody knows *The Good Soldier Svejk and His Fortunes in the War,* written by Jaroslav Hasek, with illustrations by Joseph Lada. Svejk is this slovenly, dumpy soldier with a W. C. Fields nose and an innocent smile on his face.

He looks like an imbecile and acts like an imbecile, but he manages to survive in war and peace.

Somebody would give Svejk orders to move to the front, but he would later be discovered wandering in the countryside, stopping in every tavern and sleeping in every barn. They would be about to throw him in prison when he would give them one of his lopsided salutes and say, "Begging your pardon, sir," and then he would give this long explanation about how he was really trying to find the front, but it was dark out. Nobody could ever prove Svejk was lying or plotting, so he managed to stay out of jail.

After centuries of domination by the Hapsburgs or whoever else was coming through, Czechs and Slovaks learned to get along with authority. When the Russians came in after World War II, we learned to survive all over again.

When I was a kid in school, the teachers would use the phrase: "It needs quietness," which Svejk says all the time. During the centennial of Hasek's birth in 1983, I'm told that every bookstore in Prague had special editions of Svejk, and that the national television even had a series on him—all with the proper political slant, I bet.

There was also the proper political slant on everything they taught us about America. We would hear about exploitation in the United States, but then we would see one of those Hollywood movies and we would think it was the exact opposite. And then there were the memories of the period from 1918 to 1938, when Czechoslovakia was a free, Western democracy. Czechs and Slovaks never forgot the promise of the West. They loved the idea of America; they envied it, even if they didn't always understand it.

We'd get strange visions of America. One time my sister and I found a copy of *Playboy* in my father's closet. We don't have much pornography in Czechoslovakia, at least you don't see it around, but we weren't shocked by the magazine. I thought it was kind of silly, but to me it was a sign that Americans were free. They could read this kind of stuff. The socialist, puritan attitude never got through to me on any level. I'm against anything that's restrictive, people telling me what to do or what to think.

I couldn't have been a Good Soldier Svejk because I hate the idea of a sergeant who gets in your face because you're a private. I hate the power that people abuse. When I hear someone giving orders, the hairs on the back of my neck start to crawl. And we had plenty of authorities in Czechoslovakia when I was growing up, telling us what to think.

A lot of Czechs still believe that all white Americans are rich. Somebody told me about meeting a cabby in Prague who thought all Americans drove sports cars that cost over $100,000. The American passenger told the cabby about his own $6,000 Datsun, but the cabby looked at him as if he was crazy. He couldn't believe an American would drive an inexpensive Japanese car rather than some big gunboat from Detroit or a flashy sports car from Europe.

I know my mother and sister have a hard time accepting the fact that many Americans are poor. They saw the movie *Coal Miner's Daughter* and just couldn't believe that a country-music star like Loretta Lynn could actually have grown up in a tiny house in the mountains, wearing feed bags for dresses and going to a shabby little school.

I think my family likes to believe that all Americans are as wealthy as me, that America's wealth is unlimited. And meanwhile, the Communists are telling you that most Americans are exploited, which somehow doesn't explain all the supermarkets and amusement parks and car showrooms. The next time my family visits the States, they're going to take a drive through Appalachia and visit some of the tough parts of New York. I want them to get a full picture of my adopted country.

The Communists tried to limit our contacts with the

outside world when I was little, but the American movies would somehow slip in. I always loved listening to English in the movies that weren't dubbed. It seemed silly to see the lips moving one way and hear our Czech language coming out another way. Katharine Hepburn speaking Czech? Please.

German is really the second language of Czechoslovakia, going back to the Holy Roman Empire and the Hapsburgs and of course World War II. If you thought somebody was a foreigner, you'd address him in German first—"Nemetsky?"—and it's still that way. When the Russians came in at the end of the war, they taught Russian in school and the people would learn just enough to keep out of trouble. You ask somebody if she can speak Russian today and she'll probably say no. But she can understand it.

It was a shame the Russians got to Czechoslovakia just ahead of the Americans at the end of the war. They make such a big thing of it now: I'm told that in the old synagogues of Prague there are photographs of the Russians liberating the concentration camps. The Russians were able to take over the country in 1948, but they couldn't quite obliterate the impression that America was out there.

In America, there is so much diversity that you've got Uncle Sam and Paul Bunyan and Johnny Appleseed; Betsy Ross and Sergeant York and Jackie Robinson—legendary heroes, real heroes, northern heroes, southern heroes, white heroes, black heroes, and lots of heroines. In Czechoslovakia, we've got Svejk.

Every Czech and Slovak sees a little Svejk in him- or herself—but I had a very low dosage. I just couldn't be a Svejk. I would speak my mind in school, would speak my mind at home, would speak my mind on the tennis court. In a country where people played a clay-court style of life, just to survive, I was the serve-and-volley kid.

The Interrupted
Tournament

I have to laugh sometimes when people suggest that I am some superhuman and should be barred from playing the women's tour. Where were these people when I was the skinniest little player in Czechoslovakia, competing against girls a head taller than me?

As for my forearms, nature gave me part of them, but the other part I found in the gym one day, right next to the weight machine. It's amazing what you might find if you work out a little. Besides, there is no rule that says opponents have to be the same size or weight. I mean, tennis isn't boxing.

If it were, I would have been in a class of my own when I first started playing: pipsqueakweight. I was so much smaller than the other girls. We have pictures of me that show this scrawny little thing, all ears and feet, standing in the shadow of a well-proportioned young woman, my head barely up to her chest.

I remember one time the committee didn't want to let me play in the twelve-and-under tournament because I was only nine years old. I had to get medical permission from my doctor before I could enter. But I got permission and I played, wearing the same shorts and T-shirt I wore in physical education, and in the finals I beat a twelve-year-old who towered over me, 6–1, 6–4.

Nowadays I'm the Goliath, but in those days nobody was organizing any committees to make things more equitable for skinny little girls like Martina. You played who you had to play, and you learned to survive.

My parents made all kinds of sacrifices so I could play. We didn't take a summer vacation for five straight years, and they saved money all winter so I could travel. They never questioned my going to the tournaments. When I'd come home, my mother would have dinner waiting on the table, and she would sit and listen as my father and I chattered about tennis. Sometimes we'd start arguing and she'd get nervous and try to change the subject, but we didn't mean anything by it. He was good, though. He would never let me go to sleep without settling our differences, so there were no hard feelings the next day.

I played against my mother until the first time I beat her, 7–5. I'll never forget the score. I was using a new Dunlop Maxply and was so happy with it that I played better than ever. She wouldn't play me after that, but she devoted more of her time to making life easier for me and my father.

I was doing pretty well locally, so my father decided to enter me in some summer tournaments in other towns around the country. Like most families in Czechoslovakia, we had no car. To get to the tournaments, my father would put me on the back of his motorbike, a two-seater that went up to ninety kilometers per hour. He would drive me, ten, twenty, thirty kilometers, whatever it took. I loved whizzing along the roads in the open air, never even thinking about falling. When it rained, you just kept going.

I was entered in one tournament where I never expected to win a match. The way the system worked, you got no expenses unless you won your first match, so my father drove me over and we planned to go home that night. But I beat a girl a few years older than me, and had to play the next day. We had nothing to eat, so my father had to go home to get enough sausages and bread to last a few days. Another time my mother arrived at the town with a basket of goodies just when it looked as if my father and I were going to go out of business from hunger.

Gradually people began to notice me, and friendships began to spring up with important tennis people. During the Pilsen tournament in August, I used to stay at the home of Vera Hrdinova, my doubles partner, who is the niece of Vera Sukova, the 1962 Wimbledon finalist.

Vera was then the national women's coach and she was also the daughter of the Czech tennis star my grandmother had once beaten. Years later, I would cause Vera Sukova a lot of problems because of my defection while she was still the national coach. Until her death a few years ago, we would still greet each other and exchange small talk, but things could never be the same after my defection.

The Sukova-Navratilova connection is still going strong. Vera's daughter, Helena, used to work as a ball girl at some of my matches back in Czechoslovakia. She's not a ball girl anymore. In my last match of 1984, on December 6, she beat me in the semifinals at the Australian Open, 1–6, 6–3, 7–5, to keep me from winning all four Grand Slam tournaments in one calendar year, something I had never done.

Helena is a shy, six-foot-one player who is just starting to come out of her shell as she moves out of her teens. Whenever we play a match or say hello in the locker room, I have this feeling of three generations of tennis players, all intertwined. After she beat me in Australia, I congratulated her for being the better player that day. I wondered if she thought about all the things that have happened to our families and to Czechoslovakia over the years?

Now that I'm an American, I often hear other Americans talk about "the watershed year of 1968" and all the changes and tragedies in that year: Martin Luther King and Robert F. Kennedy killed, the controversy over Vietnam, President Johnson's decision not to run for reelection, the bloody Democratic convention in Chicago, the election of Nixon.

We had something of a watershed year in Czechoslovakia, too. We were invaded.

I was eleven years old in 1968, during the biggest political upheaval since the Russians took over in '48. People were seeking more freedom to run their own country, and in January, party leader Antonin Novotny was deposed and Alexander Dubček named in his place.

A month later, the whole nation sat in front of our television sets and watched our hockey team beat the Russians, 5–4, in the Winter Olympics at Grenoble, France. Afterward, people took to the streets despite the brutal February weather to celebrate. Everywhere you went, you would see the legend "5:4" chalked on the sidewalk or on a wall.

Some people said the game was a good omen for the year. They were convinced that under Novotny our national team would not have been allowed to beat the Russians, but under Dubček they'd been free to play to their limits.

My parents are not political people; they are more interested in tennis and work and the outdoors than in politics. But you would have to have been deaf, dumb, and blind to miss what was going on in Czechoslovakia in the spring of 1968.

The people were trying to recapture the old energy they used to have, before the war. You could hear them on the radio or read things in the newspaper: people asking questions, people asking "Why?" On June 27, a statement by Ludvik Vaculik, signed by seventy prominent people, was published in four newspapers: "The 2,000 Words." It called for positive, peaceful changes without ever mentioning revolution or speaking against the Russians, but *Pravda* attacked it and Dubček and other leaders were forced to criticize it or get in trouble with the Russians.

There was a petition going around supporting "The 2,000 Words." Whether my parents signed it or not, I don't know. A lot of people did get into trouble for signing it. Lawyers wound up shoveling manure; teachers were digging ditches; television announcers would be sweeping the streets. And still are—many of them.

Even for a schoolgirl taking the train into Prague once or twice a week, there was a feeling of excitement in the air. You couldn't miss it. People were holding mass open-air meetings in the town square, promising to work harder to help rebuild Czechoslovakia, wanting only some small incentive, some reward, some freedom.

To combat this mood, the Russians would sometimes proclaim a holiday and we'd have to attend a rally in Wenceslas Square in Prague. They'd sign us out of school, take us to a parade where they played the Czech national anthem and always the Russian one, too. Everywhere we'd look, we'd see our red-white-and-blue flag hanging next to their red flag. There would be banners and billboards all over the place proclaiming "Friendshp with the Soviet Union Forever"—emphasis on the forever.

When they'd take us to one of those rallies, we'd try to slip into the arcades, which run off at right angles from Wenceslas Square, to see what movies were playing or whether they had any Western-style clothes in the stores. If you couldn't escape, they'd put a banner in your hand and make you walk in the parade.

Sometimes you'd go out in the morning and all the red Russian banners would be turned around on the buildings, a modest protest. The newspapers would be full of propaganda, dredging up the past, how the Russians had come and liberated Czechoslovakia from the Nazis in 1945.

The propaganda is still the same today. Hana Mandlikova brought a Czech paper to the U.S. Open and I took a look at it. Such baloney. It made me glad all over again that I was out of there. That was the main reason I left. Forget the tennis: by 1975 I just couldn't have lived with the propaganda much longer.

In that glorious Prague spring of 1968, there was a lot of talk that the Russians would come in if Dubček and President Ludvig Svoboda and their government didn't crack down. We never believed it would come to that, and life went on pretty much as usual.

In August, my family let me go to Pilsen to play in a junior tournament and stay with Vera Hrdinova. Vera and I were a couple of typical little tomboys, running around in shorts with our cropped haircuts, staying up late, the way kids do on vacation, giggling and talking. On the night of Tuesday, August 20, we finally fell asleep. About six o'clock the next morning her father called from work and said, "Don't go outside. There are tanks out there."

He told us the Russians had entered Czechoslovakia the night before and were rolling across the countryside. Our government was cautioning people against doing anything rash, but tempers were pretty high. A big crowd was gathered outside the Radio Center in Prague because that was one of the country's major communication centers. Dubček was telling the people to give up, not to do anything.

I had a cousin who was in the army at the time and he later told me that a lot of the soldiers wanted to fight right then and there. Maybe if they could have made the first move, the Russians couldn't have moved in so easily. But we'll never know because the president gave the order not to resist them. Some people thought the Americans might back us up from the German border, but America had its own problems in Vietnam that year and was in no position to do anything. It was just as well: it would have been a bloodbath all around, with the Czechs caught in the middle, as usual.

I was such a kid that my first reaction was disappointment over the cancellation of the tournament. We stayed inside on a beautiful morning and played cards and fumed at the Russians for lousing up our tournament. We really couldn't see much because Vera's house was on a side street.

When her father came home from work, he took us to the tennis club and on the way we saw the tanks and soldiers. People were shouting slogans at them—"Russians get out, Russians go home," stuff like that—and the soldiers would pop their heads out of the tank turrets and wave machine guns around. Nobody was shooting but you had the feeling it could start at any minute. Later we learned that there had been some shooting in Prague and Bratislava and other places.

In Pilsen, where I was, whenever one of the Russians closed the tank turrets, somebody in the crowd would pick up a rock and throw it at the tank. It would bounce off the armor, accomplishing nothing, but it made a wonderful noise. After a while, a lot of us started tossing rocks and pebbles at the tanks. Clang. Clang. Big deal.

Later we found a better diversion. Wherever there was a street sign or an arrow pointing to the next town, we'd turn it around. We figured if the Russians were smart enough to find Pilsen, they could also get to Prague on their own.

Just to try to help them, people made some new signs that said: MOSCOW—1,500 KILOMETERS.

Most Czechs spoke some Russian, whether they would admit it or not, and people would yell things at the soldiers in their own language.

"Do you know where you are?" people would yell.

It turned out that some of the Russians didn't even know they were in Czechoslovakia. They thought they were still in East Germany, or Poland, or whatever. They didn't know why they were there, whether it was just a field exercise or the real thing.

In one place where there was a little shooting, a friend of mine asked a soldier: "Why are you here?"

"Because the commander says so."

"And why are you shooting at these people?"

"Because the commander says so."

"If it were your mother, would you shoot at her, too?"

"Yes, I would."

They were so brainwashed, they didn't care what they did. They were telling the world they represented all the nations in the Warsaw Pact, and they did use some Polish, East German, Hungarian, and Bulgarian soldiers, but ninety-nine percent of them were Russian.

My father drove out to Pilsen on his motorbike to take me home. Most of the vehicles on the road were tanks or trucks, and there were Russian soldiers out in the middle directing traffic. A few days before, the road had been smooth and open, but now it was badly dug up from the heavy military vehicles. It was a very uncomfortable ride, and dangerous.

The Russians were driving around like drugstore cowboys, tearing up our roads. One guy in a truck up ahead in the left lane signaled for a left turn but turned right. Thank God, my father was being cautious and didn't try to pass him, or it would have been all over. Most of those Russian kids really didn't know how to drive.

Once in a while they'd ask us a question in Russian and we'd shake our heads as if we didn't speak a word. Or they'd ask us where a town was and we'd just point in the opposite direction. What else could we do?

I got home and everybody was worried about what the Russians would do to us. We were fearing the worst, an occupation like the Germans' during World War II, but they didn't have to get that rough. Dubček was in enough trouble already, and he put out the word not to resist.

We'd get furious when we saw the Russians shopping in our country. They had so much money, we couldn't believe it. All the things they couldn't get in Russia they would buy in Czechoslovakia. Their army regulations said they had to wear brown gloves but the Soviets didn't manufacture brown gloves, so the soldiers were technically in violation of the dress code every time they went out; this made it easy for their officers to punish them and meet their quota for discipline. In Czechoslovakia, the soldiers loaded up on brown gloves.

It told us everything we needed to know about the state of things in the Soviet Union to see a soldier go into a shoe store and say, "I want twenty pairs of shoes." They didn't even care what size the shoes were. They'd put them in their tanks and take them home when it was over and sell them on the black market or give them to relatives. They had wads of hundred-crown bills. I guess they got paid extra for the dirty job they had to perform.

We were lucky. They never came into Revnice, but the town of Mlada Boleslav was filled with them. They came and they never left. Even now, if you walk through some towns, you'll still hear Russian spoken.

When I started school again in the fall, I'd go into Prague and see them on the street. They had their own cars, so they didn't travel much on the train. But they were there. When they first came, they sent 600,000 soldiers to control 25,000 "dangerous people," which comes to about 24 soldiers with machine guns and hand grenades for every unarmed "troublemaker."

For weeks afterward, you'd see all kinds of banners:

"Ivan, go home. Natasha has sexual problems."

"Socialism, yes; occupation, no."

"The Russian National Circus has arrived, complete with performing gorillas."

"What do you tell your mother about our dead?"

"This is not Vietnam."

"Home, dogs."

People would write "Ivan, go home" on tanks or draw swastikas. But we didn't really think the slogans would cause the Russians to go home humiliated and embarrassed. We didn't think they would go home at all. We were stuck with them. And life in my homeland would never be quite the same.

Response

I turned twelve in October, less than two months after the Russians came in. Our hopes had been built up so high— "socialism with a human face"—and now we were getting a boot in our face forever, as George Orwell once described the future. The invasion definitely colored my feelings about myself, my country, my future.

Over 120,000 people defected in the first year after the invasion—many of them "the best and the brightest" my country had to offer: writers, artists, business people, teachers, athletes. Most of them were not political in any sense of the word, just people who could see that their skills and aspirations would never be realized in their homeland.

One of them was my cousin, Martin, who had been planning to study in Canada that fall. With the Russians in Czechoslovakia, he couldn't get out legally, and he knew he could never acquire the specialized education he needed back home. So he left all his money with his parents, made his way across the border, and was helped by some friendly Austrian people in reaching Canada. Today he has a good job with a major chemical company and he has a family that I love to see whenever I'm in Canada. His parents have been out to visit him, but he's never been back to Czechoslovakia.

People like Martin have made their contributions in Canada, Australia, England, all over Europe, Israel, the United States. Sometimes it makes me sad to think what they could have done for Czechoslovakia if they had stayed. But under the system, what could they have accomplished?

The invasion cost me a coach, too. Shortly before the invasion George Parma had gone to Graz, Austria, to work in a resort hotel for the summer. The normal system in the Communist countries is to not allow entire families out together, turning husbands and wives into hostages; but under the Dubček regime, those laws had been relaxed, and for good reason. People were happy with Czechoslovakia in the spring of 1968; they saw some hope, some chance of freedom to work and speak and live the way they wanted.

There was no doubt that people like George Parma would have come back after working in Austria for the summer, so his wife and daughter were allowed to join him when school was out. They were all together in Austria when the Russians invaded Czechoslovakia, and the Parmas decided not to go back, even though they had relatives there. They just didn't want to return home to Russian soldiers.

I understood completely why my coach was not coming back. We sent him a vase that I won in a junior tournament, and he wrote back to my father, outlining lessons for me for the rest of the year. So my father became my coach, and for a long time after that he could get me to do anything simply by saying: "This is how George wants it." I would think of those blue eyes sparkling across the net from me, and work doubly hard.

George worked in Austria for a year and later moved to New York, and then to California. He and his wife have never been back to Czechoslovakia since then.

We who stayed behind had to take our pleasures where we found them. The first major event after the August invasion was the Mexico City Olympics, so we rooted for our people, and when we couldn't win, we rooted for the Americans. I'd watch Jimmy Hines on the television set and I'd cheer wildly. The Communists were always telling us how blacks weren't considered equal in the United States, and it was clear they were right. Jimmy Hines wasn't equal. He was better.

When the Olympics were over, we were plunged into a winter of discontent that continues to this day. Why stoop and pick up a rock or pull out a weed if it's not your farmland? People who've been back recently tell me the only land that looks any good are the private gardens in people's backyards.

After the invasion, if you wanted to tell a political joke, you had to check the room to see who was around. If somebody did a Brezhnev imitation at a party, he had to make sure his friends weren't taking pictures. People would make jokes about our own leaders like Gustav Husak, the first secretary of the Czech Communist party:

"Did you hear that Husak has the biggest car in the world?"

"No, tell me about it."

"The seat is in Prague, but the steering wheel is in Moscow."

What else could you do but make jokes? Except it wasn't funny to be a teenager and walking past the National Museum at the top of Wenceslas Square and see the holes in the cement, left there by Russian mortar shells fired into the crowds during peaceful demonstrations in 1968.

My resentment toward the Russians made me a better tennis player. A year or two later, at the Letna Club in Prague, I was playing doubles against two Russian girls, and when my partner and I won the match, this blond Russian was so conceited, she just stuck out her hand and tapped mine. She wouldn't even shake, palm to palm, which was all right with me.

"You need a tank to beat me," I told her.

After the invasion, there was more pressure on everybody to join the Communist party. My parents would never join, but there was extra pressure on me because I was getting lessons in Prague. The officials would make the not-so-subtle suggestion that I owed the government something. They would say that if I didn't join the Communist Youth Party I would not be able to go to college, and there was always the threat that they could hurt my tennis career, too.

One government big shot loved tennis and was always pushing me to join the party and go to meetings. I ended up going to one when I was about sixteen or seventeen. They had a Russian gymnast and Olympic medalist there, but she looked so uncomfortable that I felt sorry for her. I kept wondering what it was like for her to have to stand around at this meeting. It was clear to all of us that she wasn't free to just work at her specialty—she had to promote the party line. We were supposed to be at this convention for three days, but I only stayed an hour. I wasn't very good at that sort of thing and I never could be.

Could they have kept me from playing tennis or getting an education? I believe so. They tried stuff with other people I knew, and the way they later handled my tennis career made it clear that politics was more important than results and ability to them.

We all began to realize that the rules had changed in Czechoslovakia after 1968. We had always been hardworking people, trying to survive under one foreign rule or another, operating within the law, or getting around it good-naturedly like our Good Soldier Svejk, but after the invasion people really had to hustle to survive. They became even better at converting money on the black market, paying 25 or even 30 crowns for an American dollar rather than the "official" rate, which was one-third of that. They learned to save their energy for odd jobs after work that would earn them extra money rather than waste energy on the pointless tasks at work.

By 1969 about half the Russian soldiers had left Czechoslovakia. The remainder were not as visible, but you knew they were there. Besides, they had frightened the Czechoslovakian government so much that the leaders could be trusted to clamp down on their own people.

The Czechs and Slovaks learned to swallow their feelings after 1968. We became a depressed society. You could see the difference: people just weren't optimistic about the future. It was all pretty gloomy, and from what I hear, it still is. There's nothing to laugh about, everybody looks very stern, even at entertainments like the opera or the ballet in beautiful Smetana Theatre. They're going through the motions, sitting in that gilded hall in their best suits and gowns, listening to a baritone from the Ukraine or their own opera company, watching a dancer from Soviet Georgia. But there's little joy.

There are plenty of Russians whom I like, but I still get a tense feeling when I see the politicians. I don't care where I am, in a hotel in Japan or an office building in New York, I can spot a Russian bureaucrat. The hairs on the nape of my neck will stand up. How do I know they're Russians?

Their bowl haircuts, their dark, demure suits, just like a uniform.

When I was twelve and thirteen, I saw my country lose its verve, lose its productivity, lose its soul. For someone with a skill, a career, an aspiration, there was only one thing to do: get out.

First Visit Out

In 1969 I got to leave Czechoslovakia for the first time. It wasn't for America or Japan or Australia, the three countries I had always dreamed about, but it was for West Germany, and that was pretty exotic, too. My club in Prague, Slavie V.S., had an exchange program with clubs from Krefeld, Duisburg, and Düsseldorf, and we were to play a series against their best players.

It wasn't my first big trip. I was doing pretty well against older players and I had been invited to tournaments all over Czechoslovakia. When I was ten, I had taken my first airplane ride to Karlovy Vary, in an old Tupolev-14, a Soviet two-propellor plane that sounds as if it's going down at any moment. I had been so excited at flying because I thought I'd see the clouds, but there were no clouds that day.

Although the trip to West Germany would be made by train, not by plane, it was still a big deal, and my father and

I wasted no time accepting. Not that many people could get out of Czechoslovakia for any reason in 1969 because of all the people who had defected after the August invasion.

It was very expensive and it was hard to get a visa, and the government had to be pretty sure you weren't going to defect. But with my mother and sister back home, they figured my father and I would come back, and they were right.

The kids in school were impressed when word got out that I was going to West Germany. Most of them had never been outside the country, and those who had had been to Bulgaria, Yugoslavia, Poland, where you were still under Communist rule. The big thing was to go to the ocean. Anybody who had been to Western Europe and seen the Atlantic Ocean or the Mediterranean would be the big cheese.

West Germany wasn't very far away. The trains that went through Revnice went through Pilsen and crossed the border into Nuremberg. You'd sit at the station and watch the train rolling west and see well-dressed businessmen from West Germany sitting in the cars with the visas that took them out.

With the support of the Czech tennis federation, we got our two visas and took the express train from Prague to Frankfurt. Since the train went back through my home town, my mother waited at the Revnice station to wave good-bye once again as we barreled through at ninety kilometers per hour.

I'll never forget how the pretty Czech countryside turned bleak and frightening, just barracks and barbed wire and patrol cars, near the border. We stopped at a cold, nasty-looking station, with nobody around except soldiers. Everything was eerie, quiet. Everybody was tense. Even the Westerners stopped cracking jokes and nervously fingered their precious passports. You started to wonder who everybody was in the car. Was this a normal stop or did they suspect something?

Outside, soldiers with machine guns at their hips walked back and forth, looking under the carriage of the train, in case somebody was trying to sneak out. Then the customs inspectors came through the cars, examining everything, even my racquet covers, to make sure no one was smuggling anybody or anything out. They asked us questions: Where are you going? How long? Why? How much money do you have? Fortunately, our papers were totally in order, so they didn't give us any trouble. But you could feel the fear in the car. Smell it, really. I'm sure some people in that car were afraid because they had something to hide. Outside, you'd see some poor guy being taken off the train and escorted into the waiting room because his papers were not in order.

Then we started up again and crossed the barbed wire and barracks into West Germany. You could see the difference in a minute: the neat houses, the cars, the supermarkets, the way people were dressed. The farmland was so lush and beautiful, you realized people were taking care of it. It was that way all the way into Frankfurt.

I stayed at somebody's home for the tournament and would wander around the house looking at what they had. They weren't rich, but they had a television, electric gadgets, a car. I couldn't help noticing how healthy these people looked; their skin was pink, not white like the Czechs'. To me, even at thirteen, it looked as if they ate better.

Another thing I noticed right away was that everybody washed their hair regularly. We were always taught in Czechoslovakia to wash our hair once a week, that it would ruin your hair if you did it more often, make you bald. But the West Germans seemed to wash their hair every day and they looked sleek and clean.

One warm afternoon at the tennis matches I had a culture

shock. I was sitting in the stands on a bench next to a German couple. The woman was wearing a sleeveless dress and she had her arm around her husband or boyfriend—and I noticed that she had no hair whatsoever under her arm!

I was very aware of this because at thirteen I had no hair on my body except on my head. I was very slow in reaching puberty, had no breasts, and didn't until I was fourteen or fifteen, and naturally I wondered if there was something wrong with me. In Czechoslovakia, the women all have hair under their arms, and I was so embarrassed that when we were swimming in the river I'd keep my arms down.

When I noticed this grown-up woman at the tennis matches with no hair under her arms, I felt a lot better about myself. But then I realized she had shaved her arms and legs, like a lot of the women you'd see in the Western magazines that were slipped into my country.

I was too young to think about shaving myself in those days, but as soon as there was anything to shave, I started doing it. My mother had a fit, saying, "Now you'll have more hair growing." I could probably get away without doing it now because I have so little hair, but I shave my legs and underarms because I think it looks better.

When the junior tournament started, I was the youngest player in the Czech group and I was beating the West German women players like a drum. They ran pictures of me in the West German papers and acted surprised that I wasn't better known. I was getting more attention on an international level than I ever did back home. It wasn't anything political in Czechoslovakia; I was just a late bloomer, starting to hit my potential. I came home with real newspaper clippings, proud to be able to display them to my family and friends.

Another thing I brought back from West Germany was one of the world's major collections of felt-tip pens. You almost never saw a felt-tip pen in Czechoslovakia, but I wandered into a stationery store in this town and saw a whole rack of them. My father had given me a little spending money, and I spent a lot of it on pens, all different colors, for me and my sister and some of my friends. When I got back, I was the big cheese.

I had another form of culture shock on my first trip "outside." For the first time in person, I saw American blacks. In Czechoslovakia, once in a while you might see somebody from Africa, but you wouldn't see any blacks from the States.

We were staying near an American base. No matter how much propaganda you heard about the American presence in West Germany, you really didn't believe it until you saw it. You'd drive along the Autobahn and it would seem like you were in Ohio or New Jersey or someplace, all these guys in their big American cars, twice as big as the little boxes we drive in Czechoslovakia. Of course, there were also Mercedes and BMWs and Porsches zooming by at 150 kilometers per hour.

It seemed that half the American soldiers in West Germany were black or Hispanic. We had always heard that Americans made all blacks live in the ghetto, that they couldn't have any social standing, but you'd see the blacks driving the same kind of cars as the white guys, with the same rank on their uniform, and you'd realize they didn't look at all like second-class citizens. Now that I'm an American, I understand more about prejudice in the United States, but even so, it's nothing like what they told us back home.

As an athlete, I was aware that a lot of the black soldiers carried themselves like athletes. I'd see them shooting baskets at an outdoor court or something and I'd be in awe. I still am, actually. It wouldn't surprise me if the next great female tennis player was a black woman who started her tennis lessons at nine and ten, like me.

That first trip out made me ask questions about prejudice. Growing up in Czechoslovakia in the sixties, I didn't know any Jews. The Nazis had killed many of them during the war, and the survivors went to the United States or Israel. We just weren't conscious of Jews when I was growing up. Now the government has fixed up the old Jewish ghetto in Prague as a national museum, with six old synagogues and cemeteries giving a feel of what Jewish life was like before the war. I haven't seen the ghetto, because I left before they fixed it up, but I know where it is, right off the Charles Bridge. Part of the reason they fixed it was to play up the Russians' liberation of the concentration camps at the end of the war.

When I began traveling to the West, I wouldn't know somebody was Jewish unless someone else told me, and then I'd say, "Really?" To me, you couldn't tell. Now, after living in the States for a decade, I feel as if I'm part Jewish, particularly after having a Jewish mother like Nancy's mother Renee Lieberman teach me to say "kvetch" and "oy vay." And I eat bagels as if they were my national food.

The stories they feed you in Czechoslovakia stay with you. When my parents visited me in the United States, they noticed a few black players at the tennis club and said: "What are they doing here?" I said, "What do you mean? They're members." My parents had trouble believing that not everything is total segregation in the States. It was engrained in them.

My first trip out confirmed my suspicions that the West had a style and a freedom that communism couldn't match.

Junior

Those matches in West Germany served a small notice to the Czech tennis officials that I had some potential on the international junior circuit. I was still an underdeveloped thirteen-year-old, but I had brought home some medals and some publicity for the Czech program and so I began to get more time on the courts, particularly indoors.

When I was fifteen, I was invited by the federation to play at the Sparta club in Prague, one of the most famous sports clubs in Czechoslovakia, with roots going back to 1893. Now Sparta has facilities for many sports; it's as if the New York Yankees, the West Side Tennis Club, the New York Athletic Club, and Madison Square Garden were all part of the same state organization.

Sparta's soccer team is one of the most powerful in Czechoslovakia. The stadium is one of the few places where you can see any signs of emotion from the young people anymore. They hustle up a standing-room ticket for about 30 crowns—$3 on the official scale—and get there two hours before the game, standing close together, drinking beer, and eating thick, spicy sausages. When Sparta scores, the roar is like a decade of emotion that has been waiting to erupt.

Tennis has been popular in Czechoslovakia since my mother's mother was young. We had a Wimbledon champion, Jaroslav Drobny, in 1954, but after he settled in London, they seemed to downgrade the program somewhat. When things calmed down a little after 1968, the Communists were very conscious of building a good athletic program.

To be able to use the Sparta facilities, I had to rearrange my school schedule. The first year I went to school in Radotin, about halfway between Revnice and Prague. I'd take the 7:15 train in the morning, get to school in Radotin at 7:45, then run for the 2:00 p.m. train to Prague.

When I got off the train at Smichov, I'd catch the tram to Mala Strana, change to another tram, and then walk two miles up the hill to Stromovka, a big park sandwiched between the bends of the Moldau. Stromovka means "lots of trees," and it was a nice setting for tennis in the good weather. I'd practice from 3:00 to 5:00, then hustle to catch the 6:15 train, the quick one, back to Revnice. If I missed that, I'd take the 6:40 local back. I'd be carrying all my gear and my books, too, same as always. I had no lockers either at school or at the tennis court, and there was homework every night.

I'd eat on the run and do all my studying at night. I couldn't study in the morning. I was hopeless in the morning then and I'm still hopeless in the morning today. I once heard that you remember what you learn at night. I don't know if that's true or not, but that's what I would tell myself when I'd prop my head on my two hands and hit the books until 10:30. I never saw midnight when I was in school.

To tell the truth, I liked being at Sparta more than I liked being at school. I felt part of something at Sparta, more than I ever did at school, because we were a real team. Most of the time when you get on the court, tennis is an individual game, just you and your opponent, with a crowd watching.

I always liked the team sports, passing the puck to some-body in a hockey game on a pond, kicking the ball to somebody in a soccer game in a playground. I liked the camaraderie of the clubhouse, the encouragement from the bench, talking over a game on the way home. I'm sorry I didn't have more time for team sports, but I was funneled into the tennis program and knew I had to concentrate on that if I wanted to get anywhere.

Sparta was a family of cocky, hardworking kids, all of us thinking we'd be Number 1 someday, particularly Renata Tomanova, my closest friend for a long time. When we weren't practicing, we'd hang around the clubhouse playing chess and cards, just talking and having fun. There's a level of jock humor that just doesn't work anywhere else I've ever been. You can nudge somebody with an elbow or call them some vicious name and it's funny, within the clubhouse.

In the last few years, some fans and writers have made fun of me because a few of my friends and advisors sit together and cheer for me during a match. The old Team Navratilova smear. But I got used to companionship when I was thirteen and fourteen years old, having teammates at Sparta, having some responsibility to my club. You weren't just out there for yourself—and that was fun.

I don't think any athlete can have a greater thrill than to stand on the court and see her national flag or club banner flying in the breeze. I'm one of the few athletes who's ever been privileged to play in the Federation Cup for two differ-ent nations, when I was a Czech citizen and when I became an American. I was proud to represent my first country and then my second one, and I also loved being a teammate of Chris and Pam and the others for a few days in the Wight-man Cup and Andrea Leand in the Federation Cup.

I also loved playing in World Team Tennis, hanging around guys like Mike Estep and the Australians, Tony Roche and Roy Emerson, knowing my match influenced the team outcome. And one of the reasons I continue to play doubles is that I love teaming up with my raised-eyebrows comedienne partner, Miss Pamela Howard Shriver from Lutherville, Maryland.

You notice we wear the same red shirts and white skirts and talk to each other a lot on the court. If she's playing really well, I even share my lunch with her at the change-over. My doubles game is as important to me as my singles game. It's not just Navratilova then; it's Navratilova and Shriver. She's carried me sometimes, I've carried her sometimes, but mainly we're a team. My feeling for teamwork goes straight back to those days at Sparta.

We had some really good players at Sparta. One guy, a year older than I, named Ivan Jankovsky, was winning the international twelves when he was eleven, the fourteens when he was thirteen, and so on. That had never been done before, people said. He was so talented, with great strokes, and he even beat Borg when they were both fourteen. But he got too big—his head swelled up—and the highest ranking he ever got as an adult was about Number 4 nationally.

Renata Tomanova was ahead of me on the women's side. She was nearly two years older, and if they had a blurb in the papers, they would mention Renata first. Sometimes I would be a little upset that I wasn't being recognized more, but I knew my serve-and-volley style was better suited for international play than that of most other Czech women, that I was a more talented athlete, and that my game was going to take longer to develop.

I still insisted on rushing the net, and some of those players were good enough to get the ball past me, but I felt it was just a matter of time. I was still skinny, but usually I felt that when I started to grow and got more steam on the ball, I would be ahead of them. Other times I despaired of ever growing up, but my father kept telling people I would win Wimbledon someday and that kept me going.

At Sparta, we would often play matches against other clubs. You'd have as many as seventeen matches in a two-day meet, singles and doubles. In mixed doubles I would sometimes be matched with Jan Kodes, the best male player in Czechoslovakia since Drobny, and an economist with a degree from the University of Prague.

Kodes won the French singles titles in 1970 and 1971. His serve came in sections, like a machine cranking up slowly, or a baseball pitcher with a few hitches in his delivery. Jimmy Connors used to mimic it when they were playing each other. Sometimes during a doubles match, I would turn around to get a better view of this world-level player with the unorthodox serve, but then I'd remember to concentrate on business.

Very often the meet would go right down to the mixed doubles. Jan tells people that I was "big time" from the first day he saw me, but don't believe it. I was a raw player, and scared to death of letting down the great Kodes. Yet he trusted me to take my share of shots at the net, and then we'd walk off the court together and be greeted by our teammates and club officials. I'll never forget that Jan Kodes treated me with respect when I was a little kid—and how later he went to bat for me when I had problems with the Czech tennis federation.

I went back to West Germany in 1970 and the next year I played a senior tournament in Bulgaria and junior tournaments in West Germany and then Hungary, all over the Eastern European circuit. When I was fifteen, I made my first trip to the Soviet Union, where I played an exotic-looking Rumanian named Virginia Ruzici on a sandy clay court at Sochi, on the Black Sea. Actually, the court was more sand than clay.

The interesting part of that trip was having to stay overnight in Moscow, in order to change planes. My group took a walk around Red Square, saw the famous Kremlin, and visited the Gum Store, their big department store. I was so amazed at how little they had in their shops. Things were worse there than in Czechoslovakia. Outside the store there were women in little two-by-four stands, selling scarves and socks, with pigeons flying right overhead.

It was fun seeing the different countries in the Soviet bloc. One time Renata Tomanova and I and another player drove to a tournament in Poland. The main highways were broad and well kept, with hardly any traffic on them.

I competed in Bulgaria, Hungary, Poland, and East Germany, and attended a camp in Yugoslavia one summer. The only Eastern country I never visited was Rumania. I felt a common bond in all these countries because we all spoke Russian, so you could communicate with people. I didn't feel any togetherness with the East Germans, but I always had a special feeling for the Hungarians because they had been invaded in 1956.

There was a certain sense of solidarity between all the satellite countries, but I also had a feeling that we Czechs were our own people. We had such a rich history that I always felt separate from people of other nations, even Slovaks.

By 1972, the summer just before I turned sixteen, I had received far more acclaim outside my country than within it. Maybe nobody really felt appreciated under the system. We had fun at Sparta, but there was not enough fun for praise or rewards to go around. You'd do your job and they'd pat you on the back, but you knew you were just another wing of the state program.

I still felt pretty much like an underdog when I went to play in the 1972 Czech national championships at Ostrava, near the Polish border. They paid your expenses only if you got through the first round, so it was pretty much of a gamble for an unseeded player like me. The program said Renata Tomanova and I might both make waves in the tournament, and we did, getting to the semifinals, where I beat her. That set up my meeting with Vlasta Vopickova, the married sister of Jan Kodes, who had been ranked Number 1 in the country for years.

I had a real bad cold all week and probably should have defaulted earlier, but I kept playing and got to the finals. By the time I faced Vlasta, I was as sick as a dog, with a bad case of the flu, and it never got any better all day. I kept drinking hot tea during the match, just hoping to survive. To make things worse, I scraped my right knee during the match, bending down for a low shot on my backhand side.

For all that, I got ahead of her right away and stayed there. I was really trying hard, and I remember thinking to myself how hard I could actually play when I had to. I'd never had to play this hard before, but I found myself getting to balls I never imagined I could reach, hitting the returns harder, spotting my serves. I was really hustling and playing up to my potential, and I never even noticed that I was sick or had a scraped knee. I thought to myself: You have a chance to make something of this, and I beat her, 7–5, 6–4.

Afterward, I took the train home, went to bed, and let my mother feed me chicken soup. (What did you think Czech mothers feed sick children? It's universal.) The next morning, my family went out and bought all the papers. The reporters began to call me a "promising junior" and to talk about all the potential I had. News of my championship was on the first page of the sports section, and it even made the last page of the regular news section.

That victory over Vlasta was one of the biggest in my career. It raised my national ranking to Number 2, along with Marie Pinterova and right behind Renata Neumannova, which meant I was good enough to play on the international circuit.

In 1973, while I was sixteen, I went to England for the first time to play an indoor tournament at Torquay, near Eastbourne. The matches were played on a wood surface in a hotel, and I served and volleyed my way through the whole thing and won it. The British made a big fuss over me, and Dan Maskell, the great BBC TV commentator, predicted I was a future Wimbledon champion—just what my father had been saying for years. My English was pretty nonexistent at the time, but I knew a compliment when I heard one.

That was the same tournament where I met my first Americans—just a couple of typical boys-next-door named Peter Fleming and Vitas Gerulaitis. I remember looking at those guys, with their sharp clothes and confident, almost arrogant manners, and thinking: Are all Americans like that?

States

"*I'm going to* America!"

The girl next to me pretended not to hear. Our teacher did not like talking in class.

"I said: I'm going to America!"

She smiled at me patronizingly, either to shut me up or because she didn't believe me. I almost didn't believe it myself. I was going to see Katharine Hepburn and Spencer Tracy walking down Fifth Avenue, Ginger Rogers and Fred Astaire dancing down Collins Avenue.

I was also going to play tennis against Chris Evert and Evonne Goolagong. That was the most amazing part of all. After I had won the Czech championships in 1972 and the indoor tournament in England, the Czech federation had decided to let me and Marie Neumannova play the U.S. winter circuit early in 1973.

Marie was also going to be my chaperone. She was about ten years older than I, the only Czech player on the Virginia Slims tour allowed to handle her own expenses and travel by herself without any kind of bodyguard. I was thrilled not only to be going to the States but also to be going with somebody who was not "political," who was a regular on the tennis tour. For me, that was really the big time.

I was going to play eight tournaments in a row on the United States Tennis Association tour, first in Fort Lauderdale; then in Dallas; Hingham, Massachusetts; Akron, Ohio; New York; and back to Florida for three more. There were two tours in those days: the Virginia Slims tour with Billie Jean King and Rosie Casals and the USTA tour with Virginia Wade, Evonne Goolagong, Chris Evert, and Olga Morozova.

We took off in the dead of Prague winter, snow up to our knees, long nights and short days, and after a long day in the air through Frankfurt and New York, we arrived in sunny Miami, with real palm trees and oranges, to say nothing of cars and interstates, fast-food stands and motels. It looked like Florida to me. I was in America.

Marie Neumannova and I were given an apartment right at the club where we'd be playing in Fort Lauderdale. The man who owned the apartment was staying somewhere else, but every day he would take us for lunch at the club and would insist we have this chocolate-and-vanilla ice cream at the restaurant. You have to be polite when you're in somebody else's country, so I ate more ice cream than I'd ever consumed in my life: mounds of ice cream. Ice cream in the sky. Ice cream on the horizon. Ice cream in the freezer. Ice cream everywhere.

The man's apartment faced the courts, with your typical screened-in Florida porch, so you could watch the matches. Marie and I had some time to explore the New World, so we took a walk down the road and had our first experience with American capitalism: a 7-Eleven store. We bought some food and magazines for $5, which seemed like an amazingly small amount of money for so much. I remember buying a package of ham and sliced bread, and feeling I had made a big financial killing.

My English wasn't very good because I had only taken half a year in school, and I had a hard time translating the words and cost into English. Even so, I was impressed by the variety of magazines and newspapers and food and cosmetics items. Plus, people could afford them.

Walking back from the 7-Eleven, I spotted a coconut tree. I had eaten canned coconut before but I had never seen a whole one, much less one hanging from a low branch. What can I say? It was a challenge. I plucked it off the tree and carried it back to the apartment, wondering how I was going to open it. We rummaged through the apartment until we found a hammer and a screwdriver, and I went out on the cement patio and whacked away. I was lucky I didn't ruin my hands for tennis, but I finally managed to gash open the coconut and eat a few pieces. After all that, they tasted like the screwdriver.

I had my first hamburger from the grill at the club. After that, they gave us tickets for food, and I'd go back for seconds and thirds. After sampling the American food, I went to work on the English language. My first conversation was with Michelle Gurdal, a player from Belgium, on the way to the courts. It went something like this:

Martina: "Did you play?"

Michelle: "Yes."

Martina: "Did you win?"

Michelle: "No."

Martina: "Oh, that's too bad."

I think I do pretty well in English now. I've gotten to the point where I think and dream in English, and enjoy using exotic English words. (One of my friends calls me the Joseph Conrad of tennis; other people suggest I should talk less.) But those first days in Fort Lauderdale, it was hard just trying to understand what people were saying. I couldn't understand why they were laughing.

My first impression of Americans was how friendly they were. In Europe—not just in Czechoslovakia, but in most of Europe—people don't expect to be your best friend right away. There's a little bit of space, until they get to know you. In the States, however, there's the feeling that they can call you by your first name and share secrets with you right away.

I still like that openness about Americans, but I see it a little differently now. They'll tell you about their lovers, about their breakups, about their problems, how they got pregnant two months ago and had to have an abortion. They'll tell you their life story, and I'm not used to that. But you can also be honest and be yourself with Americans, and that's a big plus. I always felt I could be me, the real Martina, from the first time I came to the States.

Let's face it, in the States anything goes, and not just in New York, either. Coming from Czechoslovakia, where people wear black and gray and *look* black and gray, I almost had to put on my sunglasses when I landed in Fort Lauderdale. People were wearing bright magentas and pinks and lavenders, all this polyester leisure clothing, some of it terrible, but people would wear it. People were expressing how they felt. And as far as I could see, they felt pretty good.

You think about the image of those "wild and crazy guys" on the old *Saturday Night Live* show, those two swinging Czech brothers wearing plaid slacks and Hawaiian shirts and going out looking for "foxes." To me, it was the other way around. I was Miss Conservative off the plane from Prague and here were all these Americans on vacation in Florida wearing Bermuda shorts like Jackson Pollock paintings, golf slacks the color of tomato soup, shirts like TV test patterns. Wild and crazy guys, all right—but from Nebraska and New York, not from Czechoslovakia.

The man who lent us the apartment owned a wig shop, and he gave me one of his $10 specials. I'd been in the States a couple of days and already I had a thick mop of wavy hair to put over my thin, straight hair, which was still brown in those days. I wore the wig to a party in Dallas during the next tournament and thought I looked sensational. Later I brought it back to Revnice and gave it to my mother, who still wears it on occasion.

My first exposure to the American tour was the qualifying round (known as "the quallies" to one and all), dozens of players competing just to get into the main event. I roared through the quallies, winning three matches, and then won my first round before losing to Linda Tuero, 6–3, 7–6, in the quarterfinals.

In Dallas I lost to Glynis Coles in the first round. Then we flew to Hingham, where I stayed with a family of Czechs who were not very well off by American standards but really wanted us to stay with them. I didn't like it in Massachusetts, perhaps because of the weather, which was as cold as Czechoslovakia but damper.

The climate didn't hurt my tennis, though. I won three

straight in the quallies before drawing Evonne Goolagong in the first round of the National Indoors. She was already at the peak of her game then, a lithe, beautiful athlete who had won Wimbledon in 1971 when she was only nineteen. It was all I could do not to stop and stare at her grace and agility, but I got my game together and gave her a match before losing, 6–4, 6–4—just one service break in each set —probably the best tennis I had ever played.

Right away there were signs that I was going to be better than anybody knew. I was only sixteen and nobody had ever heard of me, so when I was introduced at every tournament, the announcer would say, "Just sixteen years old, from Czechoslovakia . . ." I wasn't tiny anymore, and I played a big serve-and-volley game, and the fans liked me right away, so I felt at home.

It was just like being a kid, playing with George Parma back at Klamovka. I could run down a lot of balls that many players wouldn't go after. Even when I became over-weight at the end of the trip, I could still run down balls. My serve was good. Four weeks into the trip I pulled my stomach muscles and couldn't serve hard, but it was still pretty good. I had a great forehand and an awful backhand. Just by being aggressive, I could win my share of matches on the tour, right from the start. I really didn't know how to play then, but just went out there with fearless abandon.

From playing with Jan Kodes at Sparta, I had learned to love the game of doubles. Marie Neumannova and I beat Evonne Goolagong and Janet Young at Sarasota, Florida, and then we beat Sharon Walsh and Patti Hogan in the finals.

Because of my big game, I came to like the hard American courts, but one of my best early matches was on clay in St. Petersburg against Helga Masthoff, a pretty good player at the time. The temperature must have been ninety-five and the humidity about the same, and she had me, 6–1,

4–0, but I kept hanging in with her, and finally won the last two sets, 7–5, 7–5, in a match that took three and a half hours. That match told me something: I knew I could be in the top ten. I really could be one of the best, I told myself. I can beat these people.

I was learning on and off the court. One of the first things I noticed when I came to the States was how people were more openly religious than in Czechoslovakia. In one house where I stayed, the people said grace before dinner. I had never seen that done before and I thought they were kidding.

I'd had no religious training at all back home. My parents hadn't been interested and the government had been trying to downplay religion ever since the takeover in 1948. You'd see the statues on the Charles Bridge or visit the beautiful old cathedrals in Prague to enjoy the architecture, and you'd hear about the old traditions, but religion didn't stay as strong in my country as it did in Poland, for example.

I was raised a basic agnostic. I believe there's something out there, but I don't believe in the Adam and Eve theory. I was brought up on the Darwin theory of evolution; it just makes sense. I believe there are supernatural forces we don't understand, and sometimes I feel my grandmother is really close and I look forward to seeing her again, but I have a hard time believing in heaven and hell.

I couldn't help noticing how many Americans said grace before meals, prayed on television, carried Bibles with them. I had thought Americans were way ahead in science, so I was surprised to see religion so strong. Americans can build computers that put men on the moon but they still say their prayers every day, not just on Sunday. I still don't know if it's the romantic in Americans, the belief in religion.

Now that I live here, I hear so much about this born-again stuff. I was talking with a friend of mine and she was dancing around in robes, going to church four times a week.

I believe it's one thing to be religious and another thing to flaunt it in people's faces. School prayer—do it on your own time. In California, a Baptist school canceled a basketball game with a Catholic school. How ridiculous can you get!

To me, religion is fine in moderation. But this "My God is better than your God" attitude really causes problems. Look at the way Protestants and Catholics used to go at each other in Czechoslovakia, and still do in Ireland. Look at Lebanon, Iran—these people go nuts. If God is such a great guy, why are these people killing each other? Now in the States, a few people are trying to legislate school prayer. It's one thing to have a moment of silence for those who want to pray. But to have an official prayer, out loud? This country was built on freedom of choice.

Sometimes people give me religious booklets, but I just give them back. You believe in what you want; I believe in what I want.

I was a skinny little kid when I left for the States. Ever since I was twelve, I had always eaten a lot and could eat more than my father without gaining an ounce. I was all muscle and bone, as skinny as a stick. Prut, my father called me—"Stick"—before changing it to Pluto.

Here in the New World, I soon discovered pizza, hamburgers, steak, french fries, pancakes, cereal. I'd see a fast-food restaurant and I couldn't resist sampling the wares. Big Macs. Whoppers. The International House of Pancakes. Howard Johnson's. Lum's. Wendy's. It's a stale joke now, but people used to say I was on a "see-food" diet. Any food I could see, I'd eat.

My metabolism just couldn't get all that meat organized, and it went straight to my waistline and jowls. Olga Morozova, the Russian player, came up to Hingham the third week of the tour. I knew her from the Communist tournament in Budapest the year before, a really nice person. She looked at me and didn't say a word, just puffed out her cheeks.

I thought, What's her problem? I thought I looked good. I was finally filling out: Martina gets a figure. I thought I looked more like a woman because I wasn't so muscular anymore. I felt more feminine. So I didn't take the hint and kept on Big Macking my way across America, right to Akron, where the new, curvaceous Martina was matched in the first round with a player only a couple of years older.

Her name was Christine Marie Evert.

Chris

Everybody was excited when Chris and I reached the finals of the 1983 U.S. Open. It seemed fitting that she should be the obstacle to the only major championship I hadn't yet won. All the reporters were working on stories about our rivalry over the years, and at the press conference the day before our match one of them asked if I remembered the first time I played Chris.

"Sure," I said. "It was 1973. Akron. First round. I lost, 7–6, 6–3. The tiebreaker was 5–4. At 4-all, I don't remember, but she probably passed me at the net. I was just excited to play her."

The reporters nodded as if I were some kind of genius,

being able to remember the score of a ten-year-old match. But I've always had a good memory, and besides, this is my business. Does a real-estate agent remember the first house he sold? Does a lawyer recall the first case she tried in front of a judge? To me, it's no big deal that I can remember the first time I ever played Chris Evert.

When I made my first visit to America in 1973, Chris was already one of the top players on the tour. She had come along as a fifteen-year-old in 1970, reached the semifinals at the U.S. Open in 1971, and been a semifinalist at Wimbledon and Forest Hills in 1972. By the time she turned eighteen, she was well known as America's Sweetheart or America's Ice Princess—take your pick—and she possessed a two-handed backhand that could cut your heart out without your feeling it, and a warm smile that said, "Nothing personal."

I knew all about Chris from the tennis magazines that my cousin, Martin, sent me from Canada. I could read English a little, and was trying to translate sports language with the help of a dictionary, which got a little comical at times. However, I got the point of the pictures and the numbers: Chris was like a perfect blond goddess who was stalking Billie Jean and Virginia and Evonne. Before I even met her, she stood for everything I admired in this country: poise, ability, sportsmanship, money, style.

I'll never forget the first time I saw her in Fort Lauderdale, playing backgammon with Frank Hammond, who was the tournament referee. Her sister, Jeanne, was there, too. I tried not to gawk as I walked by, and Chris just sort of nodded at me. When you're shy, the way I think I am, you don't want to say hello unless you feel comfortable. A few days later I saw her in the clubhouse again and this time she smiled, acknowledging me, so to speak, but also making me feel like a peon.

Nowadays we're matched like chocolate-or-vanilla, jazz-

or-classical, two champions with opposing styles and temperaments competing for limited space at the top of women's tennis history. We're still friends, but things get a little touchy on both sides when we talk about our accomplishments. Back then it was easy for us to be friends. She was nice to me right from the start, giving little nods and smiles to let me know she knew I was around. She does not miss a thing. Maybe she felt I was just another foil for her, a visitor from the Iron Curtain sampling all the junk food in America, and not any competition.

I was excited the first time Chris said hello. In fact, I was mesmerized. When I played her in the first round at Akron, I did pretty well, but she was more experienced, and she outlasted me. I wasn't ready for her or her reserves of strength. I saw she had some friends and family rooting for her and I felt totally alone, after the team togetherness I had felt with Sparta.

The truth of the matter is that Chris had a Team Evert long before I had any support system of my own. Her father, Jimmy, who was her first coach, and who reinforced her love for tennis, didn't go on the road very often, but her mother, Colette, was often there, and so was her sister, Jeanne, a tour player herself, and a number of their friends. Chris didn't know what it was like to be alone on the tour.

Mrs. Evert is the sweetest lady, who wouldn't say anything bad about anybody. From the first time I appeared on the tour, I got the feeling she honestly felt bad when I lost and happy when I won. When Chris beat me, Mrs. Evert would walk over and say, "Nice match, Martina." For a kid a long way from home, that meant a lot. She gave me the strength to keep going.

I'll never forget how Chris patted me on the back as we walked off the court after I finally won the U.S. Open in 1983, even though you know she had to be feeling terrible.

Later her mother came over and said she was happy for me. And I believed her.

You'll notice that I refer to Chris as "Chris," not as "Chris Evert" or "Evert." I noticed from my first week on the tour that the women tended to be on a first-name basis with each other. Sure, they were all out there to win and make money, but there was none of the hard feelings and impersonality that you get on the men's tour. It's funny, the way people always say women are the foxes, the ones who'll stab you in the back. In tennis, the men are so much worse. We women speak our minds, and we have our arguments, but there's none of the backstabbing you see with the men, nothing like the way Connors and Lendl and McEnroe go at each other.

The women are good at getting along. We spend much more time together than the men, and I guess that's part of it, but we also seem to have an instinct for nurturing within us. We want to get along with people, smooth things over. Sure, we're competitive, but we're subtle about it.

Chris has always been able to live up to her sweetheart image, knowing what to say and when to say it. I didn't know how to do that when I arrived, and I still don't. I say what I feel, whether it's revealing that I was suffering from toxoplasmosis at the 1982 U.S. Open or criticizing the amount of prize money at Wimbledon in 1983, which got me into hot water with everybody. It was as if I'd insulted God. I'd be better off keeping my mouth shut or saying something else, but I can't or won't. Chris can always make her point and have it come out right in print. It's a gift.

The Chris the public sees is not exactly the Chris we know in the dressing room. In public she always seems on an even keel, whether she's joking with the male reporters or smiling at the fans. In private, she's got a great sense of humor. She's fun, and she is not exactly what you'd call a prude. The public doesn't know that if you give her a glass of wine, she can tell a good story with the best of us.

Most of all, Chris is a great competitor. Looking back, I've had my share of matches that I feel I should have won from her but didn't, because she just took them away from me. I came close to her the second time we met, in the semifinals at St. Petersburg, Florida, later on that 1973 tour, but she beat me, 7–5, 6–3.

It took me two more years to beat her, on the sixth try, when I caught her, 3–6, 6–4, 7–6, in the quarterfinals in Washington. I just happen to remember it was 5–4 in the tiebreaker. I served and hit a forehand drop volley for the winner. Not that I meant to hit a drop volley. I was just shaking so much that I couldn't hit the ball any deeper than that. That night I was so pumped up about beating her that for the first time in my life I tried a sleeping pill to fall asleep. It didn't do a bit of good.

Later that year we met in the semifinals of the U.S. Open back at Forest Hills, played on clay. She beat me, 6–4, 6–4. I was out of shape, thirty pounds overweight, and Bud Collins of the Boston *Globe* was calling me "The Great Wide Hope."

In those early years, whenever I played Chris, I always felt I had to win in a hurry. If I won the first set, I would tell myself, You must win the second now. Get it over with because otherwise you'll be too tired by the third set. And you know what? I'd lose the second and third sets.

It was so frustrating to play Chris back then. I would use up so much energy going back, going back, all the time for those lobs of hers. I knew I could beat her if I could get to the ball and hold the net, but to do it, I had to keep getting back when she lobbed over me. And I'd be so tired by the third set.

At one point Chris had a 14–2 edge over me. I had so

much else on my mind that I really couldn't get my act together to challenge her.

People don't remember that we played doubles together for a while, winning Wimbledon in 1976. Chris and I still laugh about the first time I beat her in the finals of a match: 6–3, 6–4, in Houston in 1976. Right after that, we were playing doubles together against Rosie Casals and Françoise ("Frankie") Durr, and I could tell Chris was a little down about losing to me. After we went out there and lost the doubles, I wanted to do something to lighten the mood.

Frankie had a dog named Topspin who went everywhere with her—you know the French will even take a dog into a restaurant—and she had trained Topspin to carry her racquet in his mouth at the end of a match. So they beat us and Topspin did his usual excellent job of taking Frankie's racquet and marching off the court with her. I figured, Why not? so I grabbed Chris's racquet, put it in my teeth, and walked off the court behind her. It got a laugh out of her. Actually, she laughs a lot when we're just hanging around the locker room. She's far from the ice princess people make her out to be.

When I started to win some of the tournaments, Chris was great in defeat, too. The first time I won Wimbledon in 1978, beating her in the second and third sets, she came over and gave me a big hug. You couldn't have told who won the match, except my grin was a little bigger than hers. She was really nice. The next year when I won in straight sets, she was more disappointed, but that was understandable.

Playing doubles together got to be a problem once I became competitive with Chris in singles. First I stopped carrying her racquet in my teeth, and then we stopped playing as partners.

When my game fell apart in 1980, while I was involved

with Rita Mae Brown, Chris sent out some public messages that I needed to set my private life in order or I wouldn't be able to get back to the top. I don't think she was sending me the messages just because women's tennis needs all the competition it can get. I think she cared for me as a friend.

Nancy Lieberman used to tell me I was too friendly toward Chris. Nancy said that in basketball the intimidation begins when you walk into the arena: the way you carry yourself, the clothes you wear, the way you swagger onto the court. You watch how Bernard King of the New York Knicks puts on his "game face"—a ferocious scowl—before he ever gets on the court. Nancy worked hard on me to do the same thing.

I could see doing that on the court, but even the pro basketball players don't carry their aggression off the court. When they see each other in an airport lobby, they don't scowl at each other, from what I've seen. But Nancy wanted me to keep my "game face" on whenever I was around Chris.

The problem is, I'm very emotional. Everybody always knows exactly how I'm feeling: happy, sad, nervous, confident. You can see it from the upper deck. In tennis, there's no such thing as separate dressing rooms. You usually dress a few lockers away from your opponent, and I used to find it hard to concentrate when my friend and my opponent were one and the same. Even now, I have to make a point of not catching Pam Shriver's eye before we play each other in singles. She can arch those expressive eyebrows and get me smiling, and then I won't be totally concentrating on my match.

Chris was always friendly, even on the day of the match: *Nice day today. How are you feeling, Martina? Let's play a friendly game of tennis. Pitty-pat, pitty-pat. Oops, did I slash that cross-court backhand slightly out of your reach? Sorry about that.*

Suddenly I'd be down, 4–6, 1–3, and wondering what was going on.

Nancy changed that by bringing her basketball attitude to the tennis court. I remember in 1982 at Wimbledon, when the rain and the huge field of players made it hard to get a practice court, that Chris and I were assigned to practice together. We had no problem with that. We're friends and professionals who know how to hit the shots that the other person needs and maybe, once in a while, you stroke one into the corner and say, "Oh, excuse me," just to keep everybody awake.

At this practice, people were applauding behind the fence as if we were on Centre Court. They'd shout: "Nice shot, Chrissie." Nancy was not amused. She inspected her fingernails and watched the clouds to see if it was going to rain again. (It usually was.)

Pretty soon Chris called over to me: "What's wrong with Nancy? Doesn't she like the way I play?"

Later she drilled a shot near Nancy just to see if Nancy was paying attention. (Nancy was.) Nancy just looked up and said: "Oh, hi, Chris. I didn't see you."

Even Chris had to laugh at that.

Nancy had to know you don't psyche out Chris Evert with tactics like that, but she was trying to tell me that I could have been beating Chris more steadily. Between Nancy's mental and physical conditioning and the coaching I got from Renee Richards and Mike Estep, I was ready to beat Chris pretty regularly and start evening up the record between us.

I know it had to be bothering Chris, particularly in early 1984 when she separated from her husband, John Lloyd, for a while and had to deal with all the personal questions from reporters. It wasn't easy, even for Chris Evert, to deal with that, but she showed up on the 1984 tour in better physical shape than I had ever seen her. She had been working on weights and some of the other conditioning techniques I had been using, and she was strong.

In the 1984 Virginia Slims finals, Chris hit some amazing winners off my first serve and she stretched out my game in one of the hardest matches I have ever played, but I managed to beat her in three straight sets in the first best-of-five women's championship in years.

I shouldn't have been surprised that Chris could upgrade her game at the age of twenty-nine. She has been a great champion, an example to any athlete, male or female, for a long time, and I'll never take her for granted. The next time we met, I beat her on clay for the first time ever, 6–2, 6–0, making up for the 6–0, 6–0 beating she had given me three years earlier when my career was getting away from me. After it was over, Chris said "I'm sorry" to the fans and then congratulated me as warmly as ever.

And she was gracious after I beat her at Wimbledon in 1984. Although she played one of the best matches of her life, I managed to win, 7–6, 6–2, to break even in our personal rivalry—thirty victories apiece.

Even though Chris and I don't see each other as much as we used to, as I once told Roy Johnson of *The New York Times:* "I look forward to the day when we can share a bottle of wine and talk about the old days. . . ."

Even though we're the big rivals of our time, I'll never forget that when I first came around, insecure and lonely, Chris Evert was there to say hello.

The Great Wide Hope

I kept cutting my marathon eating swath through the New World in early 1973, and when it was time to go home I knew I had gained weight because I could no longer fit into my tennis clothes. But I was proud of my newfound femininity, and deep down I felt I was the same old Martina. I wasn't looking in too many mirrors, though.

My family has two pictures of me: before and after. In the first one, I'm standing with Marie Neumannova at the airport, ready to leave for the States, looking like everybody's favorite matchstick girl. The second photo, taken eight weeks later, contains me and the airplane. I'm the one on the left.

People have written that my parents didn't recognize me, but that wasn't exactly true. They could recognize me. They just couldn't recognize the other twenty-five pounds. Their mouths dropped open and they couldn't believe it.

I didn't go on any special diet when I got back. I just went home and ate regular meals and my weight dropped down for a while. It wasn't so much that we were into nouvelle cuisine; it was just that it's hard to overeat when food is so expensive, even for people who are comfortable, like my parents.

My weight fluctuated quite a bit after that. When I was home for a while I slimmed down. And when I went West, so did my figure. I never lost all of that initial weight, though, and I would eventually balloon to my heaviest of 167 pounds in 1976. People often write that I gained weight after I defected, eating out of loneliness, but that's not true. I just didn't know enough about a healthy diet in those days —before I discovered pasta and grains and chicken and salads and fruit and laid off the animal fats, sugar, and starches.

Things were different when I returned home. I had been out of the country for two months, on my own, doing what I wanted. Now I had to go back to school and get used to the lifestyle of a sixteen-year-old high-school student again. I had to ask my parents for permission to do anything, whether it was to go out for a while or to the movies. That was a shock, not being able to do what I wanted. It wasn't that I was a troublemaker; there was nothing serious; I just wasn't happy asking permission for everything I did, from my parents, from the tennis federation, from anybody.

My first big rebellion was smoking. Being away from my parents, I'd thought I was cool. My father and mother both were smokers, but they'd always advised me not to get hooked. My mom would quit lots of times, but then she'd get nervous about something and reach for a cigaret. So while I was traveling, I took up the weed.

When I got home, I used to go running on this gravel road under the railroad tracks by the river, and I'd take a cigaret with me. That was really pathetic: here I was, running to get in shape, then sneaking a cigaret and getting myself *out* of shape. I hated the way my mouth tasted, and I'd always be washing my mouth out. I'd go into the bathroom and smoke on the toilet and my mother couldn't smell it because she was smoking herself.

I gave it up before it could become a habit, and now I hate

it when people smoke in elevators or cars. For a while, I used to reach for a cigaret to calm myself down while playing backgammon with Rosie Casals or after losing a tennis match—both harrowing experiences—but since I don't lose that much these days, I've only had about three cigarets in the past four years.

Marijuana? I know what it smells like, but I don't buy it or need it or like it or endorse it. To me, alcohol is so much worse than grass because it's so much more pervasive. Alcohol is lethal. I liked what O. J. Simpson said when Howard Cosell asked him if he had seen drugs around pro football. O. J. said the drug he had seen abused most often was alcohol.

In addition to my Western tastes acquired during my first eight weeks on the tour, I also got a sense that I could be a pretty good tennis player. The federation must have agreed, because in May they let me play the French Open. I won my first two matches on the crushed red brick, and then alongside the blossoming chestnut trees at Roland Garros Stadium, I went out to play Nancy Richey, America's second toughest clay player, right behind Chris Evert.

I was thrilled just to see Nancy in person. I had watched her at home on television, playing at Wimbledon, and we used to make jokes about the little white cap she wore, because it was just like the cap my mother wore at her first wedding. I thought she looked old, but everybody looked old to me in those days, and I knew she was still a great player.

I didn't know anything about strategy then. I had no idea that clay was her best surface, but it was a hot day and like a sixteen-year-old, I just ran every ball down, kept retrieving, thinking I was going to get sick from the heat but never even considering what it must have been doing to Nancy. I was just playing my instinctive serve-and-volley game on every surface, including clay, and it was good enough to beat Nancy Richey, 6–3, 6–3.

I was thrilled enough to beat a great player like that, and I was thrilled again afterward when Margaret Court, the woman player I have patterned myself after most, walked into the locker room. I had never realized Margaret was so tall—and she was barefoot while I had on clogs with high heels. I tried not to gawk, but she said hello and I realized she knew who I was. I had beaten Nancy and she was acknowledging me.

That was the biggest win of my career, so far, and it put me into the quarters against Evonne Goolagong. I had played Evonne twice back in the States and felt confident against her. I gave her another hard match before losing, 7–6, 6–4.

Those two showings were enough to guarantee my being invited to the greatest tournament in the world, Wimbledon. I played at Hamburg and then headed for England to play in the Wimbledon tune-up at the Queens Club. But when we got there, Marie and I discovered we were not entered at Queens. We had sent our entry forms from Rome without realizing that the post office was on strike, and they never received them.

They couldn't straighten it out, so we stayed with a Czech family and just wound up practicing at Queens every day. I remember watching Billie Jean and Rosie drive up in a car. Marie spoke to them in English, and I was really impressed. I knew all about the big players from the tennis magazines my cousin used to send me: Julie Heldman, Pam Teeguarden, Pam Austin, Mona Schallau Guerrant. Plus, I knew everybody on the USTA circuit: Chris, Virginia, Evonne.

Billie Jean and Rosie didn't give me a second look. I didn't want to be in the way. I just stood over at the side and thought, This is the big time.

I didn't get to play at Queens but I was entered at Wimbledon, the tournament I had dreamed about back in Czechoslovakia. To this day, when my parents talk about my career, it is not winning the U.S. Open or being the big cheese on the women's tour, or all the money, or Australia or France. Everything is Wimbledon. Growing up on those red-clay courts of Czechoslovakia, you dreamed about playing on the grass at Wimbledon, and I don't mind admitting that the first time I got there, I knelt down and touched the grass.

Before my first match at Wimbledon, I went out and got measured for a Fred Perry tennis dress. I thought I should look traditional. Don't ask me why. I was used to playing in either shorts or a skirt, and I was not at all comfortable in the dress. I had to keep remembering not to bend down the wrong way, and every time I reached for a ball, the skirt would catch on my bra and I'd have to pull it down again. I was a wreck anyway, just being at Wimbledon, and the dress made it worse.

Even with the distraction of the dress, I beat Christine Truman, 6–1, 6–4, in the first round on Court 1 and then I switched to a more comfortable skirt to eliminate Laura DuPont, 8–6, 6–4, before losing to Patti Hogan.

My biggest thrill of the tournament was watching Jan Kodes, my old teammate from Sparta and now the Davis Cup captain of Czechoslovakia, work his way through the men's tournament. He was helped a little when many of the top men stayed out that year because of a financial disagreement, but he was in the prime of his career and he would have had a good tournament any way you look at it.

Jan is a terrific guy, and I don't think anybody was happier than I was when he beat Alex Metreveli, 6–1, 9–8, 6–3, in the finals. All of Czechoslovakia was happy about Jan's victory, particularly because Metreveli is from the Soviet Union.

I also got to play mixed doubles with Jan, and we met Owen Davidson and Billie Jean in the round of sixteen on Court 2. I played terribly, I was so nervous, going for all these great shots, trying to impress Billie Jean, hoping she'd remember me. We lost, and they won the championship.

After winning a Czech tournament in Pilsen, I got back to North America later that summer, playing at Toronto, Forest Hills (the U.S. Open), and Charlotte, North Carolina.

I wasn't getting paid like a professional, but I was getting a professional's education. I was learning how to deal with the grind of the tour, week after week, through time changes, weather changes, mood changes, injuries and pain.

For me, the worst pain of all was hunger. I have never been able to function on an empty stomach, even when I'm in the middle of a big match. Ever since I started playing, I have needed nourishment right then and there. When I first came on the tour, I would arrange to have such healthy items as hot dogs and roast beef sandwiches with mayonnaise and mustard available for me on the changeover.

Look at it from the vantage point of my stomach: I would eat breakfast no later than ten, get to the courts and practice, take a shower and play my match around twelve-thirty, shower again, and then play doubles at three. And as the song says, I'd get too hungry for dinner at eight.

After I learned some things about diet a few years ago, I stopped putting red meat in my system, particularly while I was in the middle of a match, and I had Robert Haas, my diet consultant, make me energy bars with carob, raisins, and dates instead. Sometimes I still bring in a bagel or bread and oranges. When I'm playing doubles, I'll give Pam a piece of whatever I'm eating and the two of us will be chewing away during the changeover. Sometimes she'll get me talking and I'll still be trying to swallow while I'm walking back on the court, and I'll have to put the food on the side of my mouth, so I won't choke on it while reaching for a volley.

People laugh at my on-the-court eating habits, and sometimes they wonder whether the food and drink during a match doesn't make me want to go to the bathroom. One of the things I discovered early in my career was that your system usually shuts down while you're physically active. Sometimes you feel as if you have to go, but that's usually in the first fifteen minutes and you know it's just nerves. If you do get sick, you can ask to go to the bathroom once during the match, but it's best to save that for an emergency.

One thing that does not shut down is your menstrual system. I didn't have to worry about that as a junior back home, but once I reached puberty and started traveling outside Czechoslovakia, I learned to make sure my tampons were fresh. I've seen players who had to leave the court in the middle of a match or even play in sweatpants on a warm day, with male reporters wondering what was going on.

In my early years of playing, I had awful cramps. I would get to the point where I didn't even want to drive a car, my timing was off so much, and I was scared I'd get into an accident. I'd have one or two days when my coordination was off.

I can look back and honestly say that half my major losses in the late seventies and early eighties came during the worst days right before my period—to Pam in 1978, to Tracy in 1979, both at the U.S. Open, and a few early ones at Wimbledon. The following day I would be fine. And since I've controlled my diet, my cramps have been minimal during my peak exercise and tournament times, and my coordination is not thrown off as much. I'll just take a Motrin for the cramps and know that I'm good enough to win no matter what. But in those days, menstruation was one more thing I couldn't handle.

Another thing I learned early on the tour was the difference between trying to drill somebody on the other side of the net and hitting at her for strategic purposes. I see some of the men drilling to inflict pain, but I don't know a single female player who would do that. You do those things for strategy, not to hurt somebody.

For example, Kathy Jordan plays a serve-and-volley game, so I'll hit the ball at her because I don't want her coming in that close, and if I don't go at her, she might stab at the ball and hit a winner. I don't hit it at her just to hit her. Chris plays back most of the time, so what's the point in hitting at her? Some of the men are just mean—they drill each other—but the women are all pretty close, and I wouldn't want to hit somebody who might be sitting next to me in the clubhouse an hour later.

In my late summer trip in 1973, I lost in the third round at Toronto, the first round at Forest Hills, and the semifinals at Charlotte. The best part of that trip was when Rod Laver—the same Rod Laver my father had taken me to see in Prague when I was nine—dropped over to watch Wendy Turnbull play in the first round at Toronto.

I didn't know Laver was there, or I think I would have dropped dead instead of beating Wendy, 6–0, 7–5. Later that night, I was playing pool in the players' recreation hall and one of the other players said that Laver had been telling people I was going to be a really good player. I was so thrilled. If Rod Laver thought I was going to be good, I figured I'd better be.

I lived off that compliment during the fall, back in Prague, but I can't say tennis was my entire life at that time. I had a full-time schedule in high school. And I had discovered boys.

First Boyfriend

My new weight gave me some curves I never thought I'd have, and they gave me the idea that I was a full-grown woman at seventeen. I'd finally gotten my period a few years before, along with some lectures on sex, mostly from my father.

I had dated one guy for a while early in high school, but it was just normal hand-holding and giggling at parties. By 1973, I'd seen enough of life on the road to know that boys and girls were pairing off at my age. I was curious enough to start thinking about a boyfriend.

There weren't many candidates on the tennis tour. There was not a great supply of healthy, good-looking, wealthy guys waiting outside the locker room. You'd be in town for a week at most, and the men you'd meet were mostly tournament officials or agents or reporters or hosts from the country club. Where did all the young men go?

When I got home that fall and turned seventeen, I was no longer in the cloistered world of the women's tour. I was a high-school junior, in a city full of young men. One of them was a friend from my home town, four years older than I, an architectural student in Prague. We used to play tennis together all the time. He had started playing late, when he was around fourteen or fifteen, and I could beat him at first, but then he got better and beat me for a while.

Once I was a tour player, I started beating my friend again, and he didn't seem threatened by it. We'd have these little wars playing tennis, with him running down my best shots. He had a nice backhand. I remember that about him.

We went out quite a bit the year I was sixteen, and when I came back from the States he started taking a different kind of interest in me. I think I had more confidence in myself, felt more feminine, because I was softening up. My cheeks were all puffed out, but I thought it was good because I didn't look like a boy anymore. I didn't realize how heavy I was, even though I couldn't get into my old clothes. Anyway, I felt a lot better about myself at the time, and I think that had an effect on my boyfriend.

We'd go to Prague on dates, like all the other young people: to movies, plays at the National Theatre, concerts or opera at the Smetana Theatre; or we'd walk through the old section of Prague, eating sausages and drinking beer, standing in front of the famous clock tower, looking in the store windows, trying to find a bar with American music.

Through his work as an architectural student, he had a government job, checking the restoration work in the castle at Karlstejn, out near Revnice. He could drive right up to the edge of the stairway and leave the car there instead of having to park in the lower town like all the visitors. I'd go up to the office with him, feeling like one of the privileged few. His air of assurance about his work gave me the feeling he'd be the same way about sex.

I was comfortable with him because he was cool, four years older, an athlete, and smart. I enjoyed his company, and he wasn't threatened by my life in tennis. We started getting pretty close, and he invited me to his apartment at school in Prague.

I had gotten a double message about sex while I was

growing up. On one level, my mother was old-fashioned enough to expect I would be a virgin when I got married. But on the other hand, my father would say it was important to have sex with a boy before you married him to make sure you were compatible in bed.

My father would say: "It's a big part of marriage, but you shouldn't go to bed with somebody unless you plan to marry him." He would also say it wasn't a good idea to have sex before you were twenty-one.

I wasn't planning on getting married, but I liked the compatible part. And as for twenty-one, who could wait that long?

I was a little hesitant about going to this boy's apartment for what we both knew would be My First Time, but we kept planning it and it got built up in my mind, and one weekend while his parents were away, we kept our appointment. I was so scared.

I kept telling myself, He's been with other women, he knows what he's doing—relax, trust him. But when we got down to it, there were no bells, no stars, no flashing lights, no colors, and not a lot of affection or skill, either. I hadn't realized how painful it could be. I kept thinking: Who needs this? It hurts too much.

Making love shouldn't be painful once you get used to it, but I never got to that point with him. My first sex with him was painful, very painful. At the time, it was something I could have done without.

I can't say that my first sexual experience influenced my choices later. I wasn't in bed with him wishing I was with a woman. I was just so curious; I had to know. It was convenient to do it with him, so I did, telling myself, He knows all about this, he's been with women before.

I assumed too much. I also assumed he knew something about birth control. But if he did, he didn't act on it. Soon afterward, I was walking around the house bitchy and petrified and seven days late. I asked my father a few vague questions about birth control, but he said, "Come back when you're twenty-one and ask me about those things." Twenty-one is a long time to wait when you're seventeen and a week overdue.

I was so grouchy that my mother finally realized something was wrong.

"What are you worried about?"

"Well, I haven't gotten my period yet."

"Why should you worry about that?"

"Uh, well, I think I should worry about it."

They were pretty calm. They said: "Don't do it again," which I guess parents have to say, but they didn't carry on the way they would a few years later when they came to the States and found out I was involved with a woman.

Meanwhile, of course, I was still overdue. I didn't tell him, because I didn't feel that close to him. It was really my problem, so to speak. I wasn't about to say to him, "I'm pregnant, let's get married." The main thing I was worried about was my tennis career.

I didn't know how far it could take me, I had no idea, but tennis was the most important thing in my life at that time. I had realized that a few years earlier, when I was around fourteen and was downhill skiing. I'd loved skiing downhill, just barely in control, or maybe slightly out of control, but this time, right in the middle of a run, I thought: Hey, wait a minute, what if I fall down and break my leg? That could be the end of my tennis career. So I decided to slow down, right there in the middle of the Krkonose Mountains, and ever since then I have been skiing more slowly, always in control.

Now I had another kind of decision. Abortion in Czechoslovakia is free, but I was not thrilled with the idea, even though I believe every woman should have the right to make that decision for herself. My dilemma was whether to have an abortion or have a child and jeopardize my tennis career.

Marriage was not an option. Everybody said, "You get married, you have children, you work from nine to five." But I never thought I was going to be working from nine to five, having a boss, being in an office or a factory. No matter what happened in tennis, I always thought I'd be my own boss, which in Czechoslovakia would have taken a lot of doing.

Abstractly, I always thought I'd get married—but not because I was supposed to. I thought I'd get married late and have children, but it wasn't something I wanted at seventeen. Fortunately, a few days later I got my period without doing anything, and it turned out all right.

When I visited the States a few months afterward, I told a friend of mine about my close call, and she got me some birth control pills. I took them for four or five days, but since I wasn't having sex very often, I stopped taking them. Now that I know more about the side effects of those pills, I am glad I stopped right then and there.

We saw each other a few more times when I got back home, but by then I was traveling so much and he was spending so much time at school that we both agreed, "You go on with your life, I'll go on with mine." We stayed friends, just as I've stayed friends with other people I've known since.

I ask my parents about him occasionally. I hear he's married now. When he was a bachelor, he was so lazy that his parents and younger sister used to take care of him, clean up after him, but I hear he cleans the house for his wife now. I also hear he has four kids. That doesn't surprise me in the least.

If I could do it over again, I wouldn't. I felt I loved him, but I would say I loved him like a brother, and should have waited for somebody I really loved. Looking back in terms of age, my father was right. Why twenty-one? Why not eighteen or twenty-five? It's kind of ridiculous to put an age limit on things, but I know it would have been better if I'd been more mature, more emotionally involved, and that would be the same for any relationship. I learned a lot from my first experience. After that, I would always ask myself, How do you feel?

California, This Time

I was allowed out of Czechoslovakia again in 1974, only this time the tour began in California. When I explored the hills and shops of San Francisco and the desert and condos of Palm Springs, I began to realize the United States was even more lush and varied than I had imagined. I loved it out there: everything was so clean, and the weather was beautiful. Once I saw how beautiful it was, I knew I was getting hooked.

I didn't have any false illusions. As the tour moved on through Washington, Fort Lauderdale, Detroit, and Chicago, I was overwhelmed by the size of America, the varied climate, from heat to snow in an hour's plane ride, and the crime, always publicized in the newspapers. Back in Prague, you'd hear about crime in America, but the stories were hard to believe. We had maybe ten murders a year in Prague; more people were killed by not looking both ways crossing the railroad tracks. Only soldiers had guns in

Czechoslovakia. In America, everybody had one, so you'd need one just to keep up. (Yes, I do, in my house.)

Until I came to the States, I thought rape was a crime of overpowering, because it's the same word in our language. Later I realized how many rapes there are in the States and I wondered what was going on. All the shooting and raping. I can understand crimes of passion, but the random violence definitely gave me a dual picture: on the one hand, warm friendship; on the other, senseless violence.

One of my best friendships began with me muttering and cursing to myself during a match in Chicago. I didn't appreciate some of the calls the line officials were making, so I made a few choice comments in Czech, figuring I was safe.

After I won the match, I was walking off the court when two of the officials, a man and a woman, came over to me with smiles on their faces and one of them said: "*Dobry den. Jak se mate?*" ("Hello. How are you?") And they started chatting in perfect Czech.

"Oh, my God, I'm so embarrassed," I said, but they thought it was funny. They said they had been laughing—even when I was talking about them.

Mirek and Svatka Hoschl have a daughter about my age, and I got along well with the whole family. I went to their house for dinner—duck and dumplings, what else?—and we've been friends ever since. Whenever I play a tournament in Chicago, I stay at their house. Svatka even comes to Wimbledon or the U.S. Open sometimes and stays with me and cooks my meals. You eat a few of Svatka's dumplings the night before a match and you have enough stamina to stay on the court for eight or nine sets against Godzilla.

The 1974 tour moved east to New York, where I visited George and Jarmila Parma. George was now working as a tennis coach for a Czech man in New York. On my first visit to that city in 1973 I had found George to be as handsome as ever. But he couldn't get over the change in me. He kept saying, "You used to be so tiny."

I had never known his wife very well, but we got acquainted on this visit. I stayed with the Parmas for three nights, sitting up till all hours, talking and smoking cigarets. I wanted to buy presents for my family and my boyfriend, and Jarmila was happy to give me advice about shopping. She also had a lot to say about life in the States.

The Parmas were good about not saying too much about the Czech government. They were not political people and never tried to convince me to defect. I think they felt I was too young to be persuaded to do something like that, that it would have to be something that would come from me. I was glad for them, glad they had gotten out. I never figured he owed me or the country anything, that he should have stayed. A lot of people were leaving, and I thought it was lucky for them that they'd all been out of the country when the Russians moved in.

I realized it was not a simple thing to leave your homeland when the Parmas told me about "The Emigrant's Dream"—that they were back in the old country. In the dream they were looking for their passports but couldn't find them. They said that after a while they would wake up in a cold sweat. They each had the dream, separately. Even early in 1974, defecting was definitely on my mind, but listening to them I realized it would not be a picnic.

George and Jarmila knew they could never go back and visit their families. They would have to wait until people got old, past sixty, when the Czech government would let them out because they had no more value to the state. I thought about maybe going twenty years or more without seeing my parents, and shivers ran down my spine.

During my visit with the Parmas, I learned there were thousands of Czechs and Slovaks living in the New York area, with churches and travel agencies and restaurants catering to them. The Parmas took me to The Duck Joint, a popular restaurant owned by Paul Steindler and his wife, Aja Zanova, the former world champion figure skater who had moved to New York in 1951.

Aja is a tall, beautiful, and intelligent woman, who had toured with the Ice Follies for many years before settling down in New York with Paul, also from Czechoslovakia. In 1974 they were right at the center of New York's political and social life. I'd go to their restaurant and meet all kinds of celebrities. They knew everybody: Ed Koch, who later became mayor, entertainers, business people, and from our first meeting they gave me a sense of life in the Big Apple.

I realized from talking to Aja that there was no such thing as the "Czech community," even though there were thousands of Czechs and Slovaks in the city. She felt that many Czech-Americans expected too much of her, or were jealous because she was successful right away in America, while they had to perform menial jobs until they got their feet on the ground.

Since I moved to the States, I've discovered that some Czechs will form a network once they're out, keep in touch with what's going on back home. People try to get in touch with me because I'm Czech, but I don't encourage it. I'm not political and neither is my family. I miss the country-side, some friends, my family, my dog, but that doesn't automatically make me a lifelong friend of every Czech and Slovak in the States.

New York was the last stop on my tour of the States. I had won $3,000 in a tournament and I was supposed to give that—in cash—to the Czech federation back in Prague. They're not fools: they want American dollars just like every hustler trying to make change on Wenceslas Square. The economy was stacked against you. It was so hard to save money that ordinary people had no hope of traveling. The government would buy dollars from Americans and pay 10 crowns to the dollar, or 14 if you got a tourist rate, but people were so desperate for dollars they would pay 25 or more crowns to the dollar on the black market. Then they hoarded the dollars in secret hiding places—their shoe, their mattress, a tin can in the backyard—so they could buy something nice in the Czech tourists' shops or take a trip outside the country.

Naturally, the Czech federation wanted some of the American dollars. Because I was under eighteen, nobody in New York wanted to cash the check for me, and I had to ask Jarmila Parma's help. Jarmila was annoyed. "The tennis federation is using you as a money courier," she said. "I wouldn't make a young girl carry three thousand dollars in cash around New York with her." She finally took me to her bank and got the check cashed. It was a lot of money, but no big deal to me. I was used to carrying cash in Czechoslovakia, where you don't have credit cards or checks. I was probably pretty careless about carrying the cash and still am, really, but I told Jarmila, "It's all right, I can handle it."

She was mostly annoyed with the Czech government, and didn't mince any words about it when she put me in a taxi and made me promise to call her from the airport. I had heard the horror stories about visitors being driven all over New York and charged hundreds of dollars by unscrupulous cabbies, but I wasn't about to get taken like that—not by a New York cabby, anyway, when I could get taken by my own tennis federation.

The federation claimed I was too young to keep that kind of money—but as far as I could see, I wasn't too young to earn it on the tennis court. They also said they'd control my endorsements; imagine these bureaucrats making deals with equipment manufacturers in the West—what a mismatch.

The federation gave me $11 a day for food in 1973, and when they raised it to $17 in 1974 I was able to save money and bring it home. Of course that encouraged me to eat cheaply, the wrong kinds of food for an athlete in training, but I didn't know anything about diet in those days.

The only thing I knew was getting back to Prague and forking over $3,000 in American dollars to the federation and thinking to myself: Some day you're not taking all the money I earn.

I started to straighten out the money part later in 1974 when I met Fred Barman, a Beverly Hills business manager. His daughter, Shari, had been in the first wave on the women's tour. It was Shari's letter home to Fred, asking for some money to keep her alive on the road, that led Fred to get involved in Team Tennis and other tennis ventures. Shari and a few other women told me Fred might be able to get me a better deal from the Czech federation.

One day during the 1974 U.S. Open, I was practicing on a back court at Forest Hills when Fred stuck his head over the fence and introduced himself. We had coffee at the Roosevelt Hotel that night and he told me to think about what he could do for my career in the States. I think I surprised him the next morning when I called early—I was on Prague time, he was on L.A. time—and said, "Fred, I need you."

He said something like, "Sure, who is this?" and we agreed that he would represent me. I was impressed with his show-business background as well as his tennis contacts.

The Czech federation couldn't quite figure out who—or what—Fred was. Some of them thought he was my boyfriend, even when they saw his beautiful wife and four daughters, who were older than me. As far as we were concerned, we were just friends. I think the federation saw him as just another undesirable step in the Americanization of Martina.

The Americanization went full blast once the Czech federation adjusted my earnings to an eighty-twenty split in my favor, and as Fred Barman likes to point out, the twenty percent I paid the federation was "net, net, net."

The federation made that adjustment just in time because I was showing signs of being a big money-winner on the tour. Earlier in 1974, I had reached the finals of the Italian Open, losing to Chris, and losing to Helga Masthoff in the quarters in France. I lost to Mima Jausovec in the first round at Wimbledon, but then won two rounds at the U.S. Open before losing to Julie Heldman. I made up for that a few weeks later when I beat Julie, 7–6, 6–4, at Orlando to win my first professional tournament. We still have the picture at home of me jumping in the air after match point and hugging the light pole, since there wasn't anybody there I knew well enough to hug.

By saving my per-diem expenses the first two years out of the country, I was able to give my father some money for a car. He bought a Skoda, made by one of the famous old Czech manufacturing companies taken over by the state. Skoda used to stand for quality, but now under the socialist system it turns out mostly garbage. The color of the car was a light green, a debauched green, but it was our first car, and we were thrilled.

We had always dreamed of having a car, it cost $2,000 —about a year and a half of salary in those days. Of my father's salary, then about $100 a month, and my mother's salary, which was a little less, eighty percent went for food and living expenses.

I'd say about one Czech in twenty-five owned a car in those days, but owning a car didn't really make us a big deal. The big difference was that my father and I had been traveling to tournaments on his motorbike since I was nine, and now we could travel as a family, the four of us. My parents, Jana, and I could take rides through the country-side, go into Prague, travel to tournaments. We hadn't taken a family vacation in six or seven years, not since I started serious tennis, and it was about time.

Forcing the Decision

I began to think seriously about leaving Czechoslovakia when I went home in the fall of 1974. I wanted to be a world-class tennis player, I wanted to live in America, maybe I even wanted to become an American citizen sometime in the future. But every time I'd get to the point of actually leaving home, I got stuck.

Czechoslovakia was my home—it *is* my home—and I would have been very happy keeping my options open, procrastinator that I am. I wandered about Revnice in a trance, playing with my dog, Babeta, a German shepherd who was just a puppy then. I visited friends, saw my boyfriend, spent time with Grandmother Subertova, and took some long walks in the mountains above our town, gazing at the river and the houses and asking myself: Are you really ready to say good-bye to this? I wasn't.

I was still debating the issue with myself when the bureaucrats made up my mind for me, creating political problems that made me fear I might never be able to travel again.

One of the problems was that I was becoming more dominant in women's tennis than Jan Kodes was in men's tennis —not that this was ever a problem between Jan and me. The problem was with Antonin Bolardt of the federation, who later captained the Czech Davis Cup team. When Renata Tomanova and I helped win the Federation Cup, the female equivalent of the Davis Cup, Bolardt and some other Czech officials were jealous.

Bolardt had known my father since they were sixteen or seventeen, and now he started telling him that I was becoming "too Americanized," that I had better start behaving myself or I'd be in trouble. That was a threat that they could make me or break me. I have never liked threats. We already had plenty of those from the Russians; who needed threats from a fellow countryman?

Vera Sukova, the women's coach, was good about it. She would talk to me once in a while and say, "You've got to cool it. You'll get yourself in trouble and everybody else in trouble. Just play the game. Do whatever it takes. Be smart."

My parents told me: "You can't do whatever you want." And I'd ask: "Why not?" I was not exactly the Good Soldier Svejk. No imbecile smile. No pretending to follow orders. I was eighteen years old and thought I was a big cheese.

Despite all the vague threats, I did get permission to return to the States for the spring 1975 Virginia Slims circuit, and this time I was ready. In the third tournament of the season, in Washington, D.C., I ran into Chris in the quarterfinals and beat her, 3–6, 6–4, 7–6.

The real tipoff on my improvement came the following day. Very often, you see a player score a big victory one day and get killed the next day because all that energy and emotion takes something out of her. But I came back and beat Virginia Wade and then Kerry Melville in straight sets to win the whole thing, showing I could play a full tournament against good opposition. A month later, at the U.S. Indoors in Boston, I beat Virginia, Margaret, and Evonne, all in three-set matches, for my biggest victory yet. I was also playing doubles with Chris, and was exhausted when I got to the finals against Evonne. I had never won a set from Evonne till then, mostly because I had a hard time breaking her serve with my little dinky chip backhand. But I was improving, pretty much on my own, with some advice from Billie Jean, and was progressing almost day by day. Tennis writers like Bud Collins of the Boston *Globe* made a big fuss over this victory.

Looking back at 1975, it seems like the golden age of women's tennis, at least in depth. I can't compare one player from my era to one player from another era, but I doubt there was ever a field like the one in 1975. Billie Jean was playing mostly doubles, Rosie was a threat, and you had Margaret still tough, Virginia at her peak, Chris reaching the top, as well as Betty Stove, Olga Morozova, Kerry Melville, Dianne Fromholtz, and Nancy Richey once in a while.

We all thought we were at the dawning of a new age of women's tennis, but that was really the peak. Where are all the great players who were supposed to come along next? Tracy came along and got hurt, Andrea Jaeger has her problems, Pam Shriver and Hana Mandlikova are tough, Virginia Ruzici and Sylvia Hanika were better a few years ago, and a lot of the younger ones get to the top for a brief moment and then they fold. Now there's a real generation gap—almost nobody in their mid-twenties.

Maybe the young ones feel there's no way they can get up there with me and Chris. I'm not one to judge. Maybe it comes too easy to them. Maybe they're not willing to put in the extra work that Chris did, that I did. Or maybe they just start too young and their bodies and their emotions can't take it. Who knows? I just remember being eighteen and seeing all these great players around me, and wanting to beat them all, one by one, like Old Shatterhand picking off the bad guys when I used to play cowboys and Indians as a kid.

After my victory over Evonne in Boston, I was supposed to go back to Czechoslovakia, but there was a week off and then one more tournament on Amelia Island, so I decided to stay. It was my business. I was a tennis player, and something told me the April weather would be nicer in Florida than in Prague.

Unfortunately, I handled the whole thing stupidly, like a kid. I didn't write home, didn't ask permission, didn't even tell my mother and father. So in the middle of the tournament I got a telegram from my parents saying they were worried about me. Then they called in tears saying I had better come home, what was wrong with me. I told them I was going to finish the tournament and then come home and that was fine with them.

But it wasn't so fine with the tennis federation. They sent me a telegram saying I'd better come home immediately. I started crying. Billie Jean was with me when I got the word. "Don't worry," she said, "everything will be okay. But maybe you should go home." I didn't go home, though, and finally Edie McGoldrick, one of the tournament officials, sent a telegram saying it was all right, that I'd be home after the tournament. I ended up getting into the finals and losing to Chris, and then I went home and found out I was in big trouble.

Not long after I got home, people from the federation called me in and said I was "too Americanized." I asked what that meant and they said I liked the States too much, that I was too friendly with American players like Chris and Billie Jean and Rosie, and that I'd better start paying more attention to the Czech officials. It was true, to a point. If there was a group from the Czech tennis federation going out for dinner, I wouldn't join them. I felt I had the right to pick my own friends.

They called me *nafoukana*—"nose in the air"—and said they wanted me to be with the Czech people and other Eastern players. I didn't understand it. We were all on the same tour. We were all tennis players. Why did I have to be friendly to some people and not others? There were always different people traveling with us, keeping an eye on us, but I wanted the right to choose my friends.

They allowed me to go to the French Open and of course I was supposed to stay with the Czech players. But seeded players could get reservations and good rates at one of the fancy hotels, and since I was seeded second and playing doubles with Chris, I thought it natural for us to stay in the same hotel. I never gave it a second thought. The hotel was so expensive it was ridiculous, but I felt I had earned the right to stay there. I remember Chris sent out her laundry, and it came to $200.

After I lost to Chris in the finals, I went home and was put through the wringer again. I wondered if I'd be allowed out for Wimbledon. It has been suggested that I was suffering through a love affair in the States at that time and was afraid I'd never see the person again, but it wasn't true. I wasn't involved with anybody; I just wanted to play tennis.

They finally gave me permission, but I was getting sick of all the conflict. I kept telling my father: "I've just got to leave."

I've never told this to many people, but my entire family was going to defect together at Wimbledon. Fred Barman came over and made some legal preparations so my parents, Jana, and I would be able to go over to the U.S. Embassy right after Wimbledon. The whole time during Wimbledon, my parents and I discussed it. One day it would be "Yes, we're going" and the next it would be "No, we're not."

My father was hesitant because he figured he would have

Left: With my mother in the Krkonose Mountains, 1961. Judging by the skis, I was five years old. My mother still has the jacket she was wearing.

Below: Sitting on Court One in front of the club house in Revnice with my mother, 1961. The boy at the far right, Vladimir Lacina, later became a good friend and a sparring partner. This was my first racquet; I still have it.

Above: On a pond in Revnice, 1966. I thought I was real cool in my figure skates; my mother wouldn't let me play in hockey skates. Note the broken hockey stick.

Right: On Court One again, this time with my little sister, Jana, in 1967. The racquet with the ball on it was my first—it belonged to my grandmother. The other racquet was the first one bought especially for me.

With my coach, George Parma. I'm nine here; it is the summer of 1966.
This was the first time George came to my home town. I was so excited
that he came to see *me*. I thought he was a god.

Above: Left to right: Chris Evert, me, and Chris's sister Jeanne, Paris, 1975. I was still living in Czechoslovakia. The Czech government wanted me to stay in the hotel with the other Czech players and the officials. But I wanted to stay in the same hotel with Chris, Jimmy Connors, and the other American players.

Right: Virginia Slims tournament, Oakland, California, 1977. This was the first year my playing was consistent. I had been living in the United States for two years.

Right: The end of the day's shooting in Harry Langdon's studio in Los Angeles, 1977.

Below: The Avon tournament, Dallas, 1980.

Judy Nelson gave me a horse for my twenty-eighth birthday. We named it Grand Slam.

Puma and Yonex (Yonnie) during a tournament in the summer of 1984, Mahwah, New Jersey.

Aspen Highlands, Aspen,
Colorado, 1984.

1984.

Carol L. Newsom

to depend on me, and what would happen if I got hurt and couldn't play anymore? What would we do for money? It was strange because he had always been so confident that I would be a great player and now that I was on the verge, he was worried about whether I would make it. But look at it from his standpoint: he and my mother had always worked, and they were not used to thinking about their daughter supporting them.

It made for a few tense evenings in England, and I lost to Margaret Court in straight sets in the quarterfinals. I'd probably have lost anyway, with all her experience, but still, I would have had a better chance without all this stuff going on. And the bottom line was that we chickened out as a unit. We took a short vacation to France, to the Riviera, and then drove back to Czechoslovakia, where the national championships were being held in Pilsen, at the same club I'd been playing at when the Russians came through in 1968.

When my parents and I showed up there, everybody acted as if they had seen a ghost. They'd point and whisper when they thought we weren't looking. Everybody was so surprised to see us because, we found out later, there were rumors going around that we had already defected. So even though we came back, people were more wary of us than ever.

I was supposed to play in a junior tournament in France the next week but Vera Sukova called me up and said, "You're not going to France."

"Why not?"

"We want to give some of the younger kids a chance to play in international competition."

I realized right away that this was baloney. They still thought I was too Americanized, and they were suggesting they might not let me go to the U.S. Open. To me, that's typical Communist thinking. The Czech government had put a lot of time, and money, and energy into my tennis, and now that I had gotten to the top, they were nervous. It wasn't simply that I might defect, not completely: they just couldn't deal with a Czech being a big shot on the women's tour and starting to get ideas of her own about how to train, how to play, which tournaments to enter. They wanted total control, but the more I won, the less they could control me. They were willing to sacrifice my tennis career in order to control me. And I wasn't going to stand for that.

I was still trying to make up my mind three weeks before the U.S. Open, when I was supposed to play in the European Amateur Championships in Vienna. I was still counted as an amateur even though I was now keeping most of my prize money.

When you think about it, they were crazy to put pressure on me. With all the money I was making then, I would have been an asset to their economy. And with the money I've made since, I could have boosted their Gross National Product. But they had to pressure me. It's the only way they knew.

Back in Czechoslovakia, I applied for permission to go to New York. Jan Kodes talked to some of the big shots in the federation who were totally behind me. Stanislav Chvatal, a really nice, straightforward man, and a friend of my parents, was also on my side, but Antonin Himl, president of the federation, had the ultimate decision.

Himl was a pretty good guy, too, but he had been listening to Bolardt's predictions that I was going to defect, so he called a meeting at his office at the Ministry of Sport. It was all very civil. I told them I didn't understand why they were picking on me and that I had no intention of leaving, which was basically true. I didn't want to defect, not totally. I just wanted to play tennis.

Kodes and some of the others talked Himl into letting me go, pointing out that I would be seeded quite high at Forest

Hills, and that a good showing by me would be good for the country. Himl finally ruled that I could play the Open and the tournament just before it, in Westchester County, but then I'd have to come right back.

Even with the permission to leave the country, I could feel their control tightening. They were treating me like a little girl, telling me I had to finish high school, when I was already a professional athlete, and they wouldn't give me permission to play Team Tennis. I had no idea when I'd get out again.

I could look around and see that the Czech people weren't happy. There was a growing sadness, a melancholia, a sense of *litost,* as Milan Kundera, the writer, puts it. I began to realize there was no room in that system for me to feel good about myself, for me to make decisions about my life. If I stayed, I belonged to them. My life would never be my own.

The last night before I left for the Open, my father took me for a walk on the road near the river. He said: "Well, if you're going to do it, stay there. Don't let us talk you into coming back. Just stay. But remember: there's no circumstance under which you would be able to come back once you decide to defect."

We didn't even talk to my mother about it. I didn't tell her anything. It was pretty obvious that I was unhappy with the way the federation was jerking me back and forth. My mother knew how I felt, and I could tell by the nervous way she rubbed her hands together and smoked a cigaret that she knew I might never be coming back. She had once told me that if I were going to defect I shouldn't tell her, so I didn't—another gap between two born procrastinators who love each other so much they can't discuss it.

I don't want to sound too maudlin about leaving. I was ninety-five percent sure I was not coming back, but at eighteen years of age I was pretty confident that I could handle it. If I had been five years younger, it might have been rougher, or if I had been five years older, I might have been more sensitive, but at eighteen, you think you're going to live forever and knock the world dead. I knew America fairly well, could speak the language, and it never occurred to me that I could get hurt and never play tennis again. So I was eager and ready to get on with it. The future could take care of itself.

Still, I did not dare say good-bye to my sister or my grandmother or my friends. I packed my clothes, fussed around the house, tried to sleep, and went to the airport the next morning knowing there was a chance I would never see my family or my homeland again.

The Big Step

I made the final decision on the tennis court in August of 1975. Confused and scared, I was playing in a warm-up tournament in Westchester County, New York, when I got wiped out by Dianne Fromholtz, 6–4, 6–2, in the quarters. I was in such an emotional state, it was pathetic—so depressed, I didn't know what was happening.

This can't go on, I told myself. Every time you go home, you're going to wonder if they'll ever let you out again. It's time to make your move.

My move was to call Fred Barman. Poor Fred. Up to

now, he had merely handled the finances of some show-business celebrities, but now he was about to get involved in international intrigue.

"Fred, I want to stay over here," I told him. "I don't want to go back. Can you take care of it for me?"

He told me it was my decision and he would help any way he could. He didn't try to encourage me or discourage me. I liked that. He treated me like a grown-up instead of a confused eighteen-year-old. When he saw I was serious, he put me in touch with a lawyer friend of his in Washington.

The lawyer had never worked with anybody trying to defect from an Eastern country to the United States, so he brought the details to some contacts of his at the FBI. Fred, in the meantime, was arranging a meeting with the New York office of the Immigration and Naturalization Service to begin filling out the papers and getting my legal status clarified.

All this was going on during the U.S. Open. I was staying at the hotel with all the other players, hoping nobody would notice I was spending more time with people in business suits carrying briefcases than I was with people in shorts carrying tennis racquets.

I was worried that the Czech federation would find out what was going on. They were giving me a little more distance than in the past, but they would still come around all the time and ask me how I was. Fred and the other lawyer told me the FBI was protecting me—from what? I began to wonder. I'd go out on the court and I'd look for guys in trench coats spying on each other. Which one would be the Czech agent and which would be the American?

Even with all that going on, I had a pretty good Open, wearing my Ted Tinling original, a flowered dress with a bright print that I liked "because it's like my personality—wild!" I told people. I beat Margaret in the quarters and gave Chris a pretty good match before losing, 6–4, 6–4, in the semis.

People still talk about how I used to lose my concentration in big matches against Chris; not many people know that during that match, I knew I had a big appointment that night with Fred at the Immigration and Naturalization Service on the Lower West Side of Manhattan.

What a setting for a spy movie: *The Left-hander Who Came in from the Cold.* We got off the elevator and were shown into an office that seemed empty. There are few things emptier than a federal office building in downtown Manhattan late on a Friday night.

Fred had dealt with actors and singers like Mel Torme, David Janssen, and Peter Graves in Hollywood and Beverly Hills, but never with the FBI and the Immigration Service in freight elevators in spooky buildings. I was used to intrigue, having crossed the Iron Curtain so many times, but he wasn't.

Finally, the immigration agent came into the office and introduced himself. Then he took off his sport jacket and laid it across the table. Fred and I looked at him. Strapped under his arm was a huge pistol. What did he need *that* for?

"May I have your passport?" he asked.

Then he left the room. Fred's paranoia was working overtime.

"What if he doesn't come back?" Fred whispered.

"He'll be back," I said.

I hoped.

The man came back a few minutes later, saying he'd had the information duplicated on a copying machine, no big deal. Then he asked to talk with me alone. Fred was a little nervous about this. He was convinced that somebody was going to stuff me in a taxi, jab me with a hypodermic needle, and hustle me on to an airplane bound for Czechoslovakia.

I wasn't as fearful as he was, but it has happened to other people. They are sedated and jammed on a plane and you never hear from them again.

Nothing that sinister was going on. He wanted answers to some basic questions: Why did I want to leave Czechoslovakia? What were my plans for living in the States? He made it all sound pretty cut-and-dried.

Meanwhile, Fred fretted out in the hall. I think he was starting to see a Communist behind every post. Later, he told me that two men had come up to him and introduced themselves as FBI agents assigned to the case. One said he'd been born in Czechoslovakia and spoke the language, in case I might need an interpreter.

Fred, looking out for my interests, didn't believe them. He asked to see their identification, which they showed him politely.

"I'm still not convinced," he said. "Anybody can make a card or steal a badge."

Finally, Fred persuaded them to get on the phone with a buddy of his who knew how the FBI operated. When the friend assured Fred they were real agents, he finally relaxed.

Inside, the immigration agent told me: "We'll try to keep this as quiet as possible for as long as we can." And he advised me to attract as little attention as possible until they had the next step arranged.

I left the building at 10:30 p.m. on Friday and went back to the Roosevelt Hotel. On Saturday morning, CBS News called me and said they wanted to do an interview downstairs in the lobby. I figured it was tennis business, so I tried to be polite. "Why don't we do it out at the courts, okay?" I said. They sounded as if it was pretty urgent, but they agreed.

Five minutes later I got a call from Vera Sukova.

"Why did you do it?" she cried.

"Do what?"

"Why did you do it?" Vera repeated.

Then it dawned on me that somehow she knew I had applied for asylum. She said she was coming over to the hotel to talk me out of it. I knew she couldn't do that—my mind was made up—but I didn't want to go through any emotional scenes at that time. Besides, who really knew what they would do? I trusted Vera, but what about the man with the hypodermic needle?

"They found out," I told Fred on the telephone.

"Pack your clothes and get the hell out of there as fast as you can," he said.

I got dressed and packed within fifteen minutes, while Fred arranged for me to hide out at Jeanie Brinkman's apartment in Greenwich Village. Jeanie was the publicity director of the Virginia Slims tour at the time.

Fred and I got in a cab, carrying my tennis racquets and suitcase, and as we were racing down Second Avenue, the cabby turned around and talked to us, going forty miles an hour the way New York cabbies do.

"Hey, did you hear about that Czech tennis broad who defected?"

Fred assured him we had heard the news, and would he mind turning around and watching traffic.

After I checked in at Jeanie's, I went to Forest Hills and found out there was a story in the Washington *Post* on the front page. I was impressed. I was also mad as hell. Since I hadn't left the Immigration Office until ten-thirty Friday night, somebody must have been working damn hard on that scoop—or working hard to leak it. I still don't know how it got out in a few hours.

Since all the reporters wanted interviews, Jeanie arranged a press conference so I could get the story out all at once. I had no idea I would get so much attention. It was a zoo.

I did short interviews for all the major networks and one for the radio, and one big conference for the newspapers.

"I wanted my freedom," I kept saying.

The American sports reporters kept harping on whether I had a boyfriend in America or whether I wanted to make more money, but I don't think they were getting the point. Maybe unless you've lived in Eastern Europe, it's hard to know the difference between East and West.

I wasn't defecting for political reasons, I emphasized, but I couldn't help adding: "Anybody that complains about life here should go to Europe and they would understand. Go to a Communist country, go to a socialist country. They would understand then. And they complain it is so expensive here, let them go to France and see. All the demonstrators here, they're crazy."

Will you go to school? I was asked.

"What for?" I blurted out. My school was now the women's tour. "I just want to play the tour, whenever I want and wherever I want," I said.

Fred was still concerned that the Czechs would try to kidnap me, so I hid out at Jeanie's apartment for a few days. The first night, we went out for dinner at a local restaurant Jeanie knew, where there was a back room with only two tables. We took a deep breath and ordered dinner. After we had eaten, Jeanie raised her glass and said: "To you, Martina."

At the next table, four men turned around, raised their glasses, and said: "We toast you, too, Martina."

"Check, please," Jeanie said.

The State Department was good about getting me some protection until my papers were in order. They kept an eye on me while I went to stay for a few days with my friend Svatka, who had some friends in upstate New York.

The first story out of Prague quoted my father as saying,

"We are crushed," at the news I had defected, and my grandfather was quoted as saying, "Oh, the little idiot, why did she do that?" But that was exaggerated by the officials over there. It's true, my family had nothing to do with my leaving, and they never knew specifically that I was going, but it was no surprise.

They got through to me by telephone a day or two later, asking me to come home before I got into real trouble with the Czech government. I think they were trying to be good citizens. I told them my mind was made up, and that I would see them as soon as possible. Deep down, I knew they understood.

Two weeks later the federation issued a statement that said: "Martina Navratilova has suffered a defeat in the face of the Czechoslovak society. Navratilova had all possibilities in Czechoslovakia to develop her talent, but she preferred a professional career and a fat bank account. She did not realize that she also needed an education."

During those first weeks, I played in Atlanta and in an exhibition in Charlotte, North Carolina, and was surprised when I got standing ovations from the crowds. In the South, people thought it was a big deal that I had applied for asylum. I became a celebrity overnight and not for my tennis. But I just wanted to secure my green card, which would allow me to stay indefinitely, and get on with my business.

The next tournament was in Denver. Fred wasn't convinced I was in the clear yet, so he and the FBI man who spoke Czech accompanied me to Colorado.

While I was in my hotel room, I got another call from Vera Sukova. I hadn't known she was in town, and just hearing her voice gave me a sharp pang—was it fear or sadness? She wanted to meet with me and talk over what I was doing.

Fred didn't want me to meet with her, but I felt I owed

her an explanation. She had always been decent to me, she was a great player in her own right, and the situation was not her fault. But she had obviously been asked by the authorities to see whether she could get me to return.

"This guy from the embassy just wants one meeting with you," Vera said.

I said, "Sure I'll do it." I knew in my heart they couldn't change my mind, but it was scary, nonetheless. Fred was going crazy.

When the time came, I was to meet them downstairs at the coffee shop, on neutral turf, so to speak. Fred and the Czech-speaking FBI agent escorted me downstairs and planted themselves in the lobby, and then Vera arrived with somebody from the Czech embassy I had never met before.

We sat in a corner, and this guy kept telling me he understood, that he had a son my age. He kept relating everything to his son, but I didn't know what that had to do with my situation. He kept saying that if I came back, nothing would happen to me, everything would be forgotten. They would understand. He'd try to improve things.

In fact, he said, from now on, they'd let me do anything I wanted, as long as I returned before October 30, when my visa ran out. But if I tried to come back after that date, I'd go to jail for two years.

That told me a lot. That they could even think of talking about jail meant I would be in big trouble if I ever set foot in my country again. I remembered my father telling me: "Don't ever come back, no matter what we tell you. They might put us up to it or we would be so emotional we would beg you to return, but don't. The years will pass, we'll come see you, but don't come back."

That advice from my father was all I could think about as I sat with Vera and this man from the embassy. We talked for about two hours, and it must have been clear to them that I wasn't going back.

I was getting impatient. I felt detached, actually. I was sorry for Vera because I'd put her in this predicament but I knew I was going to do it. She was really suffering over this. She liked me, she wanted me to stay on the team, she felt she could straighten everything out, but she could tell I was gone.

In the years to come, before she died of a brain tumor in 1982, Vera and I would say hello and talk about tennis, but we never discussed the old days. I'm sure she and Jan Kodes and a few of the other officials got some flack for letting me leave the country, but it was obvious they hadn't known about my plans. I've always felt sad if anybody suffered because of something I did.

I doubt the man from the embassy ever suffered. He did his best to work on my Czech paranoia and fear of authority. The whole scene was hilarious. The embassy man said he had been tailed all the way from Washington. I figured he was paranoid, too, but it turned out there really was an FBI guy on him. Vera told me I was being followed as well, but I knew it was just Fred and the FBI agent. I was more afraid of what the Czechs would do to me than any Americans. But Vera was still thinking as a Czech and trying to implant her fear of the Americans in me.

It was very cordial. I felt I was in control of myself. I felt I could ask her to leave at any time and she would. At the end of two hours we shook hands and they did go.

That wasn't the end of it, though.

I stayed in Denver until the end of the week, finally winning the tournament. One afternoon, Fred came out of my hotel room and walked down a flight of stairs to his room. In the stairwell, near a window, he spotted a pile of sixteen cigaret butts, where somebody had obviously been on duty, like a sentry or a guard.

He rushed down and told the hotel security people, but

obviously they didn't know anything about it. After that, we wondered: Ours or Theirs? But I never saw any evidence that the Czechs were tailing me. I did have some FBI guards taking me around for a while. One of them was an American Indian. After playing cowboys and Indians back in Czechoslovakia, I felt right at home with him.

All our fears were groundless. Aside from that little visit in the coffee shop in Denver, no efforts were made to get me back. A week later I was playing in Mission Viejo, California, when I got a call from New York announcing that my green card was waiting at the Immigration Service building. Fred and I got on the red-eye, arrived in New York at dawn, drank six or eight cups of coffee, and picked up the card when the office opened at 8:00 a.m. My green card had taken thirty days to arrive, the second fastest time on record. Somebody told me that when he was Governor of California Ronald Reagan had once come up with green cards in three days for a couple of defectors.

I never thought of it as a defection. I didn't know what the word meant. I simply believed that one day I'd come to the United States and stay here. Now I had to wait five years to become a citizen, which meant five years of avoiding flights over Communist territory, just in case my plane would be forced to land and I would be taken off it. I wasn't taking any chances.

The only way of getting my citizenship faster was to marry an American. That would be all legal and nice, and I could go back to Czechoslovakia anytime I wanted to. It came up in conversation, but I didn't have anybody in mind, and I knew the press would start asking me about my husband, why we weren't together all the time, and I didn't think I could handle that.

Actually, there was another reason why it didn't seem like a good idea.

A New Life

My green card was just one of the big changes in my life that took place around my nineteenth birthday. Another change was discovering that my childhood crushes on some of my female teachers had not been "just a phase."

Once I started traveling to the States, I realized I felt more comfortable around women than men. It wasn't disillusionment over my love affair with the boy back home, or any generalized resentment toward men. Maybe I felt uncomfortable around men because I wasn't as pretty as some other girls; but on the other hand, I'd always hung around boys when I was young because I could do the things they could do. I still liked men; I just liked the company of women better.

A lot of it has to do with freedom. Once I became a regular on the circuit, I saw a lot of women doing what they wanted to do. I saw them making business decisions for themselves, tennis decisions, and smaller decisions about where they wanted to live, how they wanted to eat and dress, what movies they wanted to see. They were professionals, their lives not always defined by men.

That sounds like a political statement when I say it, yet it really wasn't a matter of dogma. I just perceived some women doing what they wanted to do, and felt comfortable in their society. Of course, not all the professionals I admired were so-called gay. Nothing so simple. But I came to realize my attractions—social, emotional, professional, intellectual, sexual—were toward women.

I guess I'd known that for a long time, going back to childhood, when I had urges to be with some of the teachers, wanted to know everything about them, their secrets, the way they did things. I had much less curiosity about men.

As I grew up through my teens, I never had any relationship with a woman, and I don't think anybody ever treated me as different. I had a family, I had a tennis life, I had a boyfriend. But I was also aware of gay people, particularly after I started traveling, and reading magazines, and looking around me in the big cities. You'd see couples you knew were gay, or meet somebody and know she or he was gay.

I never thought there was anything strange about being gay. Other people would make jokes, but I couldn't figure out why these people were "sick." I knew it was more tolerated in the West than in Czechoslovakia. There, they would put you in the sanatorium for crazy people, literally. You'd read about it sometimes in the paper, and it was considered being sick.

I knew homosexuality wasn't such a crime in the States. Even when I thought about it, I never panicked and thought, Oh, I'm strange, I'm weird, what do I do now? It was just a matter of time for me. I had to get other parts of my life in order first. Plus, my first sexual experience hadn't made me all that eager for a second one.

Looking back to when I was sixteen or seventeen, I can see I had some crushes on some women players and didn't really know it. I just liked being with them. By the time I was eighteen I knew I always had these feelings.

When it finally happened, it was with somebody older

than me, a woman I met in the States, and it seemed so natural. I was pretty much a rookie with women, and I'm shy anyway, so it took forever for me to get the hints she was throwing at me. Finally, the way she put it, I was invited over to snuggle, and it went on from there. She knew what she was doing. I don't remember any flowers and candlelight, but I do remember feeling relaxed and happy being with her, waiting for the next step.

When it finally happened, I said, This is easy and right. And the next morning—*voilà*—I had an outright, head-over-heels case of infatuation with her. When will I see you again? What will we do with our time together? I was in love, just like in the story books, and everything felt great.

At the time, although a few people knew, I never felt I would have any image problem. I was one of the up-and-coming female tennis players in the world, and I didn't imagine my sexuality would become a major issue to anybody. It seemed like *my* business somehow.

I had no idea what it was like to be a public figure. Whether I was seeing a man or a woman, I wouldn't want pictures of us in the papers. It would be nice to be able to put your arm around somebody while you're out at a restaurant, and I've tried to be guarded about my private life, but it always gets out. Look what Chris had to go through when she and John were separated for a while. Reporters gain an interview by claiming to be interested in tennis, but you know they're going to ask about your love life. People do stakeouts on your house, ring your doorbell at three in the morning.

I remember one time when Rita Mae Brown and I took an apartment near Sloane Square during Wimbledon and one of those high-caliber British journals stationed a photographer across from our building. The only picture he got was Rita Mae walking out of a grocery store. The headline was something like: "Writer Shops for Martina Love Nest."

I thought it was funny because actually I did most of the shopping.

Right from my first affair in the States, I wanted privacy but I was also uncomfortable about pretending to be something I wasn't. Somebody once said to me, "Society isn't ready for it." And I told her, "Hey, we're society, too."

The first affair lasted about six months and then it was over—her decision. I was crushed, and it was tough getting over it. When we were together, I just wanted to go off on an island and live happily ever after. And when it was over, I wanted to run away and hide on the same island. I got over it, though, even if it did cost me a few tennis tournaments, played in a haze of tears.

Other parts of my life were fine. My principal residence was Fred Barman's house in Beverly Hills. I had no interest in what was going on, financially, in those days. I didn't know where my money was going, and really didn't care. I was just interested in playing tennis and having a good time. I figured I had all these years ahead of me, so why worry about finances when there were more important things to do. Fred gave me all the cash I wanted and set up a corporation to take care of the rest.

Fred had a beautiful house with a Spanish tile roof on one of the quiet streets just north of downtown Beverly Hills. Outside, he and his wife, Rumiko, had a one-lane swimming pool, seventy feet long, great for a workout. I had the run of the house, including a den with pictures of Fred's business trips to Japan and a big pool table.

I was driving Fred's dangerous old Toyota, with bad brakes and beat-up tires, and I figured I was making enough money to afford a car of my own. I could have gone for something fancy, but I decided my first car ought to be plain and practical and basic—like me. A silver 450 SL.

I went the whole Beverly Hills route and got personalized license plates, too: X-CZECH.

I also made a few raids on the boutiques of Beverly Hills. For this, I hold Shari Barman personally responsible. It was she, after all, who had escorted me to my first American boutique in Sausalito, a few months earlier. She says I looked like "a kid in a candy store," developing my taste for Gucci, Pucci, and Neiman-Marcus, jewelry, handbags, and even sleek foreign sports cars.

There were a few "candy stores" on Rodeo Drive, too. I'd go roaming around with a couple of friends of mine, Mimi and Janet, who had a house in Beverly Hills where I could shoot pool or play tennis. They also had this servant who'd give me Polish sausages and otherwise do his best to keep me fed. I'd have lunch there and nibble somewhere else later. Before long, the expensive clothes I'd found on Rodeo Drive didn't fit me anymore.

I just couldn't keep my weight down in the States. Back home I was always running around, on the go twenty-four hours a day, but here I'd get out of shape playing tournaments. I didn't do nearly as much physically while I was on the tour as I did when I was back home, running back and forth between school and practice.

And the food was so easy to find. In Prague, they didn't have corner shops with goodies in the window that you just had to sample. Czech food had become drab and unappetizing under the Communists. But in the States, there was something everywhere you turned: pancakes, hamburgers, ice cream. At Forest Hills, where they used to hold the U.S. Open, there was a McDonald's on Austin Street, on the right side, that I could not pass without going for a Big Mac and french fries. You could have put blinders on me and I'd have found the door.

With all that I've learned about diet and exercise, I just wish I had those years back again. But life seemed pretty simple at the time. I was young, I was in America, and I was a tennis pro.

Ladies of the Evening

The melodic swell of Tchaikovsky's *Swan Lake* poured from the hotel room, for the benefit of all the other players down the hall. In the room, the 150-pound ballerina practiced her pirouettes more diligently than she had ever practiced her backhand. I was that ballerina.

In America, all things are possible—even a ballet line of swans such as you never imagined before: Billie Jean King, Rosie Casals, and yours truly with her own brief solo, a star of sorts in that infamous troupe known as the Ladies of the Evening.

We committed this assault on ballet in 1977, in the third annual Ladies of the Evening performance by the women professionals. We even had an amateur choreographer named Makarova—Dina Makarova, a photographer and translator, not the other Makarova.

We had a lot of fun on the road in those days. From the first time I was allowed out of Czechoslovakia, I sensed the freedom and camaraderie of the women players. They were just building something in those days, and they had a sense of the pioneer about them. They hung out together more than we do today, they had a good time together.

The best example was the Ladies of the Evening. Rosie

Casals was the instigator in 1975 on Amelia Island, Florida, at the Family Circle tournament. After most of the spectators had gone home for the day, Rosie set up her own championship match between Peachy Kellmeyer and Vicky (Bird Legs) Berner. There were a few interesting ground rules for this game. Peachy had to drink a beer on every changeover, while Vicky had to drink scotch. That brought the level of tennis to a height nobody had ever seen before. The rest of us got into the act, wearing grotesque outfits of the brightest colors that normally only a tourist would wear.

Chris and I were the coaches. I guess I won't soon forget her outfit: a T-shirt that said BIRD LEGS' COACH, hoop earrings, horizontal striped socks, and an orange baseball cap turned backward like a catcher's. Classy, ya know?

Billie Jean was the umpire, wearing her thickest glasses and making calls as outrageous as the ones she thought had been made against her over the years. Betty Stove and Frankie Durr were the most intrusive pair of ball girls you've ever seen. Oh, yes, and Bird Legs was wearing size forty-eight boxer shorts, to add a touch of dignity to the event.

That started the tradition, and we spent a year planning the next outing. It gave us something to think about on the road for weeks and months at a time. As Shari Barman put it, "When you always lose in the first round, you need something else to do." So she had T-shirts made up that said LADIES OF THE EVENING. The tour officials were always a little hesitant about publicizing our group—because of the name, no doubt—but we were not inhibited.

In 1976 we held our bash after the finals of a Virginia Slims event in Los Angeles. Ted Tinling was the master of ceremonies, wearing his best earring. He told the crowd they could stay if they wanted, and most of the 10,000 people sat there and watched Chris play Olga Morozova.

All of us were in a good mood because of the brownies Rosie Casals had baked for the occasion. Billie Jean and Evonne were the coaches this time, and Virginia Wade was the umpire. She did something I've never seen an umpire do: a somersault right in the middle of the court.

Later that night we had a banquet at the Beverly Hills Hotel and Bill Cosby gave out the awards. We made more of a fuss over our Ladies of the Evening contest than about our tournament.

The third version took place in 1977 at a disco in the Hilton Hotel in Philadelphia. By now we were professionals, and we put on a talent show, if you want to call it that. Olga Morozova sang a Russian song; Chris dressed up as Groucho Marx; Betty Stove dressed as a genie with a Gucci bag; Jeanie Brinkman did a tap dance; Jerry Diamond did an imitation of different players; Frankie Durr danced the can-can; and the lighter of foot performed *Swan Lake*.

Dina Makarova had simplified some ballet steps for Rosie, Vicky, Connie Spooner, our trainer, and me. Billie Jean rehearsed with us, but when the time came, she chickened out. I actually got to the point where I knew the steps so well that they let me perform a solo. I had rehearsed it, much to everybody's displeasure, at odd hours in my hotel room for days ahead. Dum-da-dum, da, da-da-da-da-dum . . . I still remember twirling. If I tried it today, I'd probably break my leg.

That's what life was like when I first joined the tour. It was more fun then because people were more willing to cut up. Even though we competed hard on the court, we had something in common off the court. Nowadays, players go their separate ways, myself included. Kids have parents or coaches or agents with them and don't mingle the way we did then.

In those days we would do things together. I remember, right after I came over, one of those beautiful dry, not-too-hot spring days in Phoenix when the desert was in bloom. Raquel Giscafre, Shari Barman, Fiorella Bonicelli, and I rented four motorcycles, not your little putt-putt motorbikes but 250s and 350s. I was playing Fiorella at eight that night but we figured we'd be getting the same amount of sun and exhaustion, so it didn't really matter. We took off around eleven in the morning, wearing bathing suits and helmets, going eighty-five miles per hour on the interstate. I wouldn't do that on my life today, but then I was eighteen, nineteen, what did I know? We went to this lake, watched people water-ski, almost did that, too, but finally we got on our cycles and roared home. Got back at six and I beat Fiorella in straight sets—just as I would have without both of us having gotten a massive case of sunburn.

It seems to me there was always something to laugh about in those days. On one tour in 1974, I lost to Rosie in three straight tournaments. Billie Jean would come by in the locker room and see me in just a bra and panties and she would tell Rosie how strong I was, that I could pick Rosie up and throw her around. They were pretending they were afraid of me, when the truth of the matter was, I am the biggest pussycat. For the first Ladies of the Evening outing, Rosie had some T-shirts made up that said NAVRAT THE BRAT, a nickname that stayed with me for years. It made me feel part of the gang, better even than back at Sparta.

In the last few years, with all the gossip about lesbianism in sports, I've read some suggestions that mothers of young players were so afraid of their daughters' being accosted in the locker room that they'd accompany them there. That's just so far-fetched. The only mother I ever saw in the locker room was Mrs. Austin, and Tracy was so shy she wouldn't walk around in her underwear.

Let's face it, if women are going to become gay, it's not going to happen in the locker room. Yes, in most locker rooms, the lockers are open, and some of us change right out in front of each other. You can also see most of us getting a rubdown from the trainers on a table right out in the open. Some of us are more modest than others, but it has nothing to do with sexual preference. When I first came along, I was petrified to change in front of anybody. I was ashamed of how I looked, too immature at first, then too heavy. I didn't even want to be seen in my underwear, much less the altogether.

After a while, it became too much trouble to change in the shower, to carry a bathrobe with you. It's not like you're an exhibitionist, but you make your living with your body and it stops having a mystique. Now I walk around the house with nothing on sometimes. I don't think Renee Lieberman is ever going to get over my going to the door naked in Far Rockaway to call my dogs back from their walk. Oops, sorry, Renee. Thought I was in the locker room.

But women's sexual preferences are not changed in the lockers. For one thing, I don't think the percentage of gay women on the circuit is that much higher than the national level—ten percent or whatever. And I'll bet it's about the same in male sports, too. The truth is, men are much more promiscuous about homosexuality. They've got gay bars, gay baths, whereas women have more stable relationships and most don't go in for one-night stands.

While we're talking about the tour, I have never seen a female tennis player who I thought had a dope problem. I've seen some male basketball players go downhill overnight and figured they must be on drugs, and then suddenly they're on rehab. I've heard the same rumors as everybody else about cocaine on the men's tour, but we're two different worlds, meeting only at a few major tournaments, and I've never seen signs of a male player going down like the basketball players. On our tour, there used to be some marijuana, but now you don't even see that. The women are so clean. The extent of their debauchery is drinking a beer or a screwdriver.

Some of the women do have emotional problems—too much, too soon, they have a hard time adjusting to life on the road in their teens. I see mood swings and personality problems in a couple of the most promising young players, but I attribute that to family difficulties, not drugs.

I hate to disappoint people, but the women's tour was much like the old-fashioned image of a college sorority, particularly back in the seventies. We played together, we traveled together, we partied together, we worried about money together.

We also had to compete against our road companions, week after week. Being on the court with an opponent is a strange business. You're totally out for yourself, to win a match, yet you're dependent on your opponent to some degree for the type of match it is and how well you play. You need the opponent; without her you do not exist.

Playing against Chris was always like battling part of your own nature. You know it so well but you can't give in to it. She was not the best athlete in the world, not a pure athlete like Candy Reynolds or Betsy Nagelsen or Hana Mandlikova, but there was always that determination.

I'd be out there on one side of the net and I'd see those eyes squinting and I'd say, "Oh, no." I knew she would be steady. I knew she would not make a mistake. She'd whip that two-handed backhand at me. I'd hit the ball back to her, and she would squint again and set her mouth and hit the two-hander, just a little differently this time. She did it so well, for so many years.

Her serve was mechanical, not a weapon. Sometimes I'd wonder why she never improved her serve, considering that she improved the rest of her game. But she had such shot-making ability. Her backhand came back so hard and she never quit on a ball, so you knew you could never quit, either. You'd always have to tell yourself, "This is Chris. Don't give up."

Another opponent who really awed me was Margaret Court, because I admired her so much when I was young. I only played her a few times at the end of her career, when she didn't serve that hard, but she was still a wonder. Even when I beat her in the Australian Open at Kooyong in 1975, by a score of 6–4, 6–3, I'd still stand on the other side of the net and watch these bombs come rocketing in on first serve.

She was so tall and formidable that I'd find myself staring at her and wondering what she had been like a few years earlier. I hate to sound like Hana, who's always talking about me being some kind of alien in size and strength, but Margaret actually amazed me with her size and strength.

With Billie Jean, it was different. In my early years, I was totally in awe of her backhand. I would serve her wide and she'd hit it right down the line to my backhand. I'd say, "Damn, how did she do that?" She wasn't the same player she had been—I never played Billie Jean at her peak—but she was still awesome. She'd try some of those little dinks and I'd think to myself, Cut the crap. But she never let on. She'd just blink at you behind those glasses, and you would wonder, What's she going to do next?

Billie Jean was the leader of the pack, no doubt about it. The queen of the hill. She was such a great player and so proud of women's tennis that she turned the sport into a big-time event. Everything she did was for tennis. She saw this new kid from Czechoslovakia and came over and gave me advice on my backhand. She had advice on every subject. She wanted tennis to succeed so much that she would even try to improve her opponents' games—to prepare us to be professionals.

The only time she didn't give anything away was on the court. I idolized Billie Jean so much that the first few times

I played her, I'd get all tense and just give away point after point. I knew my shots were as good as hers, but I also knew how smart she was and I'd start wondering what she was going to do next.

Right in the middle of a match, Billie Jean would totally change her game, and I'd think, Shoot, what does she know? I'd stop playing from strength, and I'd give away a big game to her. Other players did the same thing to me. Tracy Austin, when she came along, would lob for no apparent reason, or suddenly come in behind my ball, or she'd serve-and-volley, and I'd totally lose it. I think they watched Billie Jean play me, and watched me panic.

I've seen Billie Jean practice gamesmanship with other players: stop and argue with the umpire, tie her shoelace, anything to distract her opponent. I knew she could do it, but she never tried it with me—at least I never noticed it.

We played doubles for a while, but we were often on different tours. I didn't beat her until early in 1978, in the finals of Houston, a three-setter. Because I figured I should have done it sooner, it wasn't that big a deal.

I studied Billie Jean so carefully that I even began arguing with the officials at times. After all, I reasoned, if Billie Jean King didn't mind looking like a competitor on the court, why should I? But I don't think people took it as well from me as they did from her. She was special; she was creating modern women's tennis, by force of personality. She set the standard. She made us feel we were all in this together. She made us feel we were building something.

There's not as much of that feeling in the sport now. I know Billie Jean complains that Chris and I don't put enough back into the game. She thinks we should spend our every waking minute promoting tennis. But where do you draw the line? Billie Jean thinks you should play every week, give clinics, make public appearances, talk to the press, because that's what she did. She made this sport what it is today, and I can understand how she feels. But I've got to live my own life, too.

I'm sure Billie Jean wishes she were ten years younger. She built women's tennis up and by the time it peaked, her best years were behind her. It's too bad, but what do you say about Althea Gibson and Maria Bueno, two of the best players in history, who never got any money out of tennis?

Billie Jean had great foresight about tennis. I'm not sure she was that good in following through, in making sound business decisions. She put money into World Team Tennis, softball, a sports magazine, none of which made big profits. I don't think she'll ever have to worry about starving, but she was one of the great champions of all time and the big money wasn't there until she stood up for equal prize money for women.

I look at somebody like Ivan Lendl, who still hadn't won a Grand Slam event until the French Open in 1984, yet he was making millions. And then there was Tony Trabert, who won all the biggest tournaments and probably didn't make a dime. Wrong time, wrong place.

The money today is staggering, I don't even think about it anymore. The amazing part is that I could make even more than I do. I could play exhibitions, like Björn Borg does, and never worry about competing again. But I won't do much of that, and I'll tell you why: I'd rather be on the tour whenever possible. It's as close as I come to having a community.

Chris and I are not as close as we used to be. When Nancy Lieberman and I worked together, there was something of a wedge between me and Chris. Tracy Austin, you never saw or heard much from her. And Andrea Jaeger's got her own problems—half the time she's in a good mood and the other half she's not. But there's still a core of friendship, particularly at the smaller tournaments, where there's less press, fewer business agents around. Some of my best friends are also my opponents.

At the start, I'd have trouble mixing business and friendship. I would lose to somebody I had no business losing to. I played Frankie Durr in 1975 when I had a sore shoulder. They were timing our serves with one of those radar guns, and mine was clocked at ninety-one miles per hour while hers couldn't even be clocked because the machine wouldn't accept anything under seventy. I was so relaxed enjoying a good hit with her, that she beat me. And it wasn't the only time.

Usually, my competitiveness took over. I remember Kerry Melville Reid complaining that I could get "obnoxious" on the court, questioning calls. Kerry was quoted as saying: "She gets that from Billie Jean King, her idol. I guess she figures that if Billie Jean can get away with it, intimidating officials, then she can do it. She copies Billie Jean a lot." But Kerry added that she liked me anyway, and it was true. Most of us got along.

There were a few players who wouldn't say hello before a match, like Nancy Richey, but I always felt I could socialize and still have the killer instinct. I could do anything with Sharon Walsh before a match, she's so easygoing, or Wendy Turnbull or Betsy Nagelsen or Pam Shriver. I recently played bridge one afternoon with Marcella Mesker and then beat her in tennis that evening.

We took pride in being fair with each other, knowing that the officials were often recruited from local tennis clubs and lacked the reflexes and training needed to call a professional match. When I first came along, the press used to think I complained about my bad calls, but I would argue just as ferociously if I thought my opponent had been shorted. Sometimes I'd even double-fault on purpose if they wouldn't change the call.

Some of the players said I was the fairest one out there. The public thought Evonne was great because she was so serene and beautiful, but she never said anything about a call. Borg never said a word either, even if his opponent was getting screwed by the call. He wouldn't blink an eyelash. But I always wanted the match to be perfect, right down to the officiating.

I've never been able to treat my opponent as the enemy, particularly Pam Shriver, my doubles partner and one of my best friends. I remember only one time being psyched up against her, in Tampa not too long ago in a final, when I was out for a friendly match of tennis on a beautiful Sunday afternoon. With the score 3–all in the first set, I called a let on her serve, and she disagreed. She got upset and started smarting off, so I thought to myself, Same to you, Turkey, and played my little butt off for the rest of the match. I'm sure I would have gotten my butt in gear anyway, but she helped the cause. Later, we talked about it and cleared the air right away. "You know me from doubles," I said. "If I think it's a let, I'll call it." I also told Pam that she should be all sweetness and joking around, so she'd have a better chance. Actually, she's given me some of my biggest losses, and she constantly comes up with big matches against me.

At first it was hard being on the road most of the time. I was always glad to see friends like the Hoschls in Chicago or Aja and Paul Steindler in New York. I learned to reach out for friends when I had a free day. One time in Washington, on Super Bowl Sunday, we didn't have a match, so I called Jane Leavy from the Washington *Post* and asked what she was doing. She said she and her husband and some friends were watching the game on television and invited me over. I spent the afternoon with them and we talked football, no tennis, and I felt I had totally escaped from the cocoon for a day.

Ever since I became a pro, I have tried to balance my need for rest with my need for friends. After a while, you have friends everywhere, and you run into some fans who become your friends after you've seen them a few times. It's usually discouraging to both sides because I want to have time with them, yet I don't. On the road, I might want to go to a museum or a movie, but I learned during my time with Rita Mae Brown that I shouldn't be too emotionally spent or physically tired before a match. I now have a policy of never giving a private interview before matches because it might upset me; I don't want to be worrying while I'm on the court, thinking, Gee, why did I say that?

The one thing I learned to appreciate on the road was sleeping right through breakfast. I have a system for when I wake up: order room service, take a shower while waiting for it to arrive, eat with the soaps on television while my hair's drying, and then go out for a walk. I love being in a city like Paris or New York or San Francisco that has a real downtown, where you can drop into a bookstore or gift shop without having to take a car. In a real city, I can walk two blocks and get a lot done, but if I have to drive someplace, it's a drain on my energy. In the hours before a match, I'll read a book or watch TV, and lately I've been playing bridge with Barbara Hunter Estep, my coach's wife.

From the time I joined the tour in 1975, one of my best friends has been Lee Jackson, the chief official. But then again, Lee is a terrific friend to all of us. I know this sounds strange, but it's not like a baseball player saying he's friendly with an umpire, which could never happen. It's hard to imagine John McEnroe or Jimmy Connors hanging out with somebody they've just vilified on the court, but it's different with women's tennis.

I remember the first full year I traveled on the tour, being in New York with nothing to do and calling Lee at her home in the suburbs. She invited me to her club, where I played squash for the first time and gave the club pro a pretty good match. I also played Scrabble with Lee and sat around the club talking with a lawyer about American and European history.

I haven't been doing enough of that kind of thing since I began my full-time exercise and diet program with Nancy, but I know I've got to seek out more friendships, keep learning. In 1976 Lee Jackson's son was killed in an automobile crash and she began to travel more on the tour. She used to organize trips to Disney World or to good restaurants on a night off. I know I missed my mother, not just for her great Czech meals and her sewing, but for her emotional support, and Lee took over that role in my life. I only hope we were as much a comfort to her as she has been to a whole generation of tennis players.

I honestly don't think our friendship has interfered in any way with our work. If Lee is handling my match, and I think somebody is blowing a call on the lines, I'll stamp my foot and say, "Come on, Lee, look what they're doing." And Lee will say, right into the microphone, "That's enough, Martina." I don't want to embarrass her or her officials, so in a sense she raises our behavior level because we respect her. If that's the difference between men's and women's tennis, *vive la différence*. I will still complain about calls when I think they're wrong, even if the crowd doesn't like it. Tennis is my livelihood. We're not playing for fun like in the old days. But you don't want to humiliate people.

Hana Mandlikova broke my streak in Oakland in 1984, when I was within two matches of tying Chris's record of fifty-six consecutive singles victories. There are no surprises on the women's tour. I know Hana's a great athlete, but she's inconsistent, and if she falls behind she loses confidence. I hadn't been playing much before I went to Oakland, and Nancy was trying to get me to cancel because she wanted me to help her prepare for the Superstars competition. I couldn't get out of it, though, and Hana caught me on a bad day.

That match turned on a call by Lee Jackson. I was serving at 4-all, 15-all in the third set. Hana returned service and I hit a topspin, half-volley forehand that looked as if it would go out, but at the last second it swerved down and landed inbounds. It didn't even touch the line, and the official never even raised a hand to signify it was good, but Lee overruled him and called the ball out.

I asked Lee why she overruled a call that was never made. I mean, even if she thought it was out, she's only supposed to call it out if it's out by a lot. I didn't expect Hana to decline the call but I was annoyed with Lee for making it. I know she's a good official and she's fair, but there was no excuse for that call.

I didn't see Lee for a few weeks, until one day we were practicing in New Jersey and I could hear the clicking of her keys as she walked by. Without looking at her, I started narrating the match with Hana two weeks earlier, talking about the terrible call by the head umpire. Then I turned around and said: "Oh, hi, Lee, I didn't know you were here." "I bet you didn't," she said. And our friendship went on from there.

I need friends like Lee on the tour. She is as close to family as anybody in this country. But there were times when the tour wasn't enough, when the loneliness was too much. It took about a year for the immensity of defection to really hit me. And when it did, it hit me like a ton of bricks.

The Ton of Bricks

I thought it was going to be easy, moving to America and playing on the tour. It was so easy that within a year I was a walking candidate for a nervous breakdown, overweight and overwrought.

I started to show signs of strain at Wimbledon, in the quarterfinals against Sue Barker of Great Britain. I have always loved playing at Wimbledon, have always tried to be on my best behavior there because it's the biggest tournament in tennis, the one that Europe recognizes as the world championship. I belonged here, playing the tournament my parents had dreamed about. But I was also a lost soul, careening out of control.

Barker was the local favorite, and of course the British papers were rooting for her to upset The Great Wide Hope. I could deal with it, I thought, playing with my newfound American toughness—Jimmy Connors without the finger. I managed to win the first set, but lost the second and fell behind, 1–4, in the third set as the line calls began going against me: one, two, three, four, five, all the way up to thirty-five. You'd have to say I was counting.

"I wonder if you called it that way because she's British," I shouted.

The linesmen heard me and so did the press. After I pulled out the match in the third set, I had to answer questions about whether I thought the British officials were prejudiced against me. I had never thought so before, and I have never thought so again, but in that distempered summer of 1976 I was sure the entire world was against me.

I have never felt so alone, and I am a person who does not like to be alone. I had grown up with four in a room for part of my childhood, had always had plenty of company on my first trips out of Czechoslovakia, but now there were times when I was alone in my hotel room, alone in airplanes, not yet twenty, and very much on my own. My first couple of love affairs had gone down the drain, but I was not the kind of person who went off into a corner to lick her wounds and think things over.

Until that time, I really hadn't given much thought about who I was and what I was. I just did things instinctively, like leaving home or rushing the net. Whatever seems right, do it. But in the summer of 1976, it all started catching up with me. I was irritable, sad, lonely, with no friend or philosophical safety net underneath me.

After losing to Chris in the semifinals, I flew directly back to the States to resume World Team Tennis, the new gimmick of the time. There was enough money in it that all the good American players were concentrating on WTT in 1975 and 1976. Joe Zingale, the owner of the Cleveland Nets, had signed me in 1975 for three years; he gave me a contract reported to be $300,000, but was only half that much, and a gold "Number 1" pendant. But the sport didn't work out there, and I moved to the Boston Lobsters in 1976.

In 1977 Greer Stevens and I played women's doubles, winning something like forty sets and losing only four. We'd win and I'd win the women's singles and then we'd play cheerleader, rooting for the guys. I enjoyed being on the bench, rooting for my team. It was just like Sparta, back home in Prague.

It was also fun going out in a crowd after the match. It was easy being a woman in that company. The men had a different mentality from women. They'd take over the best corner of a pub somewhere, order some pitchers of beer. A woman would be thinking: I wonder if we can do this; I wonder if I could order that. The men would just say: "Everything's cool."

With the Lobsters, we'd be up till all hours, waiting for Emmo—Roy Emerson—to get to the punch line of his jokes. Wherever there were Aussies, we'd have a great time: Ross Case, Rod Laver, Kerry Reid. If the hotel restaurant was closed, we'd raid the kitchen refrigerator anyway. My teammate Mike Estep from Texas was quiet, but he'd throw parties at his apartment. Years later I would ask him to be my coach for the final push to the top.

But even with this rollicking bunch of teammates, I felt alone. We were constantly on the go: a few matches in Boston, then out to California and the Southwest, all spring. Then I played Wimbledon and gave a few hints that I was losing my grip, and after losing to Chris in the semis, it was back on the plane for a Monday-night Lobster match in San Francisco. We played something like twelve matches in fourteen days, including a trip to Hawaii, and when we didn't make the playoffs, I had two weeks to prepare for the U.S. Open. I needed to readjust from the indoor carpet to the clay courts of Forest Hills, but I was so sick of tennis that I didn't touch a racquet for the whole time.

Instead, I worked out one day on clay and one day on a hard court and figured I'd play my way into shape during the tournament. It was not the best reasoning in the world, but I had nobody to advise me. The World Team Tennis friendships didn't carry over into regular tournament life because we were all trying to win the same tournaments.

It was less than a decade ago, but it seems like the dark ages in some respects. Hardly anybody had a coach. Borg had Lennart Bergelin, and lots of people made little jokes about Borg being so dependent on somebody else, as if that took something away from what he did. We were lone rangers out on the court and we were expected to be lone rangers off the court, too.

Nowadays you look and almost everybody travels with a coach or advisor for most of the tournament schedule. In 1976 I had nobody in my life to say, "Hey, you ought to be out there on a clay court for a week ahead of time, getting used to the surface." The U.S. Open was important to me, but not important enough to prepare for it.

I got to Forest Hills and all the memories of 1975 came flooding over me. I kept having flashbacks of my trips to the Immigration Service, the fears of being kidnapped by Communist officials, the worries about where I would live. I had put a lid on the emotions surrounding my defection for a whole year, but as soon as I opened up my racquet bag at Forest Hills, they swarmed out like termites in the spring and they ate me alive.

We were still playing out of that crowded little dressing room at the West Side Tennis Club, and everybody was talking about the first anniversary of my defection. I got this tight, claustrophobic feeling, complicated by a hard rain that should have wiped out the entire card.

It's U.S. Open policy that as long as a few matches are played they don't have to refund the ticket money, so I knew they would manage to squeeze in some matches, rain or not. I was supposed to play in the stadium at around 3:30, but the weather kept pushing back the time for all of the matches.

My first-round opponent was Janet Newberry, a solid professional who wouldn't give anything away, but really just the kind of player you'd want to meet early in a tournament. We were sitting around during the rain and I asked Janet if we could ask for a postponement until the next day. She said she didn't think the officials would go for it.

They had installed some Har-Tru courts that dry fairly quickly, so after a brief halt in the rain, they rushed me into the stadium at 6:55 p.m. The fans, who had been waiting around since 11 a.m. with very little action, were screaming for Janet to upset me, which I understood perfectly: I was seeded and she wasn't, and people almost always root against the favorite.

I won the first set, 6–1, not even thinking about losing. But then all of a sudden, I was doing everything wrong, just lunging at the ball, and the match started getting away from me. I lost the second set, 4–6, and my body just tightened up. I was unable to do a thing as Janet played the match of her life and won the third set, 6–3. Before I could "play myself into shape," I was out.

My memories are reconstructed through a haze of tears, and the blur from a towel around my head. Newberry is a good friend, and she was nice about it, consoling me as I walked off the court. People say I looked like I was in a state of shock, just sobbing, tears rolling down my face, the floodgates open.

"I never saw anybody so miserable, so totally out of control," Janet told Bud Collins afterward.

Well, she had a good vantage point. I got to the bench and pulled the towel over my head and just rocked back and forth, moaning and crying. So much had been expected of me, so much had happened to me, and now I felt that the whole world was crashing in on me. Later I told Bud Collins: "I'm ashamed of what happened. That wasn't nice, the way I acted. And I took something away from Janet with my behavior." But I don't think I had any control over myself at the time.

Fred Barman was at the match, and he came over and put his hands on my shoulders. I didn't even know who it was because I had the towel over my head. I didn't want any flashbulbs going off in my face and I didn't want people to see me crying. Fred maneuvered me through the crowded walkways to the clubhouse, a long walk on a tense rainy night, and I took a shower, staying in there as long as I could.

We were supposed to be available to meet the press, and I knew Neil Amdur of *The New York Times* and a couple of the other regulars were waiting for me outside the locker room.

"Why don't you go through the back door?" Fred suggested.

Fred went out and talked to the reporters, who wanted to know if my new life in the States had cut into my tennis game. Fred said: "Here's a young kid who was imprisoned a year ago. She's been like a young girl in Disneyland for the first time. I've got to have a long talk with her."

So for the first time in my career I ducked the press and went back to the hotel. Once I got there, I knew I had to call off my doubles match the next day because I just couldn't face anybody. My regular partner at the time, Chris, had decided she wasn't going to play doubles anymore because of tendonitis in her finger, and I was going to play with Julie Anthony. I knew Julie wanted to play, but I called her and said: "I just can't handle this." She was good about it, and that's the only time I ever defaulted from a doubles match for any reason but injury, and I still feel guilty about it.

I still consider the loss to Janet the worst of my career, at least in the way I responded to it on and off the court. I have had defeats that meant more to me: losing to Tracy Austin in the 1981 U.S. Open was worse because I was so well prepared and should have won it, but just screwed up;

and the quarterfinal loss to Pam Shriver at the 1982 Open hurt, too, but that time I was sick with toxoplasmosis, a blood ailment, and had anticipated losing a tough three-set match if I let myself get taken that far.

But at least with those matches, I was a professional in every sense. Knowing why I'd lost, I shed my tears and I got over them in an hour or two. But that 1976 one wracked me. At the hotel, I was still crying—hysterical, shocked. If there was ever anybody who needed some help, it was me. Fortunately, I got it from someone who knew how to deal with the hard parts of being a professional athlete.

Haynie

I had met Sandra Haynie while I was participating in the Superstars competition in Florida in April of 1976. The women's golf tour was in the area, and she came over to watch. We got to talking, and I went out to watch her play a golf tournament a few weeks later.

I was fascinated by her play. As nerve-wracking as golf can be, she was so calm, so cool. When she putted, she used the same routine every time. She was so organized, so orderly, with her beautiful swing. I liked the way she handled herself on the course.

Haynie had been a pro since 1961, and she had won the U.S. Open and Ladies' Professional Golf Association championships in 1974. She struck me as different from a lot of the tennis players I knew. She was quiet, self-contained—maybe the result of years spent standing over a ten-foot putt with no opponent, no moving ball, no way to burn off her energy. You've got to have a grip on yourself or you'll never get to be a champion like Haynie. (I realize I have the habit of always referring to her as "Haynie," rather than using her first name, but this is out of fondness for a wise old pro.)

We started talking about my sport and my inconsistency on the court. Right away, I figured she could help me get over my own immaturity, but I was so busy that summer that I really didn't have much chance to get to know her.

I could have used some of her poise that rainy night at Forest Hills. But she was en route to New York to watch me play, and she never got the chance to see me in the Open —Janet Newberry took care of that. After the match, I felt so alone, without my family or friends. I called Haynie, who had just arrived at the hotel, and I said: "I lost." It was about all I could manage to blurt out, because I was still choked up with tears.

Later, she joined me and Fred Barman and started telling me about some tournaments she had lost.

"How could this happen? I thought I was prepared," I kept saying, but I knew I had not been prepared.

"You'll be all right," Haynie said. "There are always other tournaments." But at the moment, I thought the world was going to end. She told me it was hard for me to adjust to losing because I had come along so fast that I had never known what it was like to struggle.

"You've never had a bad year," she told me. "Everybody has them, sooner or later. You're young, you'll get over it. Everybody gets down. Everybody." She was right. I had never had to dig within myself. I listened to her, and it made sense.

After a day of talking with Haynie, I knew she was the

friend I needed. She was older, wiser, and a champion in her own right. She didn't need my money or my fame to feel good about herself. She was having some physical problems at the time and not playing much tournament golf, so she offered to act as my advisor for a while. The only problem was, I was still living with the Barmans in Beverly Hills and Haynie is pure Dallas, through and through. Her family is there, and she was not about to leave for anything.

So I did the only thing that made sense to me. I went to Dallas and bought a house the day after my loss to Newberry. I had only lived in L.A. since my defection a year earlier, and I had been wanting to do something else. I didn't think L.A. was my kind of town; it was a little too big, a little too casual. There wasn't a great place for me to play there, and I needed a change of climate.

Buying a house in one day is typical of my impulsive nature. I would do the same thing in 1982 after my loss to Pam at the Open. I heard about a house in Virginia Beach that was up for sale, so I went down and bought it. It was the same way with my dogs. I was going to buy one dog and wound up buying three. And I did it again recently when I saw a macaw for sale. Just had to have it, right then and there. I named it KJ because it dances and sways, its head bobbing up and down, just like Kathy Jordan does when she's receiving a serve. I admit I'm an impulse buyer.

The people of Dallas had always been nice to me when I played there on the tour. I knew the city, and now I had a friend there, so it made sense to settle in. I paid around $125,000 for a three-bedroom ranch house in the Spring Creek section on the north side of Dallas. I immediately planted some trees, put in a swimming pool and a Jacuzzi, and got to know the kids in the neighborhood, throwing a football around with them. Right away, I felt a little more at home again. I don't know how people in Dallas will take having their city compared to Revnice, Czechoslovakia, but that's how I felt.

Haynie shared the house with me, and we also used it as an office for our business. When Nancy Lieberman and I worked together a few years later, everybody acted as if I had never had advice like this before but, really, Haynie planted a lot of sound ideas in my head.

We started going to the club to work out on the machines, and she got me out running. I had always resisted exercise, ever since gym class back in Revnice, but Haynie let me know that my way of training was not helping my game. She tried to get me off junk food, too. She'd cook up a bunch of chicken and vegetables and tell me it was better to eat that than all the heavy sauces and desserts I was getting in restaurants. My weight dropped from 167 to 144 within a year.

Haynie was so easygoing that it was easy to take advice from her. She never tried to pretend she knew anything about tennis, but she did understand what it was like to compete. She didn't try to tell me what to do, like every other Tom, Dick, and Harry when things were going badly; instead, she'd urge me to listen to Chris and Billie Jean because they were both good friends.

She did question my strategy in one case. She couldn't understand why I camped at the baseline and played Chris's game, tournament after tournament. I always thought it would be a badge of honor to beat Chris at her own game, but Haynie told me to play my game, to get back to rushing the net.

Another thing Haynie always stressed was timing. She understood you couldn't lunge at a moving ball any more than you could lunge at a stationary one. After I lost weight, my game didn't get any better until Haynie pointed out that I was getting to the ball so quickly that my racquet was not in place.

A third thing Haynie told me was to stop letting my moods affect my game. She'd say, "It's fine if you want to get frustrated with yourself but turn it inward, don't turn it outward. You have to learn to direct your energy. Don't yell at the officials. Get mad at yourself, not at them." Tennis was a different game from golf, but Haynie understood the inner strength you need for either sport.

"Concentrate on one point at a time," she would say. It sounds simple, but I needed somebody to tell me that.

"If we can concentrate for five hours on the golf course, you can concentrate for an hour or two on the tennis court."

Sometimes Haynie would attend my matches. I always knew where she was sitting and I would appeal to her with my eyes if things were not going well. She had little sympathy for me. If the official had made the right call, Haynie would nod to the court, telling me to keep playing. But if I had gotten a bad call, she would never let on. Just keep playing. I needed it, all that encouragement, all that discipline.

Another thing Haynie stressed was playing almost every week. She felt I needed the work, so she'd encourage me to enter a lot of tournaments. "Put the information in your computer," she'd say.

With Haynie's encouragement, my game started to pick up almost right away. I had won only two tournaments in 1976, partially because of injuries, but I started off 1977 by beating Chris, 6–2, 6–3, in the finals in Washington. I remember some of my friends going over to Haynie and congratulating her for helping me get my act together. I wound up winning six tournaments that year, although Wimbledon and the U.S. Open still eluded me.

Then I started 1978 off by winning thirty-seven straight tournament matches, including seven finals over Betty Stove, Billie Jean, Rosie Casals, Evonne, Stove again, Dianne Fromholtz, and Billie Jean again. I was getting up to the level people had predicted for me, and this was before Team Navratilova was even invented.

Haynie and I were often in different parts of the world, but she tried to get to my major tournaments. If our schedules brought us to Dallas at the same time, we'd hang out, watch some games on television, or toss a football around in front.

I remember one time I injured a tendon in my left wrist and wound up slicing my forehand and hitting topspin backhands and chipping everything until finally I just had to get off the road. Back at the house playing touch football for recreation, I went out for a long pass and jammed my knee against the grille of a car. I shrugged it off as just a bruise. Later, on another pass, the ball took a funny bounce, and when I reached down to pick it up I stepped right on it and sprained my ankle.

Haynie had gone out to the supermarket, and on the way home she passed me and some friends in the other car on the way to the hospital for X-rays. I was on crutches for a week, which was the only way I cured my wrist—sitting there on the couch, an ice pack on my knee, an ice pack on my ankle, an ice pack on my wrist, a couple of painkillers in my stomach, and a dull, stupid smile on my face. What a mess.

Haynie calmed me down on the court and she also temporarily put some control in the rest of my life. I was already trying to live down the wild-spender image I had earned from some of my splurges in Beverly Hills and Neiman-Marcus. She had made some good investments and some bad ones in her life, and she wanted to know how my money was being handled. At the time, I was being helped by Marvin Demoff, who was Rosie's agent, and Fred Barman was investing my money for me. He had set up something called Brat, Inc., and told me I was set for life.

After I moved to Dallas, Haynie began managing my

career and my money, with no hard feelings between me and Fred. I continued to play in his tournaments in Japan and saw him and his family from time to time, and I still always have a big hug and a kiss for him whenever we meet today. But it was time to move on—a familiar feeling for me.

I loved being based in Dallas. I know the city has something of an image problem in the rest of the country because of the *Dallas* television series and President Kennedy's assassination. Many people admit to me they have a bad feeling about Dallas either from reading about it or visiting it briefly. But as somebody who has lived there, on and off, for nearly a decade, I can only say it felt like home to me right away.

I love the excitement of the East Coast, the traditions of Europe, the soft springs and falls of Virginia Beach. But Dallas has given me a sense of security, a feeling of home. Its people adopted me right away, making me a member of The Yellow Rose of Texas Society; in fact, I was an honorary citizen of Texas before I was a citizen of the United States. When I won tournaments, I received proclamations and telegrams from the governor and senators, and I never got the feeling they were just using me for publicity. They were proud to have me there—and still are. In L.A., the natives could care less who else lives there.

I like the way people are so open and friendly in Dallas. They're in the middle of everywhere and also in the middle of nowhere, if you look at the map. You drive five hundred miles and you're still in Texas. It's such a vast state, but it's different everywhere you go.

I could see real regional differences between L.A. and Dallas. In Texas, people do things in their own good time. They have no sense of urgency. Despite California's laidback façade, people out there are always thinking about work, even if they make it sound like play. In New York you know people have to get things done, but in Dallas they play it by ear. They are friendly, but it takes time to make friends. They don't tell you their life story in five minutes, the way they do in California, where people tell you their deepest, darkest secrets the first time you have lunch. I enjoyed seeing Dallas through Haynie's eyes, and I felt comfortable because she was around.

I was less comfortable when she wasn't around. I have always hated being alone, at least until very recently. I always needed somebody down the hall or in the same building or I'd start getting sad and nervous. I've never been very introspective about my feelings, so I can't say what kind of anxieties were floating around inside me. Fear of the unknown? Loss of control? Probably. I remember the first time I was by myself in my own house in Dallas. Haynie was on the road, so I went out and bought a pistol and put it under my pillow.

My poodle, Racquet, would growl at everything. It was one of those Blue Norther nights in Dallas—wind shrieking, windows rattling, lots of noises you don't notice with other people around. I got through the night cradling my pillow with the pistol underneath it, and I've kept a gun in my house since.

If I wasn't in the limelight, I wouldn't need a gun, but you never know. Nobody's ever tried to get in, but I wouldn't hesitate to use it. I know how to load it and I still sleep near it now. I don't want to sound like the coming of J.R. or something. It's not like I carry it around with me like Elvis Presley, shooting out the TV when I don't like the program. I just feel a lot safer with it.

It took me a long time to get over my fear of being alone. But after Nancy Lieberman and I stopped working together in 1984, I found I was actually looking forward to more free time alone. Today, if I'm alone with a couple of hours to kill, I like it, very much so. I don't have to schedule anything, I don't have to answer to anybody. I can read a book or listen to a record or watch television. But I would still feel strange if the dogs weren't here. They don't talk back, however, and I'm getting to appreciate that more and more. Maybe that's part of discovering Who Am I?—the big question.

I'm still evolving, still discovering, and that's how the relationship with Haynie started coming apart. She was a good calming influence on me for a few years, but I was trying to find the world outside and Haynie was happy sitting around watching TV. She was very quiet and she didn't go out—not that I was much for night life, either, but I wanted to get around a little more. She was like a guru to me for three years, and she helped me as much as she could, but I was young and I had to find out about the rest of the world.

Wimbledon 1978

When I was nine years old, I watched Billie Jean King win Wimbledon on television and I vowed that someday I would win it, too. No matter where you come from in Europe, Wimbledon is the tennis championship you honor above all others. In Czechoslovakia, we always took pride in the fact that Jaroslav Drobny had won Wimbledon back in 1954, even though they no longer talked about him because he defected and opened a sporting-goods store in England. And when I was coming along, it was a thrill to work with Vera Sukova, who had been a finalist in 1962. You'd steal little glances at her, knowing she had once curtseyed on the hallowed grass of Wimbledon.

Now in 1978 I wanted a Wimbledon championship. I was twenty-one years old, and it was about time. My father let me know that, too, when he talked to me on the phone: "You'd better win it this year. Jana is getting better and she might beat you to it."

Jana, you understand, was fourteen then.

I came into 1978 strong, rolling up my thirty-seven straight victories before Tracy Austin beat me in Dallas. Haynie's common sense and training program had been good for my head and body, and I was finally becoming the player I thought I should be. It was time to win the biggest tennis title in the world.

The year before, I had been eliminated in the quarters by Betty Stove, and although it hurt, I'd been caught up in the excitement of the Wimbledon centennial. It was a great year for Wimbledon as Virginia Wade—"Our Ginny" to the British press—won the tournament. I have never seen a more appropriate ending to a tournament. I mean, England is no longer a major power in tennis—the Eastern European countries are way ahead—but Virginia turned on a whole nation with her inspired play.

Having won the championships of my two nations—Czechoslovakia and the United States—I can appreciate what it must have meant to Virginia to win Wimbledon. I wouldn't say this about most tournaments, but Wimbledon, and particularly the 1977 Wimbledon, is one tournament I would pay to attend.

By now I've experienced Wimbledon from all different angles. I remember barely getting into Wimbledon in 1973, happy just to be around Billie Jean King and the other great players, staying at the Gloucester Hotel in South Kensington, riding out in an Austin-Healey with the other players.

You'd look out the window and feel the excitement, in a very genteel, low-key British way, of course: the fans lining up for the red double-decker buses, buying their little sandwiches and apples and box lunches, or walking in over the quiet streets and parklands in the ever-present drizzle. They'd be lined up for a dish of strawberries and cream and sugar, so I would always order one in the players' lounge. Now that I've put my eating habits in order, I have the berries plain—but the fresh spring strawberries of Wimbledon are still a treat unto themselves.

From the first time I went to Wimbledon, I was conscious of the ancient English class system that still exists there today: the sleek limousines and their occupants in sedate suits and flowery dresses being escorted to their private boxes, in the family for decades; and a few feet away, on the other side of the barricades, the patient fans from Europe and North America and the other continents mingling—all the languages, all the accents—waiting in line for standing-room tickets.

The British reserve still dominates, which is nice because you have the sense of tradition. But it's counterproductive when it precludes you from entering the matches because it's two minutes to twelve: until they open the main gate, they used to let in members but not workers or players, which meant that if you made the mistake of getting caught in the crowd by the main gate, you lost five of your fifteen minutes to warm up. And you get fifteen minutes only if you're playing on Centre Court or Court 1. I remember one time I got caught in a crush of people trying to get to the best standing-room-only spot at Centre Court. This is ridiculous, I thought. They're crowding in to see me play, and I'm stuck in the middle of them.

In the last few years, the management has gotten much

more receptive to the players' needs, but funny things still happen. In 1983, when I was already a three-time champion and working on my fourth, I rented a house a few blocks from the courts. Living near the club makes it easy to walk or bicycle home between matches and practice, and gives you a feeling of permanence. People in the neighborhood are nice, and they leave you alone, too. One day in 1983 I rode my bike through the club to the practice courts on the other side. I wasn't carrying any identification, but I figured people knew me, and the previous day a guard had let me ride right through. This time, however, a seventy-five-year-old man was posted at the gate. He stopped me and said:

"Sorry, Miss, can't get in without a ticket."

"But I'm a player. My name is—"

"Sorry, Miss."

"But I won this tournament last year."

"Sorry, Miss."

Fortunately, somebody recognized me, and the guard very politely let me in. If that had happened in New York, they might not have been as polite, and I just might have been furious. But it was Wimbledon. Sorry, Miss.

A photographer from one of the tabloids happened to get a picture of me on the bike, and that afternoon it was in the papers, with the headline: "Martina Rides Bike for Exercise During Wimbledon." This was ridiculous.

I used to get a kick out of the British papers going after every scandal and intrigue. I once said at Wimbledon: "I believe in freedom of the press—but what about freedom from the press?" You wouldn't believe the things they come up with, the rumors, pure imagination. You say some little thing at a quickie press conference and an hour later they've already scrawled the latest headline—your comment magnified a thousand times—on a chalkboard at the entrance to the underground.

The television people used to be pretty good. At least they

never followed me around the courts the way they did Björn Borg during his Teen Angel days, when hordes of teenyboppers would chase him through the flower pots. The first time the British press really harassed me was the year Rita Mae Brown and I took a flat near Sloane Square. There was one reporter who kept knocking on the door and finally bribed a maid to get in.

The thing that saved us that year was that Ilie Nastase was having problems with his wife, Dominique, a much juicier story for the British press. I thanked Nasty for helping me out and he said, "Any time, any time." The British tennis writers are all right, more like theater critics than American sportswriters. They write their little six-paragraph critiques of the match and call it in to make the next edition.

The gossip papers really got to me in 1984, when they bothered me around the clock, and I finally threatened to boycott England—except for Wimbledon, of course. Nothing could keep me from Wimbledon.

With all the bustle of Wimbledon, the gossip, the upperclass people in the special boxes, the crowds, the importance of the tournament itself, I don't think an athlete could ever feel more onstage than you do on Centre Court. It brings out every bit of competitor, every bit of egotist, that you need to win a championship. And in 1978, I was finally ready.

Haynie's influence had been helpful, and my mind and body were ready to go. I had a tough draw all the way through: Julie Anthony in the first round, Pam Whytcross in the second, Barbara Jordan, who took the first set off me in the third round, Tracy Austin in the fourth, and Marise Kruger in the quarters.

In the semifinals, I lost the first set to Evonne, 2–6, before I came back to win, 6–4, 6–4, setting up my final-round match with Chris. I had beaten her in a tough three-setter at Eastbourne the week before Wimbledon, but I knew she'd be geared up for this one.

I was nervous at the start and dropped the first set, 2–6. I was still loafing along when I ran right into a passing shot by Chris. It wasn't one of those in-your-face-disgrace slams the men go in for. Chris was aiming for an angle and I just put my temple into it. It didn't really hurt me—woke me up, in fact. After that, I began to feel the ball a little better, and Chris didn't seem so overwhelming.

I won the next two sets, 6–4, 7–5, coming back from 2–4 and 4–5 down in the third set, and for the first time, I was a Wimbledon champion, fulfilling the dream of my father many years before. I put my right hand to my forehead in disbelief, and I could feel Chris patting me on the back, smiling and congratulating me.

Four days later, the Women's Tennis Association computer ranked me Number 1 in the world, breaking Chris's four-year domination. I felt I was on top of the world, and that I'd stay there forever.

Rita Mae

All the time I was growing up, there was a part of me that had never been touched before. It was the point where my mind met my soul. My parents had loved me as their daughter, and other people had cared for me because of my athletic ability or my exotic cheekbones or my sense of humor, or what have you. But there was a part of me undeveloped, waiting to be reached.

I think a few of my teachers had tried to get to me, like the one in high school who wept when she talked about Czech literature and prodded me in desperation, because she knew I was only listening with one cylinder and practicing tennis with the other seven. When I came to the States, other friends like Lee Jackson and Aja Zanova and Svatka Hoschl tried to wake up the part of me, under the surface, that asked questions, that cared about others, that wanted to know about the rest of the world, outside the cocoon of tennis.

I certainly wasn't working too hard to find that part of me. Too busy playing tennis. Too busy playing. Then I met Rita Mae Brown, and the inquisitive little girl in me was revived.

I had read her novel, *Rubyfruit Jungle,* in paperback on a plane from somewhere to somewhere. I liked it but didn't really think her political, lesbian perspective pertained that much to me, although I'd had a few adventures of my own by that time. My self-image was that of an athlete, unconnected to the world of activism and meetings and writings and ideas. The book was fun to read, and that was about it.

We were playing a tournament in Virginia in 1978, and Wendy Overton, one of the players on the tour, said she knew a writer doing a book with a Czech character in it who would like to pick my brains. I said okay. When I found out it was Rita Mae Brown, I was a little more interested, but only a little. I had my match to think about. We talked on the phone one day and I told her a bit about Czechoslovakia, and we went on from there.

The first time we met, I felt Rita Mae wanted to know everything about me. It was exciting. She could talk about anything, and what was even more interesting, she would ask my opinion. People didn't usually do that. Either they didn't think I was smart enough, or they didn't care that much. What was the invasion like? What were the Communist teachers like? What about women's rights in Czechoslovakia? What did I feel about it all? I remember thinking, My God, nobody ever asked me these questions before.

I don't think I was suffering from tunnel vision, but I had never been stimulated intellectually like that before. As a celebrity, you are often asked about things that have nothing to do with your profession: What do you think about the Middle East? What do you think about weapons testing? What do you think about politics? But usually it's so superficial, you think the sportswriters just want a good quote for a headline.

I don't think Rita Mae expected me to be bright. She was surprised. She later said I was one of the brightest people she knew: "Once you get that mind to work . . ."

I've asked myself if she was using the book as a way to get to know me, but I doubt it very much. She was all wrapped up in planning her novel *Southern Discomfort,* and that's really all she was doing that day, picking my brain. The joke was that the Czech guy turned out to be a very minor figure in the book.

I have since seen her quoted as having said that our first meeting was "a lunch that never ended," which sounds very romantic, but that's the novelist speaking, not reality. We did have lunch, a good two and a half hours, and she was funny as hell, but that's all there was to it. I just wish *Southern Discomfort* was as funny as sitting and talking with Rita Mae, but I think they cut out a lot of the good stuff. Dialogue is her strength. I know she made me laugh the first time we met, and that's what life is all about. When people make you laugh and feel good, you want to be with them.

But a lunch that never ended? It was a long time between courses. We shook hands and promised to keep in touch. I saw her briefly in Phoenix that fall and I didn't talk to her at all. Then I ended up calling her after New Year's and we started talking on the phone almost every day, and then we finally met in Chicago at the beginning of February. That may have been the lunch she's talking about.

One thing Rita Mae made clear from the start was that she didn't care whether or not I was a great tennis player. Her attitude was almost the opposite: it's only sports. She would say, "Sports are just to keep your mind off everything else and they don't enhance culture or the mind."

It was the first time anybody had ever suggested that to me. I had always been around people who took tennis very seriously, but Rita Mae had a way of putting it down, almost to the point where if I was working hard, I was doing something wrong. She would say I could be better at other things, which I guess I believed for a while, much to my own harm. Today it's hard to imagine.

She was also cynical about the values of sports. She would tell me: "You're great when you're on the top, but people dump on you when you're not." I agreed with her then, and I agree with her now, but I've learned that's true of everything. Even a writer is only as good as her last novel, in many people's eyes.

There was something very direct, very aggressive, about her mind, something I had never encountered in a woman before. Rita Mae always saw herself as a man trapped in a woman's body. It was that seething, witty core that I was attracted to. She was the first person I ever met whom I could really talk to. Our relationship wasn't all that physical to begin with, but I was attracted to her emotionally and especially intellectually.

That's what makes me suspicious of all the sexual labels. I hate it when people have a preconceived notion of what you are. No matter what you say, you'll come out the way they want you to be. I was romantically involved with somebody who wrote and told funny stories and had a cat named Baby Jesus and happened to be a woman. Yet the strongest part of her, the part that most attracted me, was the verbal, mental, social, psychological part of her.

Suppose she'd been a man? I might be raising a child with a vicious lefty serve and a light touch at the typewriter. I'd probably be divorced, too, as things turned out. But either way, I had an affair with this person. I saw no particular rights or wrongs about her sexuality. I'm not a one-sex person, and yet I hate the term *bisexual.* It sounds creepy to me, and I don't think I'm creepy. There are times when I feel downright romantic.

The months with Rita Mae formed one of those romantic times. We started traveling together—long dinners, and glasses of wine, suede and lace and silk instead of Gatorade and warm-up suits—and I got to know her better.

I realized that a lot of her life corresponded to the woman in *Rubyfruit Jungle,* who is born out of wedlock, grows up in Florida, is thrown out of school because of her political beliefs, and winds up studying film-making and writing poetry in New York.

Rita Mae had done a lot in the thirty-two years before she met me. She had been an early member of the National Organization for Women, a founder of Redstockings, a radical feminist group, and from 1971 to 1973 she had belonged to a group called The Furies, based in Washington, D.C. She had taught part-time at the Women Writers' Center in Cazenovia, New York, and had written *In Her Day* and *Six of One, Half a Dozen of Another* in addition to *Rubyfruit Jungle.*

I used to hear her telling interviewers that she didn't want to be known as "Rita Mae Brown, Lesbian Author."

She wanted to be called "Rita Mae Brown, Author," and she would add: "I hope they say: 'She was fun.'"

I didn't go into this affair with blinders on. The first time we made contact on the telephone, I knew she was openly and proudly identified as a gay woman. I had never been identified with anybody gay before, and I couldn't have picked anybody more prominent. But I was in love with her, and you can't direct your feelings and say: You can't fall in love with this one. It might hurt your career.

When it happened, I just wanted to be alone with her. I wasn't waving any flags or trying to make a stand. I just wanted to be left alone with Rita Mae, and take my chances. It was months before the public picked up on the fact that we were traveling together. I think Europe and the States and Canada are more tolerant than they give themselves credit for. People knew and didn't write about it. And when something was written, usually it was no big deal, except for a few closet gay writers, who wrote the most vicious articles of all.

Rita Mae liberated my intellect, but I can't say she made me more liberal than I was. I was pretty radical or tolerant or liberal, or whatever word you want to use, before I met her. It was easy to be radical with her, but I wasn't trying to shock people.

My opinions were already fairly well formed on things like the Equal Rights Amendment, abortion, and the Moral Majority. I think I was always appalled that men are in higher places than women just because they're physically stronger. I don't mind men being stronger and better in tennis because it's a sport, where strength counts. But in business or politics or even in the home, authority has had nothing to do with brains or mental toughness—it's just physical strength so men can order women around.

I've always spoken out for the right to abortion, the right

to speak your mind, equal pay for equal work, gay rights —or any minority rights, for that matter. I don't understand how you can judge people by their sexual preferences. I've always been against all forms of prejudice, so I didn't need Rita Mae to teach me that. But that is why we got along: we shared the same beliefs. The major difference between us was that I'm not one to make waves and carry the banner, but at the same time I would like to get involved in the rights of minorities who are being stepped on.

I was too busy with my own career to attend many meetings with Rita Mae, but I did go to hear her speak at Chapel Hill, North Carolina, one time. She's an unbelievable public speaker, who can turn people around with her ideas. I also went with her to some women's caucus in L.A., but that was about it. She was then getting ready to write *Southern Discomfort,* so she wasn't too much into public activities at the time.

Whenever Rita Mae was with me on the road, she would try to get me out of the hotel to see what was happening in the city. If we were in San Francisco, we'd go out to the Palace of Fine Arts, or in Europe we'd go to a cathedral. In London we'd go sight-seeing and shopping. I loved visiting some of these places I'd only read about in books or heard about in high school. In my years on the tour, I had almost never heard any of the top players say, "Hey, if it's nice tomorrow, we're going up to the Museum of Modern Art," although some of the secondary players did seem more inclined to explore the outside world. It wasn't that their curiosity dragged down their tennis; they simply had more time to get out and walk because they generally lost in the first or second round.

Those of us who usually reached the quarters and the semis lived in our own encapsulated world, with barely enough time to practice, rest, travel, eat, sleep, and play. But in truth, we killed a lot of time around the courts. We'd get there early and hang out, playing cards, thumbing through old magazines. Rita Mae took one look at that life and said, "Bag this."

She started prodding me: "Don't you want to learn anything? How can you stand just playing tennis every day?" And she started regulating our routine. We'd get up earlier, leave the hotel, try to do something every day. Lots of times I was grateful for her guidance. I was breaking out of the mold my profession had cast for me.

But there were also times when I'd barely get to the courts in time for my match. A couple of times on the winter circuit, I'd be calling in and saying, "What time's the match? Who's winning? What's the score?" Occasionally, I'd get there and my feet would be tired from standing in a museum or walking the streets, and my mind would be buzzing from a movie we'd seen or a conversation we'd had. It would just happen. We'd be discussing a book and all of a sudden I'd be saying, "Oh, my God, I've got to get to work." Anybody who's ever been in love knows the feeling of rushing off to work. My work was a match against Chris Evert or Billie Jean.

We decided we could have more time together if we shared a house somewhere. Rita Mae had always loved Charlottesville, Virginia, Jefferson's home and the site of the University of Virginia. I took one look at the campus and the stately old homes and farm country around it and fell in love with the Blue Ridge. The countryside reminded me of the mountains behind Revnice, and I felt as close to my roots as the day I walked out of Czechoslovakia. So we looked around and bought a mansion on a nine-acre plot just outside Charlottesville. I felt great about my plans for moving in with Rita Mae and getting back to my rural roots.

But at the same time, my real roots were reaching out for me. Long before I met Rita Mae, I had encouraged my parents to visit me in Dallas. Now, the Czech government had relaxed its ban on travel outside the country, and my parents were seriously talking about emigrating and coming to live with me in Dallas. There was just one small problem about all this: they didn't *know*.

Family Visit

When I left Czechoslovakia, I had to accept the possibility that I might not see my parents for a long time, or even have contact with them if the government wanted it that way. But it was never that bad. We were able to talk on the telephone a few days after I defected, and I never had any trouble reaching them on the phone after that. Hearing their voices made the separation bearable, and then they let my grandmother visit me early in 1979.

In June of that year, they let my mother out to visit me at Wimbledon, the old strategy of letting one person out but not the spouse. I went to Heathrow Airport all by myself to meet my mother for the first time in nearly four years. I didn't tell anybody because I didn't want any kind of British media frenzy out there, so we were able to greet each other without the cameras clicking. My mother brought me some cookies she had baked, and we hugged and talked all the way into town.

The next day she sat in the players' box and watched me

work at defending my Wimbledon title. I always like to know where my family and friends are during a match, so I glanced up there from time to time, and noticed my mother was nervous, the way I remembered her. She was smoking a cigaret and picking her purse up and looking from side to side to make sure she was applauding at the right times. I think I was nervous, too, and I lost the first set to Tanya Harford before winning the match. A few days later I beat Chris in the finals, 6–4, 6–4.

While my mother was in England, we talked about the possibility of the family moving to the States. The Czech government had given them subtle hints that it wouldn't stand in their way if they wanted to emigrate. I thought it would be good for my parents and particularly for Jana, who was in high school at the time. I told them to do whatever they could, that I would support the move totally.

Later in 1979, my parents notified me that they would be coming over in December. We did all the legal paperwork and I made plans for them to live in Dallas. I was living by myself then, but I didn't think my house was big enough for all of us. I told them on the phone that I would buy them a house and they said, "No, no, no, we want to stay with you," but I was sure it would be better if we all had some privacy.

I had already been Americanized into thinking that everybody wants her own kitchen and bathroom. I was twenty-three years old, was traveling all over the world. I wanted to cook or sleep or have company on my own schedule. So when a house two hundred yards down the street came on the market, I bought it for them.

I met them at the airport. It was a very emotional moment, seeing my father again, seeing how much Jana had grown. God, she'd been a little kid when I left and now she looked like a grown-up, and was as tall as me.

My father was the same as always—full of ideas, full of

advice. On the trip from the airport, he was asking me questions about my finances, giving me tips about my tennis, like telling me to attack Chris's backhand and how I should bend my knees and turn my shoulders more on every shot. I guess he had seen me on West German television from somebody's house in Pilsen.

It was funny and it was familiar, like a kid coming home from college after being on her own for four years. Here are your parents, still thinking you need to be taken care of. I was still their little girl, no matter how old I was. I loved it, mostly. Two-time Wimbledon champion becomes child prodigy again.

We got to the house and they checked out all my gadgets. I don't think they believed I could be that rich. After about an hour, I said, "I want to show you something."

We walked down the street to the other house.

"What's this?"

"This is your house," I said.

"Oh, it's nice, but we'd rather stay with you," they said.

"Hey, I'm not here that much, but I want to have my space," I said.

They accepted that, but I guess they never really loved the idea. I had won a Peugeot in Washington and I had also bought a Cadillac Seville from Haynie, so they had two cars to drive, a house, all the bills paid. I bought Jana a small piano and sent over furniture from my own house.

Things went along all right for a while. My father cooked the traditional Czech carp dinner for Christmas, and I spent a lot of time at their house, letting my mother fuss over me. When I was sick she'd said, "Don't drink a cold Dr. Pepper," and when I was getting ready to play a tournament in another city, they said, "How come you're leaving again so soon?" It was hard for them to get the hang of what the tennis tour was really like. They had prepared me for it, particularly my father, but they were not ready for the long trips, the travel day before I was due somewhere else. It's not like Europe, where everything is nearby. But I made sure they could handle being alone before I went out on the road early in 1980.

Jana was attending a private school, Hockaday, very preppy and snobbish, nothing like what she'd known in Czechoslovakia. I thought it would have been better to send her to public school, but she adjusted very well to everything and she could speak colloquial English in a few months, nearly as well as me. My mother is good with languages, too, and got to know some people right away. Some kids took my parents around, but then they wanted to take them to church so my father said no thanks. I don't think my family was ready for the aggressive, proselytizing form of religion you see in the States, particularly since they had not been religious back home.

Life in Dallas must have seemed strange to them. In Revnice, they knew most of the people, could walk everywhere, and when they wanted to go to Prague, they could drive downtown or take the railroad into a familiar, historic city. Europeans are used to walking, used to being close to the center of a village or city.

In Dallas, everything was spread out. People would drive to a shopping center, get in their cars and drive someplace else. There was no center for my parents, and I think they felt the difference. You'd naturally feel a little rootless, driving around in a car, not meeting new people or seeing any familiar faces. I find myself driving everywhere in Texas, too. You've got to. But when I get to London or Paris or even New York, there's that rhythm of the streets again.

My mother took to life in Dallas right away. She had a grocery store a few blocks away, filled with a variety of food and household ingredients that she had never imagined. To somebody coming from behind the Iron Curtain, it was like a fairy tale, even though Czechoslovakia was not poor before the Russians took over. She loved dropping into the twenty-four-hour supermarket, something that just doesn't exist in Czechoslovakia. She was happy as can be, with all the meat she needed, all the seasoning.

But it wasn't so easy for my father. At the store, he might know the words but he was too shy to say what he wanted. They had picture books and dictionaries and he could have gone to school, but he just wasn't that good with languages. He speaks a little English, German, and Russian and can be very charming in them when he wants to be. I know people who've had long conversations with him in English when he was relaxed. But he didn't feel comfortable in Dallas and he was very frustrated. Back in Czechoslovakia, he was considered a big shot for being my father, but in Texas he had to rely on me and my mother.

He didn't have a job, and at fifty he wasn't ready to retire, so he announced right away that he wanted to be my coach and advisor. I didn't have anyone working with me at the time, and probably could have used some help, but I just didn't think it would work out the way he wanted it to. He had a bad elbow, so he couldn't hit with me at all, and my game had obviously gone past where it was when I was a little girl.

I understood what my father was going through. He's a proud man and he didn't want to depend on me. I told him I was doing things pretty well on my own, and that technically, he couldn't help me much anymore. His advice was pretty basic: attack Chris's backhand, things like that. He just didn't know very much about the caliber of tennis where I was playing. It's natural for somebody to think a person's backhand isn't as good as her forehand, because that's true of almost every weekend hacker. But it's not so true at the Chris Evert level of the tour.

I tried to expose them to my professional life as quickly

as possible, taking them to Japan in the spring and Chicago in the winter. But after a while, I told them I had to go out on my own and hit the tour again.

I realized things were not going to be easy when my parents called me to tell me the stove wasn't working. So there I was in a hotel room somewhere calling the repair service in Dallas, trying to explain what had to be done because the people in the house didn't speak English all that well. It was hard on me, having to take care of details like this at a time when my game wasn't going very well anyway. And it was hard on them, needing my help.

I'd be home for a week and then I'd say, "I've got to go now," and I'd call every other day and they'd say, "Why didn't you call yesterday?" They were a little possessive, and that was fine. They hadn't been with me for a long time. They still thought of me as their little girl. They had a hard time accepting me as a woman on my own. They wanted me to wear pajamas to bed when I was in the habit of wearing a T-shirt. They had a lot of advice for me, but I was dealing with it and so were they. I'm sure we could have gotten over that part of the adjustment, if they could have adjusted to my, shall we say, "lifestyle."

I hadn't given much thought to what my parents would think of my private life. They never asked questions when I had a roommate for a while, and probably nothing would have hit the fan if I hadn't met Rita Mae. I had asked my parents to come live with me in Dallas before I met Rita Mae and before I even thought of buying the house in Charlottesville, when I didn't even know if the government would even let them out for a visit.

I could afford two houses, plus one for my family, so I didn't think it was any big deal if I lived part of the time in Charlottesville. But when I told them in April that I was buying another house, they didn't love the idea. As far as they were concerned, it was like having houses in Stuttgart and Lisbon. And then they got the drift of why I was buying another house in Virginia.

"I think you and Rita Mae are living as man and wife," my father told me one day in Dallas.

I didn't want to lie to him, so I told him he was right. He seemed pretty calm about it at the time, but he did tell me I should read a book about my "sickness," as he called it. I told him he should read a book, too—that his view of homosexuality was fifty years behind the times. He started calling me names, saying he'd rather me be a hooker than what I was.

He wasn't being totally unreasonable for a Czech male. In Czechoslovakia they call male homosexuals "warm people," which is not as nice as it sounds, and I don't even think they have a word for lesbians. Women just don't come out of the closet. In Czechoslovakia they think that all lesbians are women who are so ugly they can't get a man. I tried to tell my parents that it's a bit more complex than that.

After I moved to Charlottesville, my family visited the house and my father seemed more agitated than before. He thought Rita Mae was flaunting the relationship, being too obvious about it around him and other people, and he just wasn't comfortable with it. One day while Rita Mae wasn't around, my father and I got into a roaring argument.

"I'd rather you slept with a different man every night than sleep with a woman," he said.

"That's great," I snapped back.

"There must be something wrong with you physically," he said.

"Everything's in working order," I assured him.

My father was seeing everything in black and white, and I tried to tell him, first of all, that Rita Mae was attractive enough, that a lot of men were interested in her, and that I didn't do so badly when I felt like it, either.

"I like making love with men," I said, "but at the moment I'm involved with a woman."

My father wasn't having any of it.

"The reason you're going through this is because you didn't enjoy the first time you were with a man," my father said.

I guess he knew something about my first boyfriend back home. But I insisted I was not permanently down on men; I just happened to prefer a woman at the moment.

"It's too bad you didn't like the first man," my father blurted. "Then you would have enjoyed it more."

It was a pretty unpleasant moment for us, but I tried to see it from my father's point of view. I knew his male pride was injured by having his daughter turn out in a way that he couldn't accept, and he was thrashing around, saying whatever came into his head, from a macho, fifty-years-behind-the-times Czech view. He was very upset, and he certainly didn't understand it, but hearing him talk like that made me furious, and a little sick.

Through it all, I couldn't have loved him more if he were my real father, but I hated to hear him talk against me that way. It was hard to realize that this was the same man who had encouraged me to be myself on the tennis court, but now he was trying to deny the reality of the moment.

I tried to tell them it wasn't just sex, that it was the fulfillment of being around people I like, the emotional level. But they had no idea. It's a prejudice, just like being prejudiced against blacks. I understood that my father had no real choice. It's the way he was brought up.

It was in the middle of this rational family conversation that my parents told me how my real father had committed suicide. My mother was afraid I was being used by other people, and she told me I was too trusting, too open, just like he had been.

"You're just like him, you get all involved with somebody after five minutes," my mother said.

The argument went on like a brushfire over the next few days. They would call up some of our Czech friends in North America, spreading the news, drawing other people into the conflict, forcing them to give advice or take sides. It was a soap opera, Czech style, and things were never quite the same after that.

That scene was really the beginning of the end of my family's visit to the United States. The sexuality issue made it just that much harder for them to adjust to life in the States. By April, my father was saying he wanted to go back home. He said he was always going to be indebted to me, and he wasn't sure I could continue to make that kind of money. At one point, he called my cousin, Martin, in Canada. Martin tried to tell him how much money I could make in the next few years, but my father didn't have the conviction to stay three years or five years.

Mr. Hoschl offered him a job in Chicago, and they could have moved there and fit in with Svatka and her family. But they wanted to be close to me, even though being close to me often just meant another argument, another scene.

It was sad, really. My father had put so much effort into my tennis game when I was a kid, and now here I was on the brink of earning more success and more money than any woman athlete ever had. I was going to make it huge, I knew it, but at this crucial point in my life, my father, who had always been bursting with confidence in me and in himself, suddenly lost his nerve in this foreign land.

I would tell him, "Do what you want." I went to the bank with him to open a checking account and I put in five thousand dollars, and later he would say: "How come only five thousand?" That sort of shocked me, but I don't know if he did it because he resented the money or because I didn't discuss it with him first. It just seemed like a good figure to start. It was strange, seeing this proud, intelligent man acting almost childlike. By all Czech standards, he was supposed to be the head of the family, but I was taking control of him. And not only that, I was "different."

It was difficult for him. He had a hard time ordering in a restaurant or buying things. He was too shy to talk to people. He understood things but was too embarrassed to say them.

In June, they accompanied me to Wimbledon, but he was adamant about returning to Czechoslovakia after the tournament. I was going crazy, trying to concentrate on my tennis (I lost to Chris in three sets in the semis). I knew my mother would go back with him, but Jana wanted to stay with me. She wanted to go to college in the States and see what the future would bring, but I thought, I can't take the responsibility. She would miss my parents. She couldn't travel with me. And my parents didn't want her to stay.

The way my father saw it, he had tried living in America, he didn't like it, so it was time to go back. Fortunately, my parents had not burned their bridges behind them when they left. They were allowed to come back, and they even got jobs in their old factories, although it was pretty clear they'd never have really top jobs again. At first they had some political problems getting Jana back into high school and then into a medical school to study dentistry, but my father went in and told somebody, "Hey, you know you're just doing this out of politics," and they finally allowed Jana to enter the college in Pilsen.

I sent them off with $50,000, and six months later they needed more money. They bought a Renault and said they would buy a prefab house, but they wound up buying an expensive house up on a hill, with a nice garden. In Czechoslovakia, there's no law against having a nice house if you can somehow afford it.

I haven't seen their new house, since the government isn't

about to let me back in without some heavy strings attached, but I've seen pictures of it. My father is really into gardening, with forty apple trees, nice bushes, and a lawn. He likes to go to the local tavern and sing songs with the guys and be sociable with everybody. It's a good life, knowing everybody in town, playing tennis in the warm weather, living at the side of the mountain. He and my mother would never have felt as at home in America as they do in Revnice, but it would be nice if they could have both places.

I wish I could just drop in for a visit every so often, sit at the kitchen table, drinking fresh cider and enjoying my mother's cooking, go tramping through the woods with my father, see my German shepherd Babeta, spend some time with Jana and get to know her better in her own world. We had our chance to be together back in 1980, but we let it get away. I guess we'll always wonder if we could have handled it better.

Virginia

The house in Charlottesville stirred up headlines in the national scandal magazines: "Martina Buys 500G Mansion With 'Mystery' Companion." There was no mystery at all. Rita Mae and I made no secret of living together in Charlottesville. Both of us felt we were sinking down some roots in America, satisfying our separate feelings about how we wanted to live.

Charlottesville reminded me of my part of Czechoslovakia. The stone-walled house was on a nine-acre estate, half of it built in 1850 and the other half in 1936 and looked almost like two different houses from the outside. Some of the rooms could just take your breath away: an oak library with gorgeous moldings, formal gardens with fountains, and a huge patio with statuary.

There were over twenty rooms, with six baths, and a small room above the five-car garage. There was another small house next to the swimming pool and a tennis court that hadn't been played on in years.

There were a few drawbacks to an old house like that: it was cold in the winter and hot in the summer, with no central air-conditioning, and the heating didn't work too well in the new part of the house, so you suffered through the winters. My bedroom was cold because it faced the northeast and caught all the winter winds.

There was a huge basement under the old part of the house where the heater was, and a separate basement under the new part. One of the basement rooms was big enough to hold a pool table and Rita Mae's weight-lifting equipment. I'd sleep down there in the summer when it was hot.

I was starting to decorate the house with things that appealed to me and had nothing to do with tennis. From the time I left home and became a pro, most of my rooms have been littered with racquets, socks and shorts, cans of tennis balls. In Charlottesville my room was also littered with books. I had always been interested in how things are put together, particularly skyscrapers, and had fallen in love with some of the buildings in New York, Melbourne, and Tokyo. I had once said I didn't have time to look around, but with Rita Mae, I made the time. I also began collecting architecture books from Czechoslovakia as well as the States. That's the main thing Lee Jackson remembers from her visits to my house: the architecture books all over the place.

Lee also remembers how big the house was. She still tells people about the long corridor right off the huge southern kitchen and the pantry. There were so many rooms that people would get confused. The first time Lee stayed at the house, she got up in the middle of the night for a glass of water and went to the kitchen, closing her door behind her so Rita Mae's cat couldn't get into the room. After getting the drink of water, Lee realized she couldn't tell which door was hers because all of them were white. She didn't want to wake anybody up by opening the wrong door, so she tiptoed up and down the hallway for a long time with Rita Mae's cat staring at her as if to say, What's your problem? Finally Lee picked the right door—but it wasn't easy.

We had two students from the university living there, taking care of the house, because we were away a lot. The house was pretty secluded, set back on the nine acres, and getting there was like driving through a forest. We had a gardener tending the grounds.

During the year that I lived there, I was home for about five months. I spent most of that time driving to the grocery store and cooking meals. The practice courts were two miles away and the grocery three miles. I'd work out with Phil Rogers, the pro at the Boar's Head Club, and he and his wife, Rachel, became my closest friends in Charlottesville.

We tried to be part of the community, as much as possible. Rita Mae wanted to teach English or literature at the university, but she couldn't get an opening in the English department. She became friendly with a man who had written a book about Chaucer, and he and some other people would come over and talk about books. Most of the people we knew were older than me; only the students who lived in the house were younger, and they all were very interesting people, making me wish I had more time to go to a school like Virginia.

I went to one basketball game at the university, and one lacrosse game, and we often went to the movie house where they played a different foreign or old film almost every night. It was interesting living at the fringe of a great university like Virginia. I got a sense of what life might have been like if I'd grown up in the States and gone to college here. Rita Mae used to urge me to take classes, but there was no time with my tennis schedule. She wanted to know why I couldn't cut back on my tournaments. What could I say? It's the way I support myself—and other people around me.

Some people have said the neighbors weren't exactly enchanted with me and Rita Mae, but I never felt any unfriendliness. It was no different from other places I've lived. Some people are reserved, but basically they're friendly. They pretty much left me alone.

When I'd meet people at some function or other, they'd ask what I was doing living in Charlottesville. "Why not? It's a beautiful place," I'd say. The problem was, it was difficult getting in and out of that city, with only two flights a day to Washington and one to New York. I usually ended up driving home from Dulles or Washington National, and that added at least two hours onto every trip.

After we settled in Charlottesville, Rita Mae really got down to work on *Southern Discomfort*. When she got locked in on a project, she definitely made me look like a dilettante. She'd go to her workroom and I would hear the typewriter clicking away.

I tried not to disturb her. If somebody came to the door, I'd answer it because she didn't want to be bothered. If she even saw some signs of civilization, like the mailman coming along, it would disturb her—maybe destroy her concentration for the rest of the day, depending on her mood. She felt she only had three or four hours of time each day when she could write five or ten pages. If anyone interrupted her, she'd go crazy—even if it was me just saying I had to go to practice.

She was a slow writer, but I could understand that. She would do about two years of research for every novel. For *Southern Discomfort*, she spent time in Montgomery, Alabama, going down to the train station where the main characters came and went. She'd visit cemeteries to get names off the tombstones.

She loved unusual names. People think she makes up her characters' names, but they're often the names of dead people. I didn't go with her on her research trips, but sometimes I'd find names in the obituary columns of newspapers and I'd stick them in an envelope and mail them to her. Or she'd match somebody's first name with somebody else's last name. Her workroom was loaded with names written on scraps of paper, ideas just strewn everywhere.

Sometimes we'd sit around the house trying to match up her characters with a plot. She's great with characters and dialogue, but not so great with plot. She'd ask me what I thought the characters would do next, and I'd give her little suggestions. When I was around, we would definitely discuss her career more than mine. I played sports, but she was a writer.

One of the first little warning signs came when I would sign up for practice during the day and Rita Mae would say: "Oh, no, you're going to leave again." Well, I wasn't exactly leaving. I was going to work. It was funny, really, because she was so dedicated to her own work, but the idea of making an appointment to practice hitting a ball, making plans just to sweat and stretch, boggled her. There were times I felt guilty because I had to play a match or practice when she wanted to do something else with me.

After a while, it got to the point where it was better if she stayed home instead of accompanying me on the tour. It was easier for me to go about my business, to play my matches, when I didn't have to worry about Rita Mae getting her peace and quiet. It was difficult on the road with two careers—and it wasn't easy in the same twenty-room mansion, either.

One of those careers was suffering, too. I didn't play the French Open in 1980, and I lost to Chris in the semis at Wimbledon. Hana Mandlikova, one of the great athletes on the tour, and a nice kid, even if she persists in calling me a Czech instead of an American, beat me in straight sets at the U.S. Open. Wendy Turnbull beat me in Las Vegas and Melbourne. Pam Shriver beat me in Sydney. Andrea Jaeger, another new kid at the time, beat me in Deerfield, Florida, and Kansas City. I was starting to look like last decade's prodigy—and I had just turned twenty-four. Something was wrong.

What was wrong was my attitude. I had lost the singleness of purpose I'd had when I was first coming up. I had become ambivalent about tennis, ambivalent about myself, ambivalent about my career. Rita Mae would tell me, "It's only a game," which was all right for a while, but then I'd lose a match and say, "It's not a matter of life and death," which was true, except that while you're playing it, it should feel like a matter of life and death. At the moment. I know that now, but I had lost sight of it at the time. I'd get careless and lose a match and I'd say, "No big deal."

I was gullible to let her influence me so much; I began getting tired of Rita Mae's belittling remarks. "You're the greatest," she'd say, "but you really don't need it. You should do something else with your life."

Sometimes I would say: "Would you want to do something else besides write?" We had some pretty good arguments.

Some people have asked whether she really wanted to harm my career, but I never saw any signs of that. I think Rita Mae just looked at the raw material and wanted to mold it. I didn't know enough about art or politics, and maybe she saw me as Eliza Doolittle and herself as Henry Higgins, creating something from nothing. In her mind, I was already a tennis star—why not work on the rest of me?

Even though I won some tournaments early in 1981, I realized I had to make a break or I was never going to reach the level I had set for myself. Each time I'd come home from the road, I'd make up my mind to leave, but I'm not too good at dealing with conflict. My old habit of procrastination kept winning out, and I let the problem slide and slide, which wasn't fair to either of us.

At about this time I started having some pretty horrendous dreams, too. I was in a panic during the day and it would come out while I was asleep. I told a couple of these dreams to Pete Axthelm of *Newsweek*.

The Jungle Dream: "I was with my parents and we were lost in the jungle. All of a sudden we came upon a Ferrari. It was surrounded by dinosaurs and prehistoric monsters. They were friendly and it was okay. But poisonous snakes were wrapped around the key to the Ferrari. I had to get those keys. Finally I was able to, and we all drove off."

The 747 Dream: "I was with my parents next to a hangar. The plane took off and there was a flash of lightning from inside the plane. I thought I could run away but it came right behind me. I'd run the other way and it turned and still came right at me. But finally it crashed before it got to me."

When I told these dreams to Pete, I guessed that the

dreams meant I was trying to control the different portions of my life that were careening around me. Speaking of the airplane dream, I told Pete: "It never really crashes down on me." But early in 1981, it was coming pretty close.

Nancy

The first time I saw Nancy Lieberman, I was in the middle of a match on Amelia Island, Florida. I recognized her by her flaming reddish-orange hair, which stood out in the crowd. In those days I was not always concentrating on my matches the way I should. I'd be playing somebody and I'd be thinking about dinner or an interesting conversation I'd had three days earlier.

I was in the middle of a match with Kathy Rinaldi when I spotted Nancy sitting in the players' box. I had never seen her play basketball, but I knew she was an all-American from Old Dominion who by 1981 was playing for the Dallas Diamonds in the Women's Basketball League.

What's she doing here? I thought to myself as I hit a forehand.

Isn't this the playoff season for basketball? I wondered as I shagged a backhand volley.

Who does she know on the tour? I wondered as I hit a smash for a winner.

Once I got that all straightened out, I beat Kathy, 7–6,

6–1, and headed for the clubhouse, where I was introduced to Nancy. It turned out that she knew Anne Smith from playing ball in Dallas. When Nancy's season was over, she was injured and tired, and Smitty told her to come to Florida for some warm weather and good tennis.

When Nancy arrived, Smitty introduced her to Bud Collins, the Boston *Globe* columnist and tennis announcer for NBC, who is Mr. Sociability on the tennis tour. Nancy says Bud asked her if she was a tennis fan and she said, "Nope." Then he asked her if she wanted to meet any of the players and she said, "Nope."

Finally Anne said, "Well, don't you want to meet Martina?" and Nancy said, "Not particularly."

This was Nancy's city-girl basketball attitude. Never be too impressed with anybody or anything. But I was sitting around in the press room, and Bud Collins and Mel DiGiacomo, a photographer, introduced us.

We began talking, and I was very impressed with how she looked. I had always thought of female basketball players as burly and muscular, but she was slender and graceful.

She also knew her sports. It was the first time I had met a woman who knew as much about the subject as I did. We got to talking about football, and I would say, "I can't believe the Cowboys lost," and she would say, "Yeah, can you believe that call on third-and-long?" She read the box scores and the standings; she knew about sports that women never play, like football and baseball.

We got along right away. I told her I had always thought Carol Blazejowski was the best basketball player in the country (even if I'd never seen her play), and Nancy told me she'd always rooted for Chris Evert (she probably had, up to that point).

I enjoyed the jockeying and agitation the first time we met. Male athletes are comfortable teasing and testing each other, but women tend to be a little inhibited on that score. Coming onto the tennis tour, even in my Billie Jean King period, I felt the pressure to get along, to conform, to be nice. I could tell right away that Nancy Lieberman felt none of those constraints.

The more we talked, the more I understood where she got her "attitude"—on the A train. You know, the old Duke Ellington song, "Take the A Train." Nancy had grown up in Far Rockaway in the borough of Queens, but she had to travel afield to test her basketball game in Harlem. She would get on the A train and while it was barreling from Queens to Brooklyn to Manhattan, she'd be putting on her game face.

Here was this slender, redheaded female, fourteen or fifteen years old, riding uptown to play basketball against grown men, most of them black, in a schoolyard, and she'd be fixing up her face to say: "Don't mess with me. This redhead's crazy." She says it worked on the maniacs in the subway car as well as the players on the court. She had taught herself how to be tough, and later she would teach me the same lesson.

"How come you never came over to Moody Coliseum to watch us play tennis?" I asked her.

"I didn't want to see tennis players," she said with a poker face. "They're sissies. Basketball players play in pain."

"How do you know how bad my shoulder hurt when I couldn't raise my arm to brush my teeth?" I asked. "But I still played."

"Yes, but in basketball we have contact," Nancy said.

"Well, tennis is pretty physical, too," I said. "I've taken some falls."

There was nothing physical about my final match with Chris that week, but it hurt just the same. Nancy was still around as I got through Sylvia Hanika and Mima Jausovec to reach the finals. But I didn't feel right about my tennis, and hadn't for months. I couldn't hit the wide side of a barn if my life depended on it.

My loss-of-control dreams haunted me that week at Amelia Island. The night before the final round with Chris, I had a dream about playing her. There was a huge valley on my side of the court, and you could hardly see the net when you were down at the bottom. I would serve and try to run up the hill, but she'd hit a deep shot so I'd have to run back down the hill to hit it. Then she'd hit a drop shot so I'd have to go all the way up the other side to get to the ball. I was furious. I couldn't win a point.

The dream became reality the next day. I didn't have a good night's sleep after that dream, but still when I woke up the next morning I felt fine. Everything went wrong from there, and she, of course, didn't miss a thing. It was as if Chris was playing cat and mouse with me. I was trying my hardest during the match, but when you don't put in the time at practice, it catches up with you.

Things were so bad against Chris that at one point I offered my racquet to a ball girl, telling her she could do better. Nobody could have done worse. Chris beat me, 6–0, 6–0, and it was the first time I'd ever been shut out since joining the tour. I had given the double bagel to early-round opponents seven times, but losing to Chris in the finals that way was shattering.

Trying to live with Rita Mae, I had tossed part of my career over the side, like a sled driver trying to lighten the load to outrace the wolves. I had given away part of myself, and now I had to get it back.

I won my last tournament in the States and headed for the French Open at the end of May. I was at a low ebb on my way over. Billie Jean was in the process of being sued for "palimony" by Marilyn Barnett, who had once been a hairdresser on the tour, and everybody was gossiping about it. There was talk that Avon, one of the major sponsors, was going to pull out because the company didn't want to be associated with the idea of homosexuality in women's tennis.

I was sure that any hint of scandal was going to hurt me financially and maybe worse: I had applied for American citizenship, and my final hearing was scheduled for later that summer. There are some states where homosexuality is a crime, and I was afraid my sex life could keep me from becoming an American. If that happened, where would I live?

Nancy was getting to know some of the people on the tour, and a few of them said: "Talk to Martina, she respects you, you can help her." I think people felt I'd never be able to get my emotional and conditioning problems settled by myself.

We sat around talking one night and Nancy said, "Why don't you move to Dallas? I don't know what's happening with the basketball league, and I may have plenty of time to help you get in shape. I've got a big townhouse I share with one of my teammates. There's plenty of room."

I asked her if she wasn't afraid of having an image problem by my moving from Charlottesville to Dallas, but she said she wasn't worried about it. She said she thought it would be a challenge to try to get my tennis game back in gear again, and she warned me she would work me hard. From that conversation, the basis of our friendship was formed: two kindred souls, two athletes, one of them disciplined, the other one floundering.

But I still had a relationship back in Charlottesville, and I dreaded doing anything about it. When I got back to Charlottesville, I started talking to Nancy on the telephone every so often. Rita Mae overheard one of the conversations, and we started arguing.

I had told her before that I wanted to leave, but she was shocked this time when I said I was actually leaving. I had never shown that kind of determination before.

I guess you never have enough experience or wisdom to do something like that well. I just said, "I'm leaving. I've got to get my act together." We began fighting, shouting, crying—one of those moments when you don't know if it's a dream or reality, but either way, you want to get it over with.

She probably didn't understand how strongly I felt about getting back to basics in tennis; she came from a different point of view than I did. She had been great for me, up to then. Even now I think about Rita Mae, and I know she was someone very special. God, there are times when I'm talking about something, and I can't quite get the facts right, and I think to myself, Rita Mae would have the answer. But that wasn't enough to make me want to stay.

Rita Mae watched me start to put my stuff together, and let's say she did not take it lightly. She was hurt, anybody would be, and we got into one of the nastiest, most physical arguments I ever hope to be in. We stormed around the house raging at each other, from room to room, until I couldn't take it anymore.

I raced out of the house, getting to the car before she did, and I jammed it into gear and spun out of the driveway, spewing gravel and exhaust fumes, while Rita Mae stood in the driveway, gesturing at me.

I got to a phone and told Nancy how badly it had gone, and how I couldn't go back to that house. I knew I was putting the problem in Nancy's lap, but she'd said she wanted to help me, and she told me to get out of Charlottesville as soon as possible.

A few days later, I went back to the house to collect my belongings. Rita Mae and I were both too numb by what had happened to do any damage, psychic or physical to each other. I packed and headed directly for France, where I was meeting Nancy.

When I saw her, I was still getting over the last few months. I felt numb, dead inside, with no incentive to get about my tennis again. I needed something to shock me into the next stage of my life, and Nancy seemed to be it.

I don't think I was prepared for her bluntness. One of the habits I had gotten into was buying something for myself whenever I was feeling down—expensive toys like cars and jewelry and gadgets for the house and gym. Almost immediately after losing to Sylvia Hanika in the quarters at France, I went on a spending binge, going through $15,-000 I hadn't made, to reward myself for losing. I bought two expensive watches for Nancy and me, and Nancy lit into me.

"You've got it all wrong," she said in a cutting tone of voice. "You don't buy something because you lost this tournament and you want to feel good about yourself. You buy something because you want it and you deserve it. You don't deserve something for losing. You have to earn it."

Later, I realized how habitual spending on clothes and cars could become as destructive as relying on alcohol or drugs or over-eating or starving yourself, things some other women do. I can see now that I was looking for self-respect. I felt that spending money would make other people respect me, and then I'd respect myself.

I had another bad habit. I also liked to buy gifts for my friends, to thank them for being my friend. One day we were out shopping and Nancy mentioned that she liked a bracelet.

"I'll buy it for you," I said.

"Martina, you don't have to buy it for me," Nancy snapped. "I like you. It's all right."

I had never had anybody speak that bluntly to me, but Nancy promised she would keep it up. She was already sounding as disgusted as a drill sergeant on the first day of boot camp. And she hadn't even seen my practice habits yet.

Discovering Pain

"Get up, dammit, get up."

"I can't. I can't get up."

Nancy Lieberman towered over me, hands on her hips. She was furious. I was crying.

This was our first workout session together, and both of us were making important discoveries. I was discovering true pain in my body for the first time in my life; Nancy was discovering that I did not like to exercise.

I never did like exercising, going back to grade school. I would go to any length to avoid it. I didn't mind running after a ball or skating on a pond, but once I hit the winner or scored the goal, I liked to reward my body by stopping. Exercise meant you kept going.

Nancy had gotten together with a trainer named Ken Johnson who lived in Connecticut, and they had devised a series of exercises to build up my stamina, with a belt around my waist for them to pull me back.

The first exercise consisted of ten sprints. I did five of them and collapsed.

"What do you mean, you can't do any more?" Nancy shouted. "Martina, I'm not leaving until you finish."

Her tone was caustic; her volume was high. She was leaning forward, putting her face toward mine. I had never had anybody shout at me, rupture my façade of dignity, the way she was. She grabbed my arm and pulled me up and shoved me onto the track again. Then she began running alongside me, pushing me, goading me.

"That stinks, Martina. That really stinks."

Faced with that barrage of sarcasm, I once again chose the path of least resistance. I ran. It was easier than facing Nancy Lieberman's contempt. Thus began an association that would last three years and help me reach the top in tennis. It was an association built on our dreams of being the best in our respective sports, helped along by our general interest in athletics.

As we got to know each other, we described our childhoods, how we had both excelled in sports. Nancy's parents are divorced. Her father lives in Florida and she rarely sees him. She has a brother who's a dentist, and when they were little, he was the neat one in the family and she was the sloppy jock, throwing her stuff under the bed, just getting by in school. Whereas I had always been encouraged by my family and the sports programs in Czechoslovakia, Nancy had been constantly discouraged by American attitudes toward women in sports.

She said she was constantly being told in one way or another that she shouldn't play so much ball, should play with dolls instead or learn to cook or whatever, but she wanted to play every sport the boys played. I got to know Nancy's mom, Renee, who's known to most people as "Reenie," really well in the next few years. She welcomed me into her home, and treated me so kindly that I called her "Moms." But I always felt Reenie would have been happier if Nancy had been a schoolteacher or a housewife rather than an all-American basketball player. Nancy once said that Reenie used to puncture her basketballs with a screwdriver, but that didn't discourage Nancy.

With the growth of women's basketball in the mid-seventies, Nancy found herself recruited by a lot of big colleges. However, she chose Old Dominion in Virginia because, she once told me, "I wanted to start something there. I always thought of myself as an underdog."

That's a part of Nancy that I couldn't understand at first. I wanted to win, too, but I wanted everybody to be good, I wanted everybody to have a good time, I wanted everybody to be smart. I guess I couldn't accept my having more ability than other people. Nancy never thought that she had more gifts than other people. She saw herself as an underdog, with people trying to take things away from her. I think it may have had something to do with growing up with only one parent.

Nancy was a competitor even as a little girl. Whenever we'd visit Madison Square Garden, her friend, Mike Saunders, the trainer of the New York Knickerbockers, would remind her about the summer camp they used to attend in the Catskills.

"We had this competition between two halves of the camp," Mike would tell people. "Nancy was in this race where you run with a spoon handle in your mouth and a Ping-Pong ball on the spoon. Nancy chewed a big wad of gum, stuck it on the spoon, stuck the Ping-Pong ball on the gum, and won the race."

She was always competing—with the girls she grew up with, her brother, even her own teammates. I've heard Nancy say: "I'd be diving for balls, and the other women were thinking of dressing nice and going out for tea afterward."

The Women's Basketball League folded before I could

ever see Nancy in action, but I got the point in the gym at Southern Methodist, where we began working out during the summer of 1982. I saw her get out with Rhonda Rompola, one of her best friends, and go at it tooth and nail for hours. Then they'd both come home and make lunch as if nothing had happened. To me, it looked like World War III, but Rhonda and Nancy understood each other.

I knew very little about basketball, and Nancy couldn't wait to teach me the game so she could compete against me. As soon as I got a reasonable jump shot, I became a target for the full Lieberman arsenal: elbows and hips and knees and plenty of verbal aggression, too: "Come on, Tini, get inside. Work harder. Get up there. Pass it. Shoot."

I remember when Ira Berkow of *The New York Times* came down to do a story on us right after I moved to Dallas. Ira's a pretty good basketball player, and he guarded Nancy and tried to stop her from backing in toward the basket. She gave him a quick shot with her butt, right where it hurt the most, then turned around and sank an easy layup. Ira later said he'd never been hit so hard in that area in his life. He gave her a little more leeway after that—which was her goal in the first place.

I began to enjoy basketball as an alternative to my tennis workouts. Learning a game where the hoop is ten feet high extended my tennis game tremendously. Reaching for an overhead volley was a lot easier than going up for a rebound against Nancy. Nobody would be standing on a tennis court wiping *my* blood off *her* elbow and saying, "Tini, it's not my fault if you ran straight into me."

But Nancy didn't let me ignore my tennis workouts. She would ask: "When are you going out to practice?" and I would tell her that I didn't necessarily practice every day, and when I did practice, I usually did not go more than an hour.

"You don't work too hard, do you?" she asked in her

most cutting tone. "You know, Martina, I bust my butt three hours a day and you work one hour."

She prodded me to start running a few miles every day and gave me some routines that she used, substituting tennis footwork for basketball footwork. We jumped rope and began working on weights, but I'd be exhausted after an hour and didn't feel like hitting a tennis ball after that.

"I dare you to play tennis for three hours a day," Nancy would say.

She insisted that my attention span was like a baby's, and she didn't mince words, even if we were sitting around the house, visiting with guests. She'd say: "Martina, don't you think we ought to go to the gym." I was hoping maybe she'd forgotten, or that we could put it off, but she wouldn't let up.

Some people have told me they were embarrassed by the way Nancy talked to me, and it's true that if you walked into a practice and heard her snarling, "Martina, that sucks, that really sucks, why don't you just get out of here," you might wonder what was going on. But at the time I needed it. I might cry, I might throw my racquet, I might storm off the court or curse back at her, but I always came back for more.

I had no coach, had no family in this country, no strong authority figure in my life since my father and George Parma back home. Other tennis players were starting to develop guru-disciple relationships with coaches, but I didn't have one. I worked out with some pretty good instructors, but I wasn't ready for a steady coach just yet.

I think it helped that Nancy had never played much tennis until we met. There's no way an adult can pick up the game and become a pro, so we had no competition in tennis. She knew her main value would be getting me into physical and mental shape to win, and then turning me over to a tennis coach who would refine my game.

Nancy got me in shape the only way she knew how: the hard way. I used to tell her, "You don't have to talk like that," but I guess she had heard American basketball coaches apply that kind of constant pressure, and she felt that was the way to do it. Maybe it was her style; or maybe it was exactly what I wanted and needed.

We both had a lot of adjusting to do. I had just come from a strong emotional involvement with a well-known writer, and had discovered it was hard to have two egos, two careers, under the same roof. Moving in with Nancy brought other adjustments. I had sold my two Dallas houses when I moved to Charlottesville, so I had no place of my own in Dallas. The townhouse where Nancy and Rhonda lived was a two-story condo in a quiet neighborhood just west of downtown, but the house itself was not always quiet. There were often a few basketball players around, and Nancy was going out with a guy at the time, so it was a busier household than I was used to.

It took a while for me to understand just how well known Nancy is in her sport. When we were in the airport at Dallas or Norfolk, people would call her by her first name and wave and tell her how they'd seen her play for the Dallas Diamonds or Old Dominion. I realized more and more that she was a celebrity in her own right, and I saw this as one of the main reasons she and I might have an even friendship. She wouldn't be trying to live off my accomplishments, nor I hers.

"I figured I'd made it through twenty-two years without you," Nancy once said. "And you've made it through twenty-four without me, so if we were going to be friends, we would each have to give."

I liked to tell myself that I had gone through more in my lifetime than anybody else I knew—leaving home at the age of eighteen—but Nancy had faced a few changes of her own. Long before I met her, she had become a Christian

227

after spending time with a family in Virginia. Naturally, this was hard for Reenie Lieberman to accept. Occasionally, Nancy would get invited to attend dinners and accept awards sponsored by Jewish organizations and she would politely turn them down. While I was in Dallas, somebody wrote in one of the papers that Nancy had become a Christian, and she got a lot of hate mail because of that.

Nancy was one of the first American athletes to support President Carter's boycott of the 1980 Olympics because of the Russian invasion of Afghanistan. It wasn't easy for her to do it, after working four years to prepare for the Games, but Nancy had come out in favor of the boycott because she believed it was right.

I never had any doubts about what Nancy thought. She always liked to talk about the time I came home and announced: "Guess what I got."

Nancy groaned and said, "I don't want to know."

"A massage table," I said.

"Oh, good. I didn't know *when* we were going to get one."

The truth is, we already had one, but this other one had some new fixtures, and besides, what if we both needed a massage at the same time?

Nancy also would tease me about my stable of cars. At one point I owned a Toyota Supra, a Pontiac J, a 733 BMW, a silver Mercedes, a Porsche 928, a 1965 Rolls-Royce Silver Cloud, and a white 1976 Rolls-Royce Corniche convertible, which was valued at $100,000 new.

"We're going to move into the Corniche," Nancy once told Sarah Pileggi of *Sports Illustrated.*

With Nancy keeping watch over me, my spending habits declined along with my appetite. She was just learning about diet, but her instincts were to cut down on red meat and sugar and rich sauces. Later we would both refine our diets, but the original effort was a step in the right direction.

I went from a high weight of 167 a few years earlier to 145 by the fall of 1981. A skin-fold caliper test in December of 1981 showed that my total weight was only 8.8 percent body fat, compared to the average 12–14 percent for tennis players. With my new silhouette, I felt like a new person.

The Weather Report

In 1981 it had been nearly six years since I had asked for asylum, and I was getting nervous about attaining my American citizenship. There was always that worry in my mind about whether the citizenship would be granted.

I would sometimes read about this writer or that musician being denied citizenship for being too "controversial," and I was afraid I might fit into that category. Once I got my citizenship, I wouldn't care what anybody said about me, but until then, I was frightened that somebody could decide to deport me out of the country.

That was the summer Marilyn Barnett sued Billie Jean King, saying she was entitled to some form of alimony for sharing time with Billie Jean over seven years. She also produced a packet of letters from Billie Jean, who never denied the relationship but instead called it "a mistake." All hell was breaking loose. Avon seemed likely to end a $3 million relationship with women's tennis, and we all knew Billie Jean was going to lose a lot of money in endorsements.

"I still can't figure it out," I told a reporter from *Inside Sports* that spring. "Billie Jean supposedly lost a vitamin commercial because of those revelations. On the other hand, Anita Bryant has lost all her commercials because of her campaign against gays. Now you explain that one to me."

My point was that people get nervous about anybody who is controversial. I knew that my past relationship with Rita Mae was pretty well known. Although I had never talked about it in public, I had given one off-the-record interview that was ticking away like a time bomb in one reporter's notebook.

At the time, I didn't care so much about the endorsements, but travel was a pain in the neck without a U.S. passport. My green card, which allowed me to live and work in the U.S., reminded me I was still not a citizen, and I always had to carry a re-entry permit when I left the States.

"What's this?" some of the customs people would ask when I got off a plane in the States with my official document, and I'd have to spend more time at the gate than a citizen would.

But the real problem was flying over Communist countries. I just couldn't take the chance of being grounded in any Communist country and perhaps being turned over to the Czech government. I always had to check the route maps to make sure where the plane was going. If it was going over Communist territory, I'd change my itinerary.

After nearly six years, I wanted my citizenship. My lawyers had told me to apply for it in Los Angeles rather than Dallas, because things tended to be a little more relaxed on the coast. In Virginia, where I used to live, any kind of gay relationship was against the law, technically, and I was afraid somebody might bring it up.

I was worried, even about California, because I heard

they might ask your sexual preference. To me, there is no reason why anybody should have to answer that question, but it was explained to me that the government feels it has the right to know because some people might apply for sensitive jobs in the military or defense industry or something, and homosexuality could be grounds for blackmail. But everybody can be blackmailed for something, if you think about it. In a better world, where you could be open about your sexuality, there'd be no question of blackmail.

I was scared because of the double standard: they want you to be open about it but then they can penalize you. I was sure they would ask me because there had been some publicity, maybe a picture of me and Rita Mae together at a party or an opening or something. If I told the truth, they could deny my citizenship, but since I was under oath, I didn't want to perjure myself. My lawyers told me to just be honest, that nobody was going to give me a hard time.

My hearing was set for the end of May at the office of the Immigration and Naturalization Service in Los Angeles. The lawyer who accompanied me to the proceedings told me that she had known the hearing officer for years and that the woman rarely ever smiles, but that day she was smiling and friendly. I took it as a good sign.

One of the first things I was asked to do was write a simple sentence in English. I wrote: "The weather in Southern California is wonderful," and that seemed to satisfy them. Then the officer asked me a few questions: What's the color of the flag? Who was the first President of the U.S.? Who is the President now?

Another question was: Can the President alone declare war? I thought about it for a while and said, "Yeah." Actually, that was wrong because the President needs the consent of Congress, but I figured if there's a bomb on the way, you're not going to have time to call Congress and take a vote. I guess I was wrong but my logic was right, and I don't think they held it against me.

Then the officer asked me a few brief questions about whether I had a criminal record or a drug habit. There was also something very quick about my sexuality, and I just gulped and said I was bisexual, and she never even glanced up from the form she was reading, just went on to the next thing. When it was all over she was very friendly but didn't tell me whether I had passed or failed.

My lawyer told me it would be three or four weeks before I found out, so I went back to tennis and my conditioning drills with Nancy. In early July the lawyer called and said: "You've got it."

I was so thrilled because now I could finally unpack my emotional luggage and really feel at home. I wanted other people to recognize me as an American, although I realize some people never will. It still annoys me sometimes when people say: "I'm an American, I was born here." I say to myself: Well, what did you do to get here? What did you do to deserve it? Nothing.

It even bothers me when people say, "Where are you from?" because of my accent, which is really pretty slight these days. Sometimes people ask, "Are you from South Africa or Australia?" It shouldn't bother me that people can tell I'm not a native-born American, but it does.

Becoming a citizen was an important legal barrier for me, and also a psychological one. But I still had to face the people who judged me differently because I was born somewhere else. I know there are differences. My old coach, George Parma, says he used to wonder why Ivan Lendl got such bad press in the States for a while. Later George realized that Ivan was trying to translate his somewhat sarcastic Czech sense of humor—answering a question with a short, sardonic question—into English, and it just didn't work.

I think some of my "hostile" image had to do with the fact that I was not afraid to speak my mind, and that my answers came out with a slight foreign accent. A lot of Americans are not comfortable with different languages and accents, while in Europe you deal with them all the time. The longer I stay in the States, the more I understand how important it is to smile and seem like a nice guy. Like Ronald Reagan. Your image seems to count more than what you do. I've always wanted to be liked for myself, and I hoped that becoming a citizen would help that happen.

The swearing-in ceremony took place on July 20 in Los Angeles. As I recall, the judge was an older black man and there were around fifty or sixty people in the group: the typical Los Angeles mix of blacks, Orientals, Caucasians, and Hispanics. The judge read the proclamation, and I recited it after him.

Then he said: "I now pronounce you citizens of the United States." I felt like cheering and clapping and giving high-fives, but the other people were already filing quietly out of the room. I felt like saying: Hey, I've been waiting a long time for this. One little boy slept right through his own naturalization ceremony and I thought, Hey, this kid doesn't even know what's going on.

When I got outside, Larry King was there, along with Linda Dozoretz from Rogers & Cowan, my public relations firm in L.A., and my old friends Mimi and Janet. There was no fanfare, no crowds, and only one photographer, because Linda had done a good job keeping it a private affair. Everybody was hugging and kissing me, and I was crying. I wished my parents and Jana could have been there, too.

I got my passport the next day, but it didn't really sink in until a few days later when I was heading for an exhibition in Australia. I was searching for my green card in my pocketbook, when the customs man said: "Do you have your passport?"

"Do I have a passport!" I said, flourishing it proudly.

I was so cool. I was an American. And the weather in Southern California was wonderful.

New Image

I had a new dress size and a new passport by August of 1981, but I still didn't have the U.S. Open championship, the only Grand Slam title I had never won. My slump of the past year had long ago been chronicled by the tennis writers but now all the columnists and feature writers were doing a "What's Wrong with Martina?" story. I thought I had already straightened my life out considerably, but good news travels slower than bad news.

To combat that image, Nancy and I gave an interview to a local columnist as soon as my citizenship was official, explaining that I had moved to Dallas to get myself in shape and try to regain my Number 1 ranking. We made the point that Nancy was helping me, and that people shouldn't make any assumptions about our relationship, particularly since Nancy had a boyfriend in Dallas at the time.

I said that I was bisexual but Nancy was "straight," and then I added: "I don't care what they say about me, but Nancy shouldn't have to suffer just for being my friend."

Looking back, that might have been a mistake, since people are going to think what they want to think anyway. It might have been better not to call attention to anything, to deny nothing and not throw anything in people's faces. But we did what we thought was right.

As the U.S. Open approached, the whole tennis world was quaking because of Marilyn Barnett's so-called palimony suit against Billie Jean King. To make things worse, I had granted an interview with Steve Goldstein, then with the New York *Daily News,* a few months earlier, saying how much I feared further publicity about my relationship with Rita Mae. I had spoken openly about my fears and they became a self-fulfilling prophecy because once our conversation was in his notebook, it was doomed to get out.

Steve waited until I'd received my citizenship, then he called me in Monte Carlo and said it was time to use the interview. I told him I still didn't want it in print, that the Billie Jean stuff was just too big. He told me his editors knew he had the story and that he was under pressure to use it. So he did.

I still maintain that the publication of our conversation was a betrayal of a trust, but I also blame myself. It was gullible and naïve of me to have shared my strongest feelings with a reporter who had other priorities than my security, my happiness. But you live and learn. I've always been candid with the press—ask Jane Leavy of the Washington *Post* or Steve Jacobson of *Newsday* or Sally Wilson of the Dallas *Morning News* or Peter Bodo or Susan Adams—but after that episode, I cut back on intimate conversations.

In that same article, Chris was quoted as saying: "Her tennis isn't going to straighten out until she straightens out her life. Martina is in a slump right now. Two years ago she was playing real well. I don't think she's really working that hard right now, not practicing the way she used to. I think she's happy living in America, being an American citizen, enjoying the luxuries. If she wants to be Number 1, she has to change something."

She was legitimately concerned about me. How was she to know I had already changed my training so drastically that within two years she would be unable to beat me on any surface, even clay?

At the time that article came out, Rita Mae told another newspaper: "She fell in love with someone else. It happens all the time."

It was really a joke, if you think about it, people drooling over little tidbits about whether I'm this or that. It made me realize that women and men are treated differently even in something as private as sexuality. Sportswriters have no problem asking a woman, "Is it true you're sleeping with other women?" but they'd never ask a man whether he was sleeping with other men—and God knows there are some well-known male athletes who are doing just that.

You know that if a reporter asked that question of a man, he'd get a knuckle sandwich and he wouldn't wake up for a week. But if a woman smacked a reporter who asked insinuating questions about her sexuality, that would only prove the point, wouldn't it?

It really shouldn't matter that much, but I am told that image counts a lot in the world. Advertisers and sponsors pay a lot of money because of image. At the time of the Billie Jean revelations, there was concern about Avon dropping sponsorship if they felt there was too much bad publicity. They denied they were getting out—but they were gone within a year.

Fortunately, there were a lot of tennis sponsors with more courage and vision than Avon. I could see that if I regained my form, I could make a fortune in endorsements for equipment and apparel. Still, I was really concerned about my image—not so much who I thought I was, not so much what the public thought, but what the gnomes and the gremlins in the business world thought. The unseen "they" who decide how the public feels.

Who makes these decisions? Mark Spitz won all the swimming gold medals at the 1972 Olympics, but people reacted badly to his personality in the commercials. That's one thing—I was more worried about the prejudices some people might carry around before they ever got a chance to see me in a commercial.

The whole idea of image is so confused. On the one hand, Madison Avenue is worried about the image of the players in a tennis tour. On the other hand, sports events are often sponsored by the makers of junk food, beer, and cigarets. What's the message when an athlete who works at keeping her body fit is sponsored by a sugar-filled snack that does more harm than good? One out of two deaths in car crashes are caused by drinking, yet people watch football games on TV and laugh at the funny beer commercials, then have a few drinks and crack up their cars.

Let's be honest, one of the major forces in women's tennis is Virginia Slims, a great sponsor, a first-rate company, but one whose product carries a warning about its danger to your health. They probably should warn people about eggs, too, considering the cholesterol levels. And if you could see what goes into red meat, you'd never eat it. I am proud of being sponsored by Virginia Slims, but I only smoke a couple of cigarets a year, usually when I'm getting beaten in bridge or backgammon, and I'd never want to have my picture taken with a cigaret in my hand because of . . . the image.

Part of my image was formed during the Navrat the Brat stage, when I was doing my Billie Jean get-on-the-officials imitation on the court, and wearing five bracelets and three necklaces off the court. And on the court I thought I was just perfect, but I'm sure I overdid it.

It's funny. These days I go around promoting some of my sponsors and people meet me and say: "You're not anything like I thought." The wife of a sports columnist met me for the first time recently at the big party Virginia Slims threw during Wimbledon at the Inn on the Park. I was wearing a gown and my hair was long and I had some eye makeup on, and she said to me, "You're *pretty.*" We both laughed, and it was cool, but what do people expect?

One of the first things I did in the summer of 1981 was start to pay more attention to my hair. I had done some fairly strange things with my hair in the past, including getting my first perm from Marilyn Barnett back in 1975—the frizzy look you see in the classic flowered-dress, Great Wide Hope pictures. That round head of hair was exactly what I needed with my round face and round body of the time—made me look so much bigger!

I never had another perm after that, but I did try to lighten my natural brown color by using a spray that lets the sun bleach your hair. That was a disaster, too, because it just dried out my hair and was terrible for the texture. In 1981, Al Frohman, who was Nancy's manager, was talking to me one day, and he casually suggested that I would look great as a blond, so I got my hair highlighted and had a makeup lesson at Vidal Sassoon's in New York.

My mother occasionally does her nails, but women in Czechoslovakia rarely use makeup. Now I was using a little eye liner and blush to heighten my high Slavic cheekbones, which people are always raving about.

I also began caring about how I was photographed. There's nothing you can do about photographs taken during a match, of course, but if a photographer was working on a feature article, I'd ask him to wait until I'd showered after practice. Most of the photographers are great about this, and really enjoy taking pictures that make me look the way I feel. And after a shower, and with some makeup and a nice outfit on, I feel a lot more like smiling.

I'm not like Andrea Temesvari, with all that makeup and

her hair done, who even on the court always looks as if she's going directly to the Magyar Ball. These days my taste tends toward understatement, whether for myself or my surroundings. I don't relate to Marilyn Monroe, talking like a little girl and letting her blouse hang open, or Joan Collins, the way she throws it at you. My idols are actresses like Greta Garbo, for her beauty and also for her sense of privacy, and Katharine Hepburn, for her strength and calmness. I understand she was once a very fine golfer and tennis player. You can tell just by the way she moves. I hope I can have that courage and inner peace at her age—or next week.

I've been a Hepburn fan ever since I saw her in *The African Queen* when I was a kid in Prague. It was one of the first American films I ever saw. From then on I wanted to be like Katharine Hepburn.

My big hope was to meet her someday. One time I was playing a tournament in New Jersey and I sent a message to her at the Broadway theater where she was performing in *West Side Waltz*, inviting her to the matches, but her assistant called and said Miss Hepburn was sorry but she couldn't make the tennis matches.

But I kept trying, and after the 1984 U.S. Open, she invited me and Judy Nelson to her apartment in New York for a visit. She was exactly the way I'd imagined: very poised, very intelligent, more interested in other people than in herself. She wanted to know about tennis, and what it was like to be out there on center court. She seemed to know all about my career, and I tried not to sit there and gawk. I could just visualize her in all those great movies.

The African Queen. . . . In the old movies, when the film board said you had to be fully dressed with at least one foot on the floor, a three-second kiss was so sensuous. Now everybody's undressed and it's not nearly as much of a turn-on. Bogart and Hepburn. Fred and Ginger. Tracy and Hepburn. Such mystique. Nowadays, directors can't believe it when the actress doesn't want to do a nude scene. If I was an actress, I wouldn't do it.

I started liking the way I looked in the summer of 1981. I was a far cry from the little girl her father called Prut ("Stick"). I remember the time I went to the movies with my grandmother and the ladies'-room attendant sent me to the other room because she thought I was a boy. I said: "I'm a girl," and she said: "Are you sure?"

People judge you by appearances, and since I was all woman underneath, I finally figured I might as well start dressing the part. I think it helped to be in the best shape of my career. When you feel good about yourself, you look better and you perform better, too. The confidence shows. It affects you on the court. I don't feel masculine on the court. I know I'm stronger than other women and faster than most, but I'm not bigger than a lot of them. I was working out and eating better and I felt confident and healthy and feminine. Put it this way: I liked standing out there in front of 18,000 people in my bright new orange and gold outfits, with a touch of blusher on my cheeks. I felt good about myself, better than I ever had.

I was getting to like the new me—makeup, blond hair, and frilly clothes—but I was afraid that reporters at the U.S. Open were going to ask me about the article about my relationship with Rita Mae. Normally, I am the most cooperative interviewee in tennis. I will sit and dig out real answers, try to be funny, and tell the truth, for as long as they ask. The reporters who deal in depth know I'll bleed for them, because I respect that part of my business.

This time I was prepared to say: "If you want to talk about tennis, fine. If you want something else, forget it." But I never had to say that. Instead, I had to answer questions about another part of my image: the choker, who still hadn't won the U.S. Open.

The Other Opponent

By the time the 1981 U.S. Open rolled around, I was more than ready to win it. I was in great shape and feeling competitive. This was the only major tournament I had never won, and it was getting more noticeable every year. Most of my major traumas had come here: the defection in 1975, the loss to Janet Newberry in 1976, semifinal upsets to Wendy Turnbull in 1977, Pam Shriver in 1978, Tracy Austin in 1979, and a fourth-round loss to Hana Mandlikova in 1980. I'd never even gotten to the finals, and now this was my national championship.

What made it worse was being paired with Björn Borg, who hadn't won the men's title. It was a natural: two great athletes from other countries who fell by the wayside every September. Some people saw great significance in the fact that it happened in New York—as if it were some test of character. Our losing streaks had begun at the gracious but crowded West Side Tennis Club, first on grass, later on artificial clay, then continued on the hard courts of the National Tennis Center at Flushing Meadow.

Fans and reporters chewed over Borg's negative comments about the hard courts and night lights of Flushing Meadow and my complaints about the swirling winds, humidity, glaring sun, and jets that roared overhead on certain flight patterns when the wind was blowing the wrong way.

Once again, I had provided a reason to root against Martina. For years I had given my honest assessment of a tennis environment that resembles the hurly-burly of a medieval marketplace: fans shouting their lungs out, various adventures of love and hate being played out all around you, a cornucopia of food and drink, the blare of the jets, and somewhere in the middle of all this, a couple of vagabonds trying to hit a tennis ball. There is no place like it, so typically New York.

The truth of the matter is, I love New York: I finally have an apartment there, and I love the U.S. Open as the embodiment of my adopted country. But until I won the tournament, my assessment of the Open's lusty character was going to be held against me: "Martina Can't Win Big One in Big Apple."

Well, 1981 was supposed to be my year. We got through the early stories about Nancy working with me, and my mind was totally on tennis. I had been hitting with Renee Richards, who'd been a friend of mine for years, and she was starting to give me some technical advice, something I really hadn't had since leaving Czechoslovakia. My old doubles partner, Billie Jean, and my Team Tennis coach, Roy Emerson, had given me some pointers, and I had practiced with friends like Phil Rogers in Charlottesville and David Ericson in Dallas and other teaching pros, but I really needed somebody who knew the women's tour and could work with me consistently.

Renee and Nancy were sitting together in the stands—this was the birth of the Team Navratilova tag—as I breezed through the early rounds, losing one game to Nerida Gregory, five to Ann White, three to JoAnne Russell, and one to Kathy Jordan. I was extended to a 7–5, 6–4 victory by Anne Smith in the quarters, and that set up a

242

semifinal match with Chris on Friday, the day before the finals.

I had played Chris only once at the Open, in 1975, the day I sought asylum in the States. This was the first time I would be playing her at all since the double bagel at Amelia Island, and I don't mind admitting that it was on my mind before the game. It was just like Nancy's description of a playground basketball game in Harlem. Somebody goes over you for a basket, the crowd starts stomping its feet and chanting "Getback, getback, getback," and all you want to do is score a "getback" on the other end of the court.

I went after my getback on your basic brawly afternoon at Flushing Meadow. I took the first set, 7–5, and Chris took the second, 6–4. I fell behind one service break, 2–3, in the third set and then we had to wait a few minutes while guards went into the stands and ejected two guys who were making a lot of noise. I don't know what the interruption did to our concentration, but I came back to break Chris in the eighth game and I broke her again in the tenth to win the set, 6–4, and the match. When it was over, I leaped in the air, thrilled to have made it to my first U.S. Open final.

Maybe I should have saved the energy from the leap. Tracy Austin had won an easy, early victory over Barbara Potter, 6–1, 6–3, while my match with Chris didn't end until late in the afternoon. Although maybe that had nothing to do with what happened on Saturday afternoon.

I felt so *ready* on Saturday. I felt as festive as my orange and yellow shirt, sure that this was the day I'd break through the last "Can't-Win-the-Big-One" barrier.

Tracy had been the youngest player to compete at Wimbledon, fourteen years old in 1977, and she had won the U.S. Open at sixteen in 1979 and beaten me in the 1980 Avons. She was still only eighteen years old, but she was already coming back from her first serious injury, sciatica, which had kept her off the circuit for much of the year. She had changed coaches, from Robert Lansdorp to Marty Riessen, and was fighting off the suggestion that she'd broken into the business at too young an age. We all have our labels.

I really never knew Tracy very well because she didn't spend much time with the other players, so it wasn't hard to play impersonally and methodically against her. I did exactly what I had to do with her baseline game—rushed in on her serve and just demolished her in the first set, 6–1 —and I was convinced it was going to be my day. A record crowd of 18,892 felt the same way. I heard them roaring for my smashes and volleys, and for the first time ever I felt myself to be the favorite at the Open.

By the second set, the wind was swirling around the court, and I was having trouble getting my big first serve in. I shouldn't have, but I was, and that gave Tracy just enough confidence to dig in and play her baseline game for a while. Even at that, we were tied, 4–4, 15–15, when she hit a forehand approach down the line and it caught the let cord and dribbled over the net for a big point. Still, I thought I had her, but I let her off the hook, and she won the set in a 7–4 tiebreaker.

In the third set, Tracy surprised me by hitting the ball down the line to my forehand, and I couldn't get there because I was already too tired. I had never seen her try so many passing shots and aggressive forehands, but she was definitely on to something. In the end I just didn't have as much energy as I would have liked, but still, I won my serve while I was down, 5–6, saving three match points.

I'll never forget that tiebreaker, how I wanted to crush the ball on a couple of forehand volleys, make it bounce over the stands on one ferocious, final swing, get the last monkey off my back. It was like a baseball hitter trying to hit two home runs with the same swing, swinging from his butt, strictly from the East Bronx. I was so far off technically that the ball just wasn't staying on the court.

Actually, I'd been making the same technical mistake all through the tournament—sticking my elbow out too far—but the added power I summoned up in this last game just magnified the error. Five minutes after the match, Renee would tell me what I'd been doing wrong. I'm convinced that if she had been my coach before that tournament, the fiasco with Tracy would never have happened. But I dug a hole for myself and double-faulted at 1–6 in the tiebreaker to lose the match.

I wanted to cry, but I held it in, biting my lip, feeling as bad as I did when I lost to Newberry in 1976. The photographers were all around, and I wanted to crawl into a hole. I thought about bolting from the court, but I'm glad I didn't.

I was still crying when the announcer called my name for the runner-up trophy. But then something marvelous happened: the crowd started applauding and cheering. Their ovation lasted for more than a minute, and I stood there and finally started to cry, but I cried tears of appreciation, not of sadness. I knew they were cheering me as Martina, but they also were cheering me as an American. I don't think they were cheering me because I lost. I think I would have been a popular winner that year, too. People say it did a lot for me to have lost, but I would rather have won.

I stood there and watched the fans applaud me. I was trying not to cry as they kept clapping and clapping, and I thought, Oh, rats. You've got to stop crying.

Finally, I stepped up to the microphone and said: "It took me nine years to get the silver ball. I hope it doesn't take me nine years to get the championship cup." And they started cheering again. It was really strange, not like tennis at all, but really something you expect to see in opera, where the soprano steps out of her role on the stage for a curtain call, and the crowd cheers and throws roses. That's how I felt. They weren't cheering Martina the Complainer, Martina the Czech, Martina the Loser, Martina the Bisexual Defector. They were cheering me. I had never felt anything like it in my life: acceptance, respect, maybe even love.

I know how fickle the New York crowd can be. In the old days they didn't like Chris because she was so "cold." Now they loved her for being so "warm." When I beat Chris in the semis, I knew the majority of the fans would rather have had her win. Still, they'd applauded my guts and determination for winning and now they were applauding me after losing, and I took it as a compliment. It was one of the best moments of my life, the moment I discovered New Yorkers are emotional, just like me. It was that moment, standing drenched in this shower of tears and applause, that I decided a little bit of me was a New Yorker, too. I felt a tremendous burden had been lifted from my shoulders. Those people in New York accepted me, not only as a tennis player but as a human being as well.

Later I told Jane Gross of *The New York Times:* "All those Americans going crazy. It's so great when the people are behind you. I tried too hard. I think I tried so hard that I froze on a couple of forehand volleys when I could have put it away. It would have meant so much to me to win here, being an American."

The loss and the response totally drained me. Pam and I lost our doubles semifinal to Rosie and Wendy Turnbull, and I went back to Nancy's mother's house, just wiped out. I can't say I got over the loss easily, either. I had suffered a lot of defeats in the past year, and at one point I might have said I was getting used to losing. But with my new attitude and my new conditioning, I was not expecting to lose, and it hurt more than any other loss ever had.

The one thing I regretted after the Tracy match was knowing that for the next year I would have to put up with the old "Can't Win the Big One" label. Actually, by that time I had won all the big ones except the Open, but in sports, if you haven't won *every* big one, there's always the suspicion that you get the lump in your throat, you take the apple, you "spit the bit," as George Steinbrenner once said about a pitcher of his.

To me, choking is not being able to win, period. Yet you hear the "choke" label used mainly against athletes with good records who haven't won a certain honor or certain tournament. It's like I told Sally Wilson from Dallas: it's only a big deal if you don't win at all.

Sportswriters made a big deal about the fact that Ray Meyer's De Paul team never won a national basketball championship. Yet the man was a great coach for forty years. And then there's Julius Erving—one of the greatest competitors and finest human beings in sports, a total gentleman. God knows if the Philadelphia 76ers would have won a basketball title if they hadn't traded for Moses Malone in 1982–83. Julius had had better years, yet suddenly he "won the big one." The way I see it, the more wins you have, the greater the percentage, the more people zero in on your isolated failures.

It's an easy way out, to say that I choked in 1981. There might be technical reasons why I lost. If I miss a shot, that's not a choke to me. You want to hit it so bad you can taste it, but you miss it. If I do it over and over again, that's choking. But to miss one shot, or one last-second shot, is not a choke.

But the label stays on. The year I lost to Kathy Horvath in the French Open (1983) I'd been playing the best tennis any woman has ever played, but I messed up a match and lost. That's not choking, that's losing. When I was playing Chris at the U.S. Open in 1983 and the Virginia Slims and Amelia Island in 1984, she kept suggesting that she'd have an edge in mental toughness if she could stay close to me. I can understand Chris saying that. She's a great competitor and she's got to keep telling herself she's got a chance. But the way it gets translated, it sounds as if I'm going to take the apple at any given moment—because I'm too emotional.

I still think the loss to Tracy was one of the toughest of my career because I had felt so ready to play and had no physical problems. I usually bounce back quickly after a loss, but this one was a real low. I was still convinced I was going to win the next year, and I felt really good about myself, but I couldn't believe I had lost again.

Renee

The best thing that came out of the loss to Tracy was Renee Richards. We started working together unofficially during the tournament and she became my coach right afterward. She made a big difference in my career.

How much difference? Well, we broke up twice over financial disputes, and she has now resumed her medical career, but when I finally won the U.S. Open in 1983, I thanked not only Nancy Lieberman and Mike Estep, my current coach, but I also remembered to thank Renee over the loudspeaker, too.

The first time I met Renee Richards was in 1977 when she was trying to become certified to join the women's tour. There had never been a controversy like it, in which a male had gone through a sex-change operation and then wanted to compete at the top level of women's sports.

I hadn't heard of Renee in her first life as Dr. Richard Raskind, an eye specialist in New York. But we soon learned that Richard Raskind had been a highly ranked player in the East, captain of the men's team at Yale, and all-Navy champion while doing his military service. I've sometimes wondered how he would have done as a male player if he had totally ignored his education, like almost all the top players on the tour today. By 1974 Raskind was thirteenth in the national men's 35s ratings, and an established eye doctor, but he was growing more uncomfortable with his role as a male.

Renee has since written about herself in a book called *Second Serve*, which I found fascinating. Even though Richard Raskind had a seemingly successful life, eventually he gave it all up, had a sex-change operation, and took a new name and identity in California. Anybody who reads Renee's book will shudder at some of the medical and psychological traumas Richard/Renee went through. One thing that really moved me was his attempt to reduce the prominent male Adam's apple, and how the drill cut right through into the trachea, nearly choking the patient on the operating table. All I can say is that Renee must have wanted to become a woman very badly, to go through so much.

Once she was settled in California, Renee couldn't stay away from tennis, and eventually people discovered her true identity. After the publicity, Renee Richards became an international celebrity and the object of legal suits as she tried to get into the women's tennis field.

The public, the press, the tennis officials, and some of the players were more disturbed about Renee Richards than I was. I couldn't believe how all of a sudden all these people had become experts on the subject overnight. If the real experts said she was a woman, I figured, let her play. Besides, I took one look at her warming up one day and knew she wasn't going to dominate women's tennis—and she certainly wasn't going to dominate me. I also couldn't envision a wave of men having that operation just so they could become the twenty-third best female player in the world, or whatever. Renee Richards looked like, and played like, a pretty good forty-year-old male player, but her main assets were her height and her intelligence.

I was introduced to Renee by Betty Ann Stuart, a player and mutual friend, who knew I was in favor of Renee's playing. We got along right away, I think because Renee and I could relate to each other as outsiders—she for what she was going through, I because of my defection from Czechoslovakia.

Renee says she can remember when she joined the tour in 1977, "with the paparazzi chasing me all over the place," how I beat her in the first round at São Paolo, 7–6, 7–6, then came up to her in the dingy dressing room afterward and said, "Stay with it, Renee, you'll make it."

To tell the truth, I remember the match but I don't recall saying anything in particular to her. If I did, it was no different from Chris Evert comforting me after a loss, or Evonne Goolagong consoling Chris when she found her crying in the bathroom after a bad day. Most of the women on the tour are pretty supportive. My feeling about Renee Richards was that if she was legally certified as a woman, she had the right to play in the tournament, and I wasn't going to make life any more difficult for her.

I was glad to have her on the tour because she was older, she was smart, she had a background outside tennis, she spoke several languages, and she knew things that most of us just didn't know. We'd go shopping and have a meal together, and it was a reminder to me that there was a world outside the courts. I remember going with her to buy gifts for her son; and we talked a little about what he was going through, knowing his father had undergone a sex change.

Renee knew more about teaching tennis than most people I'd met. We used to talk strategy, and I realized she was beating some of the younger, more agile kids with her brains. She thought about the match before it happened; that was a revelation to me. However, I never really considered Renee as a potential coach while she was playing on the tour.

After I lost to Tracy in 1981, I looked around and saw that most of the men and women players seemed to have somebody coaching them. Ion Tiriac would be leaning over the fence and encouraging Guillermo Vilas, Björn Borg never went anywhere without Lennart Bergelin, and Tracy always had one coach or another, while Pam Shriver had Don Candy. I basically didn't talk tennis with anybody. I just went out and played—part of my mystique, but not always the best policy.

During the 1981 Open, I was having trouble arranging for a practice court, and Renee said she would take care of it for me. She was eliminated in the first round, so we hit together a few times, and I realized I liked the idea of somebody giving me a little help. I'd been on my own for a long time, and I was tired. I saw how much difference Nancy had made in a few weeks, and I wanted to help myself as much as possible. So I asked Renee to work with me on and off throughout the year, and she began overhauling my game.

It was Renee who first gave me the glimmer of an idea about preparing for a match. What did the other player normally do? I wondered. What were my strengths? What were her weaknesses? What were my best percentages? Renee knew the other players, and told me things about them I had never noticed.

She also added a topspin backhand to my slice backhand, and worked on my forehand volley by getting me to stop swinging as if it were a groundstroke. Then she showed me how I'd been sticking out my elbow in the final games against Tracy. She also got me to jump into my serve for added power, and to stand a little closer to the sideline, the way John McEnroe does.

We worked together for a few weeks and she really picked up my game. I roared through my next tournament in Bloomington, Minnesota, winning ten straight sets, including a 6–0, 6–2 final over Tracy. I also won at Tampa and Melbourne before losing to Tracy in the finals at Stuttgart and to Chris in the finals at Sydney, and then I beat Chris at the Australian Open to win it for the first time.

Then came the last tournament of the 1981 season, the Toyota championships in New Jersey, where Tracy and I met in the finals with the year's Number 1 ranking at stake. I thought I had her after a 6–2 first set, but once again she came back and beat me, 6–4, 6–2, for the title. Once again the crowd cheered me, but this time I told them: "You're trying, but you won't make me cry again." I was mad this time, not sad.

The choke label surfaced again a few months later. I had won five straight tournaments when I met Sylvia Hanika in the finals of the Avon championships at Madison Square Garden. I took the first set, 6–1, and was up, 3–1, in the second when my game just fell apart again, and she beat me, 6–3, 6–4. I was disappointed, but I knew the only person who could beat me consistently was myself. And those days were coming to an end.

I felt good about Renee coaching me. I thought we had a sound financial agreement and things were going along fine between the two of us. But Nancy was also around, as my "motivation coach," and I think Renee was uncomfortable with that from the start. Renee and Nancy would sit together and everybody would turn to stare at the transsexual tennis player and the all-American basketball player rooting for the Czech defector. We all had our own labels, and the collective label was Team Navratilova.

The joke was that people made it sound like one happy little family, but meanwhile Renee was annoyed by Nancy's cheerleading from the seats while Renee was trying to concentrate on the technical and mental part of the game. Nancy, as a basketball player, thought her best contribution to my game was to focus on the emotional aspect. Sometimes I'd turn around for encouragement from one or both of them, and see them studiously avoiding each other. Some team.

Maybe the biggest impact of the so-called Team Navratilova was its effect on a few susceptible souls like Roland Jaeger. I would turn to Nancy after a point and she would clench her fist to tell me to be tough, or Renee would point to her temple to tell me to be smart. Very deep coaching. But Roland is a former boxer who approaches tennis with all the subtlety of a left hook to the ribs, and he was convinced we had some huge supernatural edge over his daughter, Andrea. He used to get this sour look on his boxer's face just watching Renee and Nancy.

Our juggernaut rolled into Paris on a two-tournament streak. I hadn't played there in five years, not since losing to Chris in three sets in the 1975 finals, but Renee made me feel that I could beat anybody on any surface, even the crushed clay of Roland Garros. I had a good tournament, beating Candy Reynolds, Lisa Bonder, Kathy Rinaldi, Zina Garrison, and Hana Mandlikova to reach the finals against Andrea, who had beaten Chris in the semifinals.

The temperature in Paris was 95° that day. Andrea had me, 5–4, and was serving for the first set, but I broke back and won the tiebreaker, 8–6. The second set was much easier: 6–1. Afterward, we shook hands and I congratulated her on giving me a good match in her first Grand Slam final.

A few minutes later I was under the stands, preparing for the press conference, when a TV reporter warned me to look out, that Roland Jaeger had told his daughter to complain about Nancy and Renee coaching me. So I wasn't surprised when Andrea came in and said: "It sort of blew my concentration. It's difficult to be playing three people at once. I was trying in the whole first set to deal with it, and I was doing fine. But it was annoying. They've done it in other matches. It's not very good for tennis. She played well and I lost. But it shouldn't happen. I might win, love–love, or lose, love–love, but I want to win by myself or lose by myself."

The rule is that coaching is illegal during the match if it bothers your opponent. She's supposed to complain about it to the umpire, who then warns you, and you tell your coach to stop whatever it is that's annoying the other player. But Andrea never said a word during the match, never even looked over. It was her father who told her to complain—after the match.

When the reporters asked me about it, I said: "This is a shock. All I can say is that I never looked at Renee except for encouragement. Here I have won the final of one of the biggest tournaments in the world. Thank you very much, Andrea. I didn't have to look up at them. Before I played, I went over the match twenty times with Renee. I could have recited it in my sleep what I had to do against her. I didn't need to look at Renee."

Renee did her share by giving a press conference in French and telling everybody how silly it was. She said: "I sat impassively, like I always do. I gave no hand signals. I didn't coach her. Nancy, of course, was screaming her lungs out: 'C'mon Martina! Let's win!' "

That was Renee's way of letting it be known she did not consider Nancy's "screaming her lungs out" to be coaching in any shape or form.

After I won at Eastbourne in the grass tune-up for Wimbledon, Renee came over from New York with news that an eye doctor had died and that his practice was available for $50,000. She had taken a refresher course at Harvard that winter and was eager to get back into her profession again, which basically was a good idea. But she wanted to borrow the $50,000 from me—and my accountant said it was not a great idea to lend money to a friend.

Renee then said she was going to earn that much money from the bonus I would receive for winning tournaments in the Playtex competition, but I said, "Whoa, that's bonus money, not prize money, and I'll decide how much I'm going to give you." So there were some hard feelings between us.

Things got worse at Wimbledon when Renee was not invited to a surprise birthday party for Nancy, planned by some friends of Nancy's. Renee thought it was Nancy's idea, but that was ridiculous. I knew the party was being planned, but I had other things on my mind—like playing in the tournament—and never being much of an organizer, I forgot to write Renee. Nancy didn't know there was a party, so she couldn't have been responsible for overlooking Renee. Nancy doesn't like to be surprised about anything. She likes to be in total control, and she almost left the party.

Anyway, Renee was upset about the party, and although she continued to prepare me for each match, she was definitely unhappy. I beat Chris, 6–1, 3–6, 6–2, in the finals, and after I won, some of my friends ran into the bathroom and poured cold champagne all over me while I was soaking in the tub at the rented house near the courts.

After I got back to New York, even though my accountant didn't like it, I lent Renee the money so she could buy the practice. We agreed that she wouldn't coach me anymore. That parting was amicable. If she had to choose between me and her medical career, I'd be the first to tell her to choose medicine.

At the U.S. Open in 1982, everybody made a big deal about Renee not coaching me anymore. Peter Marmureanu, a former Rumanian Davis Cup player, was coaching me, but Peter didn't really know the women's game. He would give me advice like "Throw the ball higher," which was fine, but it wasn't the kind of strategy Renee had offered me.

Few people know this, but Renee was watching me from a seat in the stands during the 1982 Open and, strictly out of friendship passing along some tips. But neither she nor Peter could influence the outcome of the 1982 U.S. Open; that tournament had already been decided, weeks earlier, by something that had happened three thousand miles away.

The Million-Dollar Illness

When I eventually won the U.S. Open in 1983, everybody talked about how I'd finally gotten my act together, but nobody mentioned that the year before I had my act together only to get sick before the Open. I'm still hearing people say: "She'll lose because of her nerves," but nerves had nothing to do with it in 1982. I had a frightening illness that came at exactly the wrong time, yet people talk about my "cat virus" episode, making it sound weird and exotic, or like some kind of character flaw.

In 1982 all I could think about was the Open, the only major tournament I had never won. I had been in suspended animation since losing to Tracy in the finals the year before, knowing I was ready to win it. I won at Roland Garros, I won at Wimbledon, and I helped the U.S. win the Federation Cup in San Francisco that summer, but all the time my mind was on Flushing Meadow.

The Federation Cup was a thrill because it gave me the rare chance to be on the winning side for two nations. I had helped Czechoslovakia win in 1975 and now I was representing my new country. Plus, of course, it was a great feeling to be on the same side as Chris for a change. I played pretty well and we won the cup.

The visit to San Francisco was also a good chance to see Rita Mae Brown and iron out some details about the disposition of the house in Charlottesville. She and I were listed as co-owners, and our lawyers were making things worse instead of better, so I called her up and said, "Look, as long as I'm out here, why don't we just talk it over and tell the lawyers who gets what?" She agreed, so I went over to her apartment.

We talked for a few hours and settled everything. As usual, Rita Mae had some cats running around the house. She's very devoted to them and, in fact, when she wrote a novel about women's tennis—I'm told the main character is a tempestuous left-hander from Argentina—she put one of her own cats, Baby Jesus, into the novel. When I went to visit, Rita Mae had put out some snacks, bowls of peanuts and whatever, and every so often one of the cats would tiptoe through the cashews.

I didn't think much about the cats for a while because they go with the franchise, but I did think about being sick. I was supposed to play a tennis tour in Australia and I was hanging out in Los Angeles, practicing, but I felt terrible. I couldn't move. I had played some tough matches for the Federation Cup and thought I might have strained some muscles going from clay to grass to cement in a short period that spring. But that had never bothered me before. My muscles were so tight.

I called Nancy on the phone and told her I didn't feel like working out. At first she tried to motivate me by saying, "Dammit, what's the matter? The Open is coming up and you don't look like you even care." But she realized something was wrong a few days later when I called again and started crying, saying I just couldn't get on the plane for Australia. This wasn't like me. I love playing tennis, and I had never been so negative about a trip and playing in my life.

I remember going into the Los Angeles office of Marty Weiss, my accountant, and saying I couldn't get on the plane for Australia the next day. I did try to back out of it, but he said the sponsors had already put up the money and it would be a disaster for everybody if I didn't show up.

Seven other players were there already, and I didn't want to have them on my conscience, so I ended up getting on a plane to Hawaii, resting in a hotel room for half a day, and then continuing on to Australia.

I still felt rotten when I got there. I practiced with Andrea Leand and quit after fifteen minutes. We were supposed to play three days in Sydney and two in Perth, but I just played two days in Sydney, beating Sue Barker the first day and dropping the last two sets to Andrea Jaeger indoors after winning the first, 6–1. After one set, I could run all right, but I had a hard time stopping and changing directions. I defaulted the next match.

Because of the insurance, I had to be examined by doctors, to make sure I wasn't faking. They never gave me a blood test, but just kept asking me about my reflexes. Meanwhile my glands were about three times their normal size —from my neck to my armpit and into my chest—but these doctors didn't seem to notice. Nevertheless, I guess I convinced them I was really sick and the insurance company eventually paid off the promoters. All I wanted to do then was go somewhere and sleep—but the U.S. Open was looming ahead.

I got to New York the week before the Open, staying with Nancy's mom, sleeping half the day. I'd get out of bed, start to practice, and feel the energy seeping out of me. Nancy would mention stickball or basketball and I'd groan. When I wasn't sleeping, I just wanted to lie down and read a book. I figured it was time to see a doctor.

We're fortunate to have two excellent doctors at the U.S. Open. One is an orthopedist, Irving Glick, who has worked with basketball players from St. John's University as well as most of the tennis players. The other is an internist, Gary Wadler, who has a great variety of medical interests and, along with his wife, Nancy, recently wrote a book about herpes entitled *How to Cope*. Both doctors are good guys, easy to talk to.

It's not hard to find Gary Wadler in a crowd at the Open. He's the one wearing a jacket as red as a tomato. I think he wears it so he'll be easy to find in a crowded locker room or at the edge of the court. At least, I hope that's the reason he wears it. Anyway, I went to him and described my symptoms and, unlike the doctors in Australia, he took them seriously.

My nodes were really swollen under my left armpit and they dropped to the side of my breast, particularly on the left. In the back, they were really hard and crunchy. Dr. Wadler told me that unless they got smaller in a hurry he might want to have a biopsy performed. At first I didn't know what a biopsy meant, but then it was explained to me

259

that they'd be cutting a piece out of my skin to test for cancer.

He took a blood sample right away and shipped my blood into the city. He told me that the problem could range anywhere from a virus to a serious blood disorder—perhaps even a form of leukemia.

My problems were complicated on the day before the Open when I came down with a regular virus, the twenty-four-hour variety. The rumor was going around Flushing Meadow that I had a virus, and for once the rumors were correct. But Dr. Wadler felt the size of my glands and looked concerned. Knowing I hadn't been feeling well for two months, he warned me that my illness was not just a quickie virus.

He told me his preliminary diagnosis was toxoplasmosis, a disorder caused by a parasite that weakens people and is much more common than anybody realizes. Most people afflicted don't even know they have it. The symptoms include: swollen glands in the neck and armpits—leading people to think they've got mononucleosis—and fatigue, muscle pain, low-grade fever, rash, headache, and sore throat. That definitely sounded like me. But Dr. Wadler explained he had to leave room for other possibilities, too.

I was scared, even though I figured it was probably toxoplasmosis. I realized that cancer does happen to people even younger than me, but I tried to keep from dwelling on the thought. I've always been aggressive about things I thought I could affect—the outcome of a match, personal relationships, some kind of injustice. But in broader things, life and death, things you can't change, I've usually been more accepting. I don't know if that's a Czech mentality or not, but when I was told I could have something really serious, I told myself that life goes on. The sun would still come up tomorrow.

Dr. Wadler sent my blood sample down to the Centers

for Disease Control in Atlanta, and when the report came back it said I had one of the highest counts of toxoplasmosis they had ever encountered. He explained that toxoplasmosis is caught by one out of a thousand people each year: that's two million Americans.

There are two main causes: consumption of raw or undercooked meat, and exposure to cat feces. It is actually a cat disease that humans catch, and it is not a virus, as most people think, but rather acquired through the eggs of a parasite.

"Been around any animals lately?" Dr. Wadler asked.

I thought about my own dogs and then I remembered Rita Mae's cat doing pirouettes in the mixed nuts. I told him about it and he said, "Maybe the cat transmitted the disease to you." But he said I could also have gotten sick from eating uncooked meat, and I told him I had eaten rare hamburger a few days before going to Rita Mae's. Dr. Wadler said it might be a long time before we knew exactly how I got it. But I definitely had it.

"A third of the population probably has toxoplasmosis at some point in their lives, but most people never realize it," Dr. Wadler said. "They just think they have a virus and they keep plugging away until it runs its course. But a highly tuned tennis player like you, with one of the worst cases we've ever seen, will find it hard to go about business as usual."

I started crying because I knew this was going to hurt my chances at the Open. I had waited long enough.

Dr. Wadler looked at the lab reports and said he couldn't believe I wasn't in the hospital, with that high a count. In fact, he said, it wasn't a bad idea. According to him, the only reason I was still on my feet was because I was in such great shape generally.

"My advice to you is to drop out of the tournament, go

away for a few weeks and rest," he said. "I don't think you should play here."

I had two major goals at the Open. I had won the first three Playtex tournaments that year, worth $500,000 to me; a victory at the Open would be worth $500,000 more. But I wanted the Open just for itself, to win my new nation's championship, to get it done.

"You know I want to play here," I told him. "What happens if I do?"

"One possibility is that you'll get too tired and put stress on other parts of your body. You could hurt a knee or a shoulder or an ankle quite easily by falling. The other likelihood is that you'll be able to play for fifteen minutes or half an hour, but if you get into a tough match that goes into a third set, you won't be able to get off the chair."

I believed him. I thanked him for his advice and promised to see him every day. I wouldn't be far from his office at the Open. I'd be out on the courts, trying to win every match in two sets. I'd gone too far to sit this one out.

Weak in the Knees

Even with my secret about the toxoplasmosis, I felt this was the year Chris and I would finally meet in the finals of the Open. With my new physical conditioning and my new mental attitude, and Chris remaining at the peak of her game, it was inevitable that both of us would claim to be the best female player in the world.

It was also inevitable that our attitudes would get into the papers. No country in the world holds bigger and more frequent press conferences than the U.S. In most other countries, press conferences are a formality, to give the writers a tidbit or two; but in the States, the sports reporters ask questions and follow-up questions. Some of them want sensationalism; some of them want depth. Some of them want blood.

In one of the early press conferences, I said I wanted to be the greatest player of all time, and the press made a big deal of it. Although I also said, "But I have a lot more time to go," they didn't bother to report that part.

Naturally, Chris came back with: "Martina's had one great year and I've had seven." Actually, I had been rated Number 1 in four different years, but I could see her point. By 1982, though, I felt my record for the past year was better than anything she had ever done.

While we each made our points at the press conference, in person it was the same as always: "Hi, how are you?"

Nancy was not as calm. She was working on a master psyche job, right from the schoolyard, and she wouldn't even acknowledge Chris's presence in the locker room. Chris would say "Hi" to her and Nancy would say: "Are you talking to me?"

I always felt that Nancy really respected Chris as a competitor, but she believed you had to hate your opponent, an attitude I couldn't understand.

I got through the first four rounds all right, just trying to survive and not let people guess about the toxoplasmosis. Meanwhile, Chris was drawing all the attention for being visibly sick. One day there was a big drama about whether she would be able to emerge from her hotel room to play

Kate Latham, but I never had any doubt that Chris would give it a try.

She was pale and drawn-looking as she walked through the locker room, but she went out and won. She even appeared at the post-match press conference, where she explained that she had eaten dinner in an Italian restaurant and that the cheesecake hadn't tasted good but she'd eaten it anyway, and now she had food poisoning.

Everybody wrote supportive articles about Chris suffering from stomach cramps, beating Kate and Zina Garrison before she felt better again. Everybody—players, press, and public—had accepted Chris's problem before she won or lost.

Chris has always been able to live up to her image of America's Sweetheart, knowing exactly what to say—and when to say it. She even manages to smile at the male reporters and not annoy the female reporters in the process. If one of the guys in the press asks, "Chris, what did you do last night to prepare for the match?" she'll arch her eyebrows, wink, and say, "I'm not saying." And everybody laughs. If I tried that—well, I wouldn't try it.

Anyway, for a few days there was the drama of Chris and the cheesecake, and I was thinking to myself: What do I do about the toxoplasmosis? I don't like talking about injuries. I've had sore shoulders and never even let on. We all play with pain, every one of us, and it gets boring to hear about injuries. I didn't want to say anything beforehand because people would say I had an excuse prepared, a crutch. I thought I had a chance to win, to blow right through the tournament with nobody being the wiser.

The only people who knew the whole story were Dr. Wadler and Nancy. The doctor had warned me not to play doubles if I insisted on playing singles, but I didn't think I'd use up that much energy in doubles and I just didn't want to change my routine or let Pam down by dropping out.

I never mentioned a word about my illness to Pam. Playing doubles with somebody sets up a strange relationship, in which you are friend, teammate, and competitor. Pam had been my doubles partner after Billie Jean, and she had also been in the top five in women's tennis since reaching the finals at the 1978 U.S. Open at the age of sixteen.

Pam's an ideal doubles partner for me, and not just because she's tall and covers so much of the court. She's a great competitor, thoughtful, insightful, warm, and funny —very funny. During the match, we talk constantly, from the moment we get out on the court. One time we were watching our opponents walk onto the court, one of them known for her elaborate hairdos, the other one for her girth.

"Here come Beauty and the Beast," Pam whispered.

We've got nicknames for a lot of our opponents that only Pam and I know about. Something hits us and we'll say it, before, after, or during a shot:

"I wonder what I'll wear to the party on Sunday." (Whap)

"I like that outfit you had on the other day." (Smash)

This is not to say we don't talk tennis. If somebody makes a good shot against us, one of us might make a strategic comment like: "Lucky bitch." Or "Next time I'm gonna hit it down her throat." Or, if you insist on tactics, "I'm going to lob this time," or "I'm going to cross."

We're always apologizing to each other for the previous bad play.

"I'm sorry I screwed up."

"No, no, no, it was my fault."

A lot of the top players have stopped playing doubles, but Pam and I agree with John McEnroe that doubles keeps you sharp and provides an element of fun and teamwork that isn't there in singles. It's a nice feeling, knowing that on the days when it's my turn to play lousy I'll have a teammate slapping her hand on the racquet, saying, "Come on, snap out of it, let's go."

Sometimes one of us is down after losing a singles match, or sometimes it's hard to get back up there after winning a big singles match because your mind's not quite there. Pam is really great at prodding me after I lose. And after a few years together, we're psychically very close. We often know how the other one is feeling without a word being said.

This was one time when I couldn't share something with Pam, when I had to pretend to feel strong and confident. There was a good reason—and it had nothing to do with doubles: she and I were bracketed in the same quarterfinal round, which meant it was almost inevitable that we would wind up playing each other.

That match took place on a warm, sunny day on center court. I had practiced with Virginia Wade earlier in the day, taking a fairly easy workout. I remember somebody asking, "Do you always practice so hard?" and I thought to myself, Oh, if you only knew. I felt pretty good walking over to the stadium, but I could remember Dr. Wadler telling me that tiredness could be a factor in a long match. I pretty much knew I needed to win in two sets.

I was all right in the first set, winning it 6–1, but I could feel my legs go soft in the second set. Technically, we weren't doing anything different. I just couldn't get to the ball and hit it as well or as hard as I had in the first set. She'd make the same forehand shot to my backhand, I'd take one step and dig in my feet, then hit the ball into the net.

After a while I felt exhausted just getting out of the chair. It was as if somebody had turned the hourglass upside down. You could just feel the sand trickling away. I staggered to a 5–4 lead and was serving for the second set at 30–15 when I mis-hit a forehand volley. I wound up on the losing end of a tiebreaker. The third set was ridiculous. I kept thinking, If they only knew. I felt helpless, and mad as hell.

The longer I stayed out there, the worse it got. Every shot, I'd ask myself, Why can't I hit it harder? My approach shots were floating so much that Pam actually stepped in and volleyed them for winners. A couple of times, just chasing balls took so much out of me that I didn't have enough strength to do anything when I got to them. Then it got as bad as it had been in Australia, where I couldn't bend down low without getting weak. It was so frustrating.

Pam could see I wasn't getting to the net very well and she was hitting short, but that's an instinctive reaction. I'm sure she didn't think, Something's wrong with Martina, I'll hit short. After you've been playing as long as we have, you don't really have to reason it out, you just notice it, and you respond.

I was feeling sorry for myself because I couldn't believe, after all the work I had done to get ready for this tournament, that here I was sick. There was nothing I could do about it, nothing the doctors could give me. Out on center court, it was all falling apart.

I never considered walking off after two sets, or midway through the third. That would have been worse, an insult to Pam, a disgrace for me. The only way I'd ever default would be if I sprained my ankle or something. You always think maybe you'll come back, something will happen, but my legs told me nothing good was going to happen that day.

Toward the end, I thought about what was going to happen when it was over. I knew it would be a big deal—"Martina Chokes Again"—and I wasn't eager for the questions. I put it out of my mind as Pam closed me out, 6–2.

The match was over, Pam rushed to the net and put her long arm around my shoulders. I was crying and it felt good to feel her concern. She still didn't know anything was wrong with me, and I didn't think it was the right time to tell her.

I sat down and started sobbing to myself, put a towel over my head to block out the photographers who were crowding around, the television people poking cameras at me. When I stood up on my weak legs, I felt as if I were inside a tornado, just being buffeted back and forth.

I brushed past the TV cameras, putting a towel over my head for a moment. The crowd applauded and I waved, but this was nothing like 1981, when there had been some consolation in defeat. This was just sick—sick and sickening, to think I had to wait another year.

Underneath the stands, a few photographers jostled me as I tried to find some privacy. (Later, one of them would claim I destroyed his film, which was ridiculous, but he later tied me up in a lawsuit that went on and on.) I wanted to escape this scene, but I had only ducked one press conference in my whole tennis career—the time I'd lost to Janet Newberry in 1976, and I wasn't about to do it again. On the men's tour, a lot of the top players routinely duck an interview after they lose. It gets to be a joke watching Vitas Gerulaitis or Jimmy Connors speed off into the night, laughing about paying the $500 fine to the men's tour for the privilege of not being interviewed. I really don't believe in doing that, but I was tempted after losing to Pam.

The interview room at the Open is right under the stands. Tour officials told me I'd have to wait a few minutes until Rodney Harmon was finished with his interview. Rodney is a pretty eloquent guy and he was happy about reaching the quarterfinals, so he went on for a few minutes more while I slumped down in the officials' dressing room, just sobbing.

"Losing never is easy for me. Never!" I kept saying.

Nancy was holding my racquet covers. She said, "It's okay, Martina. It's okay."

I felt the walls were closing in on me. Mary Carillo, a

former player who works in television now, and a few reporters were also in the crowded locker room. I'd peek out from behind the towel and see some of the officials toweling off and staring at me. Every few minutes the door would open and I could hear Rodney talking. I was happy for him, but I kept thinking, Get it over with, let me out of here.

All I could think about was serving for the match and mishitting those forehand volleys.

"It just never got better," I said. "It never got better after that."

Nancy and Mary put their hands on my shoulders, as if trying to put some of their strength into me.

"Tell them you're sick," Nancy said.

"I can't do that," I said.

"If you don't tell them, I will," Nancy said.

"Nancy, I can't make excuses."

"You didn't choke. You're sick. People have to know that."

The choking thing was important to me. I just didn't want to hear people say I choked. I knew how mentally prepared I had been. So when they finally signaled it was time for my interview, I made up my mind to tell the whole story. I could see over a hundred journalists packed into the small room, and dozens of microphones taped to a podium up front.

"What do you think about losing five hundred thousand dollars from the Playtex Challenge?" somebody asked.

"Believe me, money is the last thing on my mind. I can buy a lot of bras without the Playtex money."

That drew some laughs, and I began to feel better.

Somebody asked if I was disappointed, and I said: "It is the most disappointing thing. Pam said she was sorry she beat me. She was ready to cry. I was ready to cry. She played better and she beat me by attacking me."

Somebody else asked me how I felt about not winning the

Open and I said: "I still have to win this tournament. It will still hang over my head. People will still say to me, 'How come you haven't won the U.S. Open?'"

Then somebody asked how I felt physically. I remembered Nancy's advice to me and I took a deep breath and said: "Well, here it comes. This may sound like sour grapes, but it is not. My problem is that once the match got tougher, I was running out of strength."

And I told them about the toxoplasmosis, and how they thought I had caught it: "It was either from a cat or undercooked meat." They seemed to focus more on the cat angle than on the medium–rare hamburger that might have been the culprit. Sure enough, the next day some of them would be calling my illness a "cat virus," although it is technically not a virus at all.

I could see from their faces that some of them thought I was making excuses and some of them believed me. I explained how I'd known I would have to win it in two sets and how my legs had turned to jelly in the second set. I told them I wasn't trying to cheapen Pam's victory, but I just thought I should tell the truth.

After the press conference, a few reporters bothered to check with Dr. Wadler, who explained the medical aspects of the disease and added: "She's going to feel weak for another month. I've got the hard copies to prove it," waving the medical reports from the lab.

The response in the press the next day was mixed. There was some sympathy for me, and some jokes. Sample:

"What is toxoplasmosis?"

"You get it from a cat and you play like a dog."

From what I read in the papers, Pam wasn't too happy to learn about my illness at her post-match interview. I can understand why she was upset, finding out in public like that, but my illness didn't take a lot off her victory; she still had to hit the shots and keep her composure. All I know is that Pam was gracious to me after the match, when I really needed an arm around me, and she was concerned about my playing doubles. Our friendship never missed a beat.

That night I went back to Nancy's house. I was pretty depressed and really didn't want to do anything the next day, either. Dr. Wadler didn't think I should play doubles, because I might have a cumulative letdown from all the exertion. I figured that if I didn't default, people would say, "How sick is she, anyway?" but I also figured that doubles matches are much easier than singles matches and, besides, I had an obligation to Pam to not cancel unless I had to.

I had a day off to think about it. People were calling Nancy's house, leaving messages, saying they loved me and supported me. I didn't want to talk to anybody. Nancy was full of energy, though, so we went out to a playground near her house and played a little one-on-one. Going one-on-one against Nancy is just what the doctor didn't order for somebody with weakened muscles. I got beat, I got more tired, and I jammed my left pinky just trying to dribble the ball.

Jammed pinky, "cat virus," and all, I decided it wouldn't be fair to Pam to default from the doubles, so I went back and played the next day, played terribly, and we lost. I had a hard time even seeing the ball, I was so light-headed.

After that, I figured I'd better take the illness more seriously. I asked Dr. Wadler what I should do about my next scheduled tournament in Philadelphia a few weeks later: the first leg in the next Playtex series.

"You can't win by going there," Dr. Wadler said. "If you win the tournament, people will think it was sour grapes at the U.S. Open, even if we know it wasn't. And whether you win or lose, you'll still be taking the chance of getting hurt. Aside from the money, I can't think of any reason for you to play there."

I took his advice and skipped Philadelphia. I won the

next three Playtex tournaments after that, winning $500,-
000 but not the million dollars for the sweep. Add it up: the
toxoplasmosis cost me $500,000 in 1982 and $500,000 in
1983—a cool million—but Dr. Wadler convinced me it was
the wisest money I ever spent on a vacation.

My decision made, I headed down to Virginia Beach,
turned on my answering machine, and did little but sleep
and eat for days. I emerged only to buy a house. The only
good thing about the 1982 Open was that while I was in New
York a real-estate agent from Virginia Beach came up to
Nancy and said: "I hear Martina is looking for a house. I
have one that's just right, and here are the pictures." The
house was gorgeous and modern, right on the water, and I
loved its name: Shibui, Japanese for "serenity." I ended up
buying it and enjoying it for almost two years.

The toxoplasmosis did not go away easily. I visited Dr.
Wadler once a month for the rest of the year, and even went
for some tests at North Shore University Hospital on Long
Island because my glands didn't return to normal right
away. He was getting a little worried and there was some
more talk about a biopsy, but then everything settled down
and the scare was over.

Where did I get the disease? Rita Mae's cat was tested
and found not guilty, so you can blame it on the hamburger.
And people wonder why I don't eat red meat anymore.

The Long Wait

I had to wait another year for the U.S. Open, but I vowed I'd put the time to good use. If people thought the 1982 model Martina was in good shape, they would see a better one in 1983. There are so many ways an athlete can improve herself, particularly in tennis, where coaching and conditioning and diet are still almost fads.

That's one of the reasons I resent people making jokes about me being some kind of bionic athlete, as if I were bigger or stronger than the rest of the women on the tour. It's just not true. Look at me in a crowd and I don't tower over everybody. Sure, my forearms are bigger than the other woman players', but I didn't get them in a five-and-dime store—or a drugstore, either. I got them partially from my genes and partially in the gym. If anybody wants my forearms, I can direct her to the nearest exercise machines. It's like the advertisement says: I got my muscles "the old-fashioned way." I earned them.

I also realized my tennis game could still stand a lot of improvement. Despite the fallout that Renee Richards and I had after Wimbledon, I knew she had helped my game, so when she called me during the Open, we decided to go back to work again. She would continue to keep her ophthalmology practice on Park Avenue in New York, but she would attend a certain number of my workouts and tournaments over the year.

After doing without a coach for so long, I realized the value of a good one. During a match, the main reason we need a coach is for support—to know that somebody cares. You're really alone out there on the court, and nobody wants to feel totally alone. I certainly don't. Of all the women on the tour, I think Wendy Turnbull is the only one who doesn't have a coach.

When Pam Shriver beat Hana Mandlikova in the quarterfinals of the Virginia Slims tournament in New York in 1984, the first thing she did was wave at Don Candy, her coach, who was sitting a few rows up in the stands.

"I put Don through a lot, and he's always there, and when I win, I want him to feel part of it," Pam explained to Mary Carillo during her post-match TV interview.

A coach can do so much for you: arrange practice time, come up with courts in a strange town, hit with you, take you to dinner, bolster your morale. If something goes wrong, you don't have to worry—the coach will take care of it. But let's face it, the main reason players hire coaches is to learn from them.

If I had been working with Mike Estep or Renee in 1981, I never would have lost the U.S. Open. Either coach would have spotted my elbows-out tendency before I ever faced Tracy in the finals. A good coach can spot things like that right away. But no coach can help you that much during a match, except to provide moral support, eye contact. And Renee would be making notes during a match, so there wasn't really all that much eye contact. The most she would do was signal me to calm down.

The time to talk strategy is before a match, not during it. Getting back together with Renee in the fall of 1982, I realized all over again how meticulous she is. It would take her half an hour to prepare me for a match and half an hour to go over the last match. Sometimes it would seem like overload to me. Nancy and I would be watching a ball game on television and Renee would be telling me how to play somebody I'd played half a dozen times before. In the old days, I never thought about the game until I was actually on the court. I always felt I was going to win, so I played by instinct.

Sure, there's room for a little subtle advice: work on her backhand, come in more. There could be signals for that, but generally we've gone over all that before the match. If we aren't prepared by the time we're on the court, we never will be. I needed Renee mainly to put me through practice and prepare me mentally for a match, and by the fall of 1982, she had raised my game a few more notches.

Practices were always a double-barreled adventure with Renee serving as my tennis coach and Nancy as my "motivational advisor." Renee liked the idea of my practicing with male players, and so did I, because they would push me further than any female player could. Renee would have me trying to return the serves of somebody like Ricky Meyer, a fringe tour player, and they would be a lot harder than anything Chris or Hana could serve up. Renee would be nodding on the sideline, telling me how to jump into that first serve. Meanwhile, Nancy would be standing there shouting, "Martina, that stinks. That really stinks. If you can't do better than that, why don't you just quit?"

Sometimes I'd mutter, "Why don't you just shut up?" Sometimes I'd cry. Sometimes I'd heave my racquet and walk off the court. Sometimes I'd just play twice as hard. And Renee would look down at her notes and shake her head.

It got to the point where Nancy became a negative influence during practices, putting too much pressure on me and getting in Renee's way. I knew it, I resented it, and yet

Nancy was my closest friend at the time. We had so much in common in some ways and we always had a great time together when I wasn't on the court. I knew Renee didn't want Nancy around at practice, but I wasn't about to ask Nancy not to come around. I just hoped Renee wouldn't ask me to make that decision.

I could also see that Renee wasn't comfortable sharing my time or attention with other people who could help with other parts of my game. By this time I was also consulting Robert Haas, a dietician I had met after Dr. Wadler got me through the toxoplasmosis scare at the 1982 Open. I've read that Robert cured me of toxoplasmosis; that isn't true. I had medical attention first, then consulted Robert about my diet.

Nancy, and Sandra Haynie before that, had taught me to eat sensibly—long before I met Robert. I had first heard his name from Sabina Simmonds, one of the women on the tour, who had lost some weight and got into better shape on Robert's low-fat, high-carbohydrate diet. Nancy and I met him after the 1982 U.S. Open, and started following his diet: no fats, no oils, no butter, no red meats, no sugar, and plenty of vegetables and carbohydrates. Instead of the heavy Czech dishes I loved, Robert had me eating pasta, grains, bread, skimmed milk, certain cheeses, and vitamins. A lot of people eat that way normally, but I guess I needed a dietician to tell me what was good for my body.

It was hard to get rid of butter. I know it slows me down and I know it builds up the wrong chemicals in my system, but I do love it on pasta. I used to slip a spoonful—one rotten spoonful—into a potful of pasta, and if Nancy caught me, we'd fight about it through dinner. She could taste a gram of butter in a pound of pasta and make me feel guilty about it for a week.

But I could feel the difference the new diet made in my body. I felt so much lighter, so much stronger, without those oils and fats in my system. I stopped being so moody, particularly during the days just before my period when I'd always gotten really low in energy and morale. In fact, my increased workouts and rigid diet reduced my periods considerably.

Robert has been quoted as saying that his diet "became a religion, a way of life" for me, and people picked up on that as if I were totally dependent on his advice. I don't know if I'd go that far, but my blood chemistry was changed because of the diet, and for a while he did measure my blood and carry certain vitamin supplements in a suitcase to my tournaments.

Some people have asked me what goes into my energy bars, the cakelike mixture I eat on the court sometimes. Robert has never told me, except to assure me that it contains no shortening, chocolate, sugar, or cholesterol. It keeps me going on the court or in the locker rooms, where sometimes you can only find mass-produced junk food. As for the contents of the bars and the vitamins he gives me, I can only say: I trust him, unless proven otherwise.

The commonsense diet that Robert taught me was incorporated into his book, *Eat to Win*. The book has already sold well over a quarter of a million copies. Nancy and Robert and I discussed it on the *Phil Donahue Show* one morning, and the publisher said that within a few hours you couldn't find the book in a bookstore anywhere in America.

Recently, Robert has been criticized for calling himself "Dr. Haas." As I understand it, he has a doctorate from an unaccredited institution. And medical experts have objected to the mention of ginseng in his book, since ginseng can be toxic in large quantities. But none of the experts deny the common sense in telling people to eat a lot of carbohydrates and drink a lot of water. I'm not worried about doing harm to myself from the diet. Besides, I cheat a little on it, anyway, so I'm not overdoing anything.

Robert annoyed some tennis people when he said, "Martina will be the first bionic tennis player," which made me sound like something slightly different from the rest of humanity. He used to sit at courtside with one of the latest models from ComputerLand and keep track of every move my opponents and I made.

The only opponent I really needed to know about was Chris, since she was usually the one to beat in the finals. She had been quoted as saying computerized knowledge takes some of the fun out of tennis, and maybe it does, but we did pick up on a few tendencies of hers through the computer.

Renee told me: "You have to keep Chris guessing whether you're going to hit it short or long. If Chris knows, she'll camp on the baseline and hit those magnificent passing shots." In practice, Renee had me alternating spins and drop shots, even hitting a few lobs designed to keep Chris off balance. In the past I had stubbornly tried to play a baseline game with Chris, to beat her at her own game, but Renee persuaded me to poach on her crosscourt passing shots and try to out-run her.

I think I learned a few things from the computer, but basically nothing more than what Renee and later Mike Estep knew instinctively from their years on the tour. Eventually we abandoned the computer, but some people still think I'm programmed, like a robot.

I began spending even more time on the exercise machines, weight-lifting, running, and other drills. I started to work with Lynn Conkwright, a former champion bodybuilder from Virginia, who set up my daily weight program: one day on the triceps, biceps, and legs; the next day on the chest, shoulders and back. Lynn also showed me how to implement my tennis strokes into workouts on cable machines and dumbbells. I installed the weight machines in a special reinforced room in my house in Virginia Beach, and would work out four or five times a week when I was home.

I also was getting help from Rick Elstein, of the Syosset Health Club on Long Island, who puts athletes through reflex drills to improve their hand-to-eye coordination and their footwork, a system called "tennis kinetics." He had worked with the late Dr. John Marshall, a famous sports physician, to develop a movement dynamics system, based on better footwork and positioning. He gave me drills for balance, drills for reaction time, drills to develop parts of the body that he said were used by tennis players and hockey goalies in particular.

I sometimes got the feeling that Renee didn't think these new programs were necessary, but I learned a lot from Rick. Robert Haas used to claim that with all the work I was doing on myself, I could be winning Wimbledon at the age of forty. People scoffed, but that's really not unreasonable when you look at Billie Jean King, who reached the 1982 and 1983 semifinals at Wimbledon at age thirty-nine and forty. Barring an injury or lack of motivation, I can see myself doing it.

After tuning up my body and my mind in the fall of 1982, I lost to Chris in the Australian Open, which was a jolt, but Renee had me ready for Chris at the Toyota championships in late December.

As somebody who loves to eat, I began to experience the joys of my new diet: I could load up on all kinds of goodies, provided they were the right kind. The day of the finals against Chris, my breakfast consisted of a croissant, some oatmeal, and a waffle. For lunch I had pasta, bread, a honeydew melon, apple and orange juice. I was thinking of going for some more pasta, but I held back.

That night I felt as if I could stay on the court with Chris forever. I was disappointed that the tennis writers were still debating who was Number 1, that I had to prove myself one more time. Even with my loss at the Open, I felt I had earned the top ranking for 1982. Here was my chance to prove it.

I didn't execute well in the first set, trying some things that weren't in Renee's game plan, but I went back to the plan in the second set and wound up beating Chris, 4–6, 6–1, 6–2. Chris was the good sport she has always been, saying afterward: "She's Number One now. I concede." She meant for that year, not forever.

Between Renee's coaching and Nancy's motivating, I was beginning to feel I could win anything. But Renee and I did not have long to work together. She had built up her practice to the point where she was working a full week in the operating room and her office, and was fitting me in between her appointments.

Our relationship really came apart at the 1983 French Open. I had lost only seven games in my first three matches. Renee got off the plane at ten o'clock the morning of my fourth-round match against Kathy Horvath, and came out to the courts.

Without having seen how I was playing, she advised me to stay back and wait for Horvath to make the mistakes and then later in the match for me to become aggressive. She said I should just keep the ball in play, but what was the point of that? I was at the peak of my career, so far I was having a good tournament, and I'd just had a great practice against Andrea Leand. I was hitting my backhand better than my forehand, I was in great shape, and the worst that could happen was that I'd come in and miss a few volleys. And if I had established a good rhythm already, why slow it down?

I lost the first set, 6–4, but came back to take the second, 6–0. In the third set, I could see Nancy was no longer sitting with Renee, but had moved closer to the portal and was shouting: "Come on, Martina, stay up," or shrugging her shoulders to tell me to turn my shoulders more on my backhand—the usual encouragement. I kept wondering why Nancy had moved, and never did get into the flow I had felt in my first three matches. I lost the third set, 6–3, and was out of the tournament, my chances for a Grand Slam postponed for another year.

After the match, I felt there was no way I should have lost and I wanted to know what was going on between Nancy and Renee. Right away, Renee accused Nancy of giving me signals and of trying to undermine her as coach. She said she had been giving me good advice until the third set, and she blamed Nancy for moving up front during the third set to give me signals. Nancy said she had left the seat next to Renee to go to the bathroom; and when she came back, she didn't want to walk in front of people so she took the nearest seat to the portal.

I didn't know who to believe, but I did know I'd been doing fine until Renee arrived and told me to hang back against Kathy. It was the first time I had ever doubted her judgment, but I think I could have gotten over that, if Renee hadn't gone right back to New York, leaving behind a note for me.

She said she couldn't handle the Team Navratilova concept anymore, that it had to be only her. She wanted to undo everything everyone else was teaching me. She didn't think Rick Elstein's reflex training or Robert Haas's computer studies were helping my tennis strategy, and she felt she was being undermined.

She said: "I know the pressure you're under, and I know the timing of this is not very good, but I feel for me to coach you, this is the way it has to be." It was only a few weeks before Wimbledon, and Renee was giving me an ultimatum. In Czech we have a saying: "like going from mud into a puddle." Either way, I'd lose, but I didn't think I had any choice but to break off the working arrangement with her. But I said it then and I'll say it now: Renee was a good friend of mine while she played on the tour, and her coaching made a big difference in my game.

I lost on Saturday, and on Sunday morning I boarded the Concorde and got to the States in time to hit the beach that afternoon. I knew I had to be back in Paris Tuesday night for the International Tennis Federation's annual party, but I just didn't want to be in the same town, the same country, or the same continent after losing a match. So I played on the beach at New Jersey, caught a Monday night flight back to Paris, went to the party, and was back in the States Wednesday afternoon. And by that time I had a new coach who would take me the last step on my journey to the top.

My New Coach

The best thing that happened to me at the French Open was seeing Mike Estep at the I.T.F. party. When we were teammates with the Boston Lobsters in World Team Tennis, Mike was one of those solid guys you appreciate the more you're around him—not a star on the tour, but a smart player. Later he met his future wife, Barbara Hunter, one of the first women to work in television sports, while she was covering a World Team Tennis tour in Russia, and they form one of the brightest couples around tennis, people with a life outside the sport.

Mike was nearly thirty-four when I ran into him in Paris

in 1983. He had missed two seasons on the tour because of tennis elbow, and then had needed sixteen throat operations to remove some little growths, called papilloma, from his vocal cords. He had fought back in 1982 to earn the ninety-fifth spot in the computerized ratings, but he knew he couldn't keep going indefinitely. He has good credentials: he's a former all-American at Rice University, an officer in the Association of Tennis Professionals, and he gave lessons during his injured period.

When we ran into each other at the party, we began talking about how both of us felt we were at a crossroad. Mike told me that he thought I could be the greatest female player ever, but that I wasn't playing up to my potential. Now that I was in better physical and emotional shape, Mike said, my strategic game could be improved.

More or less on the spur of the moment, I asked Mike to help me at Wimbledon, and we'd see about the future. He agreed. He and Barbara said it was a funny coincidence, that they both had felt he could help me but would never have said anything as long as Renee was my coach.

The first time we got on the court, Mike told me he was going to work me for thirty minutes. Mike's not a very big guy, only five-eight, 150 pounds, but he's one of the fastest players on the tour and was coming off his best season in years—a top male athlete who could run down anything I could hit. This was a direct contrast to Renee, who is a great teacher but was never able to really compete with me on the court as my coach.

The first time we worked out together, I got through three minutes and couldn't locate my lungs anymore. I staggered to the net and gasped: "Time out. How long is this going to last?"

Mike just grinned at me from below his baseball cap and started slugging tennis balls at me, letting me know he could kill me slowly or quickly.

I could feel my game picking up each time we played after that. I zipped through Eastbourne, losing seventeen games in six matches, and was in great shape for Wimbledon.

There were more than the usual distractions at Wimbledon. Some members of the press noticed that Nancy was in New York at the start of the tournament and began writing that we were no longer together. They were more right than they knew. She had actually stayed in the States to conduct some business, but when she did come over to England, we began fighting more than ever.

Part of the dispute was about her influence on my business. I had gladly put Nancy on salary, for her value in conditioning and some aspects of my tennis work, but now she was trying to expand her influence. She was often at odds with the International Management Group, who had been acting as my agent for years. Sometimes she may have been right about details, but she kept trying to put a wedge between me and my management, and I wasn't ready to go that far.

Right in the middle of Wimbledon, we started arguing about how much influence she had over me. It was an open secret at Wimbledon after a while, with people talking about our quarrels. I had more than one tearful scene with friends, where I would sob and say, "I've got to do something," but I'd always been afraid of change, and didn't know how to do it.

I tried not to let our quarrels distract me from my tennis. After just a few weeks with Mike, my serve and backhand return were incredible. I had never broken serve the way I did at Wimbledon, and tennis people would look at my game and say, "Is she really getting better?" With Mike Estep around, I was.

Chris was looking for another shot at me, but she lost to Kathy Jordan while she was sick with the flu. Tracy was out with a shoulder injury and that opened up the whole tournament. Billie Jean roared through to the semifinals until Andrea Jaeger reminded her she was forty, and I beat Yvonne Vermaak from South Africa in my semifinal.

The night before the final with Andrea, Nancy and I had one of our worst fights. She knew I was getting worried about the relationship, and she began telling me I would fall apart without her around. She accused me of not caring, of having a bad attitude. Then she put her hands on me, and I pushed back, and it went on from there. We were up until two in the morning, raging at each other, and by the time I went out to play the final I felt physically and emotionally drained.

Yet somehow it never showed in public. My match with Andrea was a breeze compared to my fight with Nancy a few hours earlier. I had more peace on Centre Court in front of a full house and a worldwide television audience than I did in the privacy of my rented house. Now I understood why performers feel more at home on the stage than in the dressing room. This was what I did best. I could walk onto Centre Court, perform a competent curtsey to the royals, and play a Wimbledon final. It was the arguments at home that were hard.

The worst part of the match with Andrea was feeling my skirt unraveling as I rushed to the net for a forehand volley. I knew that shot would be the last of the point, because I was not about to chase a ball with my skirt around my ankles. I was long with the forehand, and I clutched my skirt string for dear life. As I tied it back again, I remembered that when the tournament began, Trey Waltke had come out looking like the Great Gatsby in long white pants and shirt, and I had promised—threatened?—to come out in a bikini.

Well, I thought, you almost did it.

You've heard the cliché about taking time to smell the

roses? I took the time to watch a small airplane circling overhead, with a trailing banner that said "Use the Postal Code." Right in the middle of the match, I was wondering why anybody would pay tax money to hire a plane to fly over Wimbledon with that message, and then I started thinking about all the letters I owed people, and trying to remember people's zip codes.

While my mind was wandering, Andrea won a few games in the second set, but I finally ended the match in fifty-five minutes, winning my fourth Wimbledon, 6–0, 6–3. I noticed that Roland Jaeger didn't accuse Mike Estep of coaching from the stands.

Somebody asked: "Do you think you're just too good for the women?"

"I hope so. I want to try to make it as boring as I can."

I'll never win too many Wimbledons. It will always be the biggest tournament to me. I love every minute of the ceremony, the purple and green outfits on the ball boys and ball girls, the lush grass, the spectators' formal suits and dresses. To me, Wimbledon is tennis, the center, the hub.

But in 1983 there was a bigger goal, the last barricade. Until I won the U.S. Open, and did away with the whispers that I let Flushing Meadow get on my nerves, I could not claim to be one of the greatest female players in history. Champions should win everything.

We returned home, and things with Nancy were better for a while after a few weeks off. I began working with Mike again at my house in Virginia Beach; he slept on the couch in the den while my mother and sister were visiting. They loved being at Virginia Beach because they could get right down to their tiny European bathing suits and soak up the sun at the beach. My mother and Jana would also go shopping, and when they came back they would bustle around in the kitchen, making enough soup and chicken to feed an army, which is about what we had in the house.

Nancy was busy with her basketball projects, so there were always some very tall people wandering through the house. We were also having some renovation work done, so there were often builders and cleaning people around. With all this going on, I didn't have much time to spend alone with my mother and my sister. After they had returned to Czechoslovakia, I realized I hadn't sat down and asked Jana how she liked school or hit any tennis balls with her. It was just too frantic. My little sister was a lovely young woman now, and I had so many business deals going on that I didn't have time to talk with her.

In all the confusion, Mike would work out with me on the court behind the house. It was the perfect place—my own court, my own house, at the edge of the water, no strangers going by, nobody listening to Mike and Nancy telling me what to do or watching me get blasted around the court by this tough little Texan.

It was a joke. Some people were making me out to be some oversized monster looming over the women's tour, but Mike, ranked eighty-sixth by the computer in his best year, was able to pound back anything I hit. I'd smash a ball into the corner and Mike would chase it down and send it back to me. At first I had a hard time accepting that, and if I over-hit, I'd get mad at myself and throw the racquet. At which point Nancy would say cuttingly, "Nice, Martina, really nice," and my mother would start fretting and tell me in Czech, "Don't get mad." Mike would grin from under his baseball cap and say, "Hey, if I'm only beating you 6–4, imagine what I'd do to the women on the tour?"

He wasn't being obnoxious about it. Mike had come along in the sixties, he wasn't an old-fashioned male supremacist, partially because of his wife's career in broadcasting, but he was realistic about the difference between men and women.

Mike was supportive of the whole women's tour, glad to

see us making money, respectful of the players. But he didn't mince words about it: he thought I should be the best player on the tour, that I should almost never lose a match.

"I don't like to say 'men's tennis' and 'women's tennis,' " Mike would explain. "Why not just say 'tennis'? If you diagram the plays, it's all X's and O's, not male or female. Look at John McEnroe: you both play serve-and-volley, you're both left-handed. What's the difference between his game and yours?"

I couldn't help remembering how John would sometimes tell me that he liked to watch me play because our styles were somewhat similar. Mike also said: "Don't underestimate the value of being left-handed." He reminded me that my forehand cross-court shots play to the backhand of my right-handed opponents. He also encouraged me to vary my serves: slice serve to the ad court sixty percent of the time, flat serve twenty-five percent, and a kick serve that twists away from the receiver in the deuce court.

Mike also thought I had been conditioned to hang back on the baseline by playing on the women's tour so long. He said: "The baseline player is the counterpuncher, and women are taught to be counterpunchers, to react to things." I think he meant in life as well as in tennis.

We'd work in the hot sun for a couple of hours, then sit around the air-conditioned house and talk tennis. Mike was challenging a lot of the patterns that I had picked up in nearly a decade on the women's tour. For many years people had tried to talk me out of my natural impulse to rush the net, citing the success of more conservative players like Chris.

"The best play is the right shot, not the fancy shot," Mike would say. "Coming to the net is not impulsive. Often it's the right shot. If you came in on the net every point, I wouldn't be disappointed. Always ask yourself: Can I come in on this ball?"

Mike told me that although I'd won a lot of points from the baseline in my Wimbledon victory over Andrea Jaeger, I could have won those points even more easily by coming to the net.

"But what if I rush the net and Chris or Andrea passes me?" I asked.

"You've got to be pretty sure they won't," Mike explained. "But you're always going to leave them some kind of low-percentage shot. If they can pass you into the corner regularly, more power to them. Then you switch to something else for a while."

The nicest part about working with Mike was that even though he thought I could be better, he was willing to work with what I already had, who I already was.

"I'm not changing your grips, nothing structural," he said. "The main thing is strategy. I think it was Pancho Gonzalez who said: 'Rod Laver won't beat us until he learns the percentages.' Well, you can improve your percentages."

There are two theories in tennis: work on your weakness or work on your strength. Mike subscribed to the latter. He felt I had the best volley on the women's tour, but there was still room for improvement. He also told me to cut down on the backswing for my backhand. The shorter the backhand, he said, the less of a timing problem there is, fewer errors.

Mike told other people that I learned more quickly than anybody he had ever seen. One time he told me not to hit a backhand overhead, but rather to move to my right and hit a regular overhand instead. The first time he hit a ball to me, I did exactly what he said. I don't want to sound as if I'm bragging about my learning ability, but once Mike told me something, it just stayed with me. And with that bit of advice, Mike took away one of the staples of the tour, the backhand overhead volley. It would never be missed by me.

Another time he gave me a simple chip-and-lob drill to see how long I could go without making a mistake. On the sixth shot, I tried to hit a drop volley, which Mike said meant I was either impatient or running out of gas. No more drop volleys. The next time he ran the drill it took eighteen shots before I made an error. And the time after that, thirty. Mind over matter, basically.

We'd play a set and I'd say: "Hey, the girls couldn't have gotten that ball."

And Mike would grin and say: "So?"

Mike told some people: "I try to teach her the way I would play against her opponents. Tennis is a lot like chess, but a lot of the women are playing without a couple of pieces. Some of them can't hit an overhead or a topspin forehand. She happens to have all the pieces on the board."

Any time I'd get frustrated, Mike would tell me: "You're not just trying to be Number One. Your goals are beyond that."

One of Mike's strengths as a coach was his attitude toward me. We were old teammates who had spent time together on airplanes and in hotel bars and at parties. He wasn't mystified by me and I wasn't afraid of him. We could talk so openly. One time I was practicing to an Elton John tape, singing the songs as I hit the ball—and getting out of breath. Mike said: "Hey, you'd better concentrate." I didn't get grumpy the way I might have if Renee or Nancy had told me the same thing. I realized I was getting too involved with the lyrics, so I picked up my tempo.

Mike's not as much into technique as he is into mapping out strategy. His court strategy involved action, whereas Renee's game had stressed *re*action. Planning for Chris, Mike would say, "Attack her serve," whereas Renee's advice was always, "Get the ball in play, get the return deep, follow it up."

Mike broke down a lot of the patterns I had picked up on the pro tour. Women's tennis was so safe—to where you were afraid to lose a point. Only come in when you won't lose the point. With Mike it was "Charge, take a little chance." I appreciated that because I had a chance to show my athleticism. Go out and have fun. That's what it's all about.

Mike was one or two steps more aggressive than Renee. That's the men's game, where the pressure is so much greater. If you take two even players, and one is more aggressive than the other, he will win nine times out of ten. If you're a good enough volleyer, the other guy will make mistakes. It's easier to hit a winner from the service line than from the baseline. Sure, the men are bigger and have a bigger reach than I have, but there's no reason I can't play their game—play tennis—to the best of my ability.

Mike understands one part of me: I'm impatient. I'm not one to wait for others to make mistakes. I want things to happen fast. As I once told Jane Leavy, if I'm going to take a photograph of a flower, I'm not going to wait for it to open. I'm probably going to bring the sun over to it.

Mike reinforced my impetuosity by telling me I wasn't really a gambler, just an aggressive athlete. He said: "Gambling is when you play against the odds." He realized I was inclined to try to finish off my points with something artistic, creative, something final, and he thought a sharp rush to the net would be fine, too. I realized that wanting to win the point was the main thing, not the artistry of a hard shot. But even so, there were plenty of opportunities to show what I could do.

Another thing I liked about Mike was that he tried to stay out of the limelight. So many people had made bad jokes about Team Navratilova that I was scarred by it, but Mike wasn't looking for publicity. He wanted me to feel that I was out there for myself, resourceful and confident. And after a summer of playing against Mike, that's just how I felt.

Off My Back

I felt so wonderful throughout the 1983 Open that I almost had to ask myself what was wrong. I felt as if I had willed away all the problems of the past. The weather was hot, but there weren't the swirling winds of earlier Opens. The airplanes had been routed onto another flight pattern for the entire tournament—just a matter of prevailing winds, but I felt it was an omen. There was no blood disorder to make my knees tremble. And it seemed just about everybody at the brawling, sprawling Open was my personal friend, smiling benignly at me and asking what they could do to help.

Maybe they saw something in me. I went around with a smile on my face, enjoying things. During the press conferences, when reporters brought up the past, I just smiled. Everything was in slow motion. Now I could look around and smell the roses.

After I beat Emilse Rapponi in an early round, one of the reporters asked me if I considered the Open to be a jinx. I said: "No, I don't feel jinxed at all. I like the city too much to feel jinxed here."

Somebody else asked me about pressure and I said: "I've never won this tournament before, so I'm really the underdog."

Asked if it was stimulating to have easy matches, I said: "This is the U.S. Open, so everything is stimulating, including the practices. First- and second-round matches are fun here as opposed to other tournaments. I always find myself more nervous before my first match in a big tournament because I want to get it under way. It's a good nervous, though. I'm excited—excited nervous, not 'Oh, my God,' nervous."

We did everything to avoid the tensions of the past. I had rented a house in Little Neck, a few miles east of Flushing Meadow, to insure my privacy. The whole two weeks went by like a dream. Quick matches, friendly faces, peace and quiet at home. We even discouraged friends from dropping in so I could relax between matches.

The only people at the house were me, Nancy, and Pam Derderian. For the entire two weeks, we kept this joke going about the magic number, like in baseball, where you only need a certain number of games to win the pennant. Every day they'd say: "Well, Tini, the magic number is four now," or whatever.

Nancy wanted me to be in a good mood during the Open, so she told me not to watch the evening highlights of the Open. I guess she was worried I'd hear something controversial that would interrupt my peace of mind. She would say: "All right, Tini, the highlights are coming on now. Leave the room." And I would leave the room while she took mental notes on who said what.

The only thing that went wrong during those two weeks was when some kids stole the sponsor's $40,000 Porsche

944 from right in front of the house. It was discovered a few blocks away the next day, with the kids driving it. They weren't too smart, driving a car like that near the house.

I cruised to the finals, beating six opponents without losing a set. Against Sylvia Hanika in the quarters, I played some of the most overwhelming tennis I've ever played, winning the first eleven points on smashes and aces. In the semifinals, Pam and I got to stage a rematch of the previous year's Toxoplasmosis Cup. Early in the match, Pam pulled even with me at 2–all and I could hear people saying, "Here goes Martina again," but I just smiled to myself and said out loud: "Wrong."

Pretty soon I was so far ahead that one loudmouth down near the court started to pick on my partner for not making it closer. I confess, I felt like making the schoolyard salute at him, but I concentrated on beating Pam, 6–2, 6–1. Afterward Pam went into the press conference and with her usual arched eyebrows told the reporters: "If she comes in here and says she has anything, I'll kill her."

When somebody asked Pam if she thought I could get any better, she said: "God, I hope not."

Pam said the match with Chris would be "a big test" for me, adding: "When you're twenty-six years old and have won as many tournaments as Martina has and you've never won here, that's not easy for anybody."

Someone asked Pam if I could be beaten, and she said yes. But she added: "I wouldn't bet my house on somebody else besides Martina."

Later that day, Chris was asked the same question. She replied: "I'd bet my three houses on it," but then she added: "I wouldn't bet my life on it."

Chris also said: "I have confidence I can beat her, I don't know how many other people can. It's up to me and the other players. There's no reason she should get worse. Even if she gets stale or drained, with her physical ability there are only three or four people who can beat her."

This was to be the thirty-ninth time Chris and I would meet in a final, and we were even at 19-all. She was still ahead of me, 30–24, in overall matches since our first meeting in 1973, but I had won nineteen of the most recent twenty-nine, including three Wimbledon finals.

Remembering all the hokum between me and Chris the year before, I tried to avoid comparisons this time. But Arthur Ashe said of me: "She's still not as good as Billie Jean or Margaret Court. Her record is not yet as good as Chrissie's." Going into the final, I had merely won all but one of my last sixty-six matches and 155 of my last 159. I thought I was having the best streak of tennis any woman had ever had. But I know how people don't like to hear women talk assertively about themselves, so I held back my responses.

Saturday, September 10, 1983, was a day I'll remember all my life: good weather, good vibrations. I got to the courts early and was working out with Mike when I spotted my friend Jane Leavy of the Washington *Post*, leaning over the fence. Jane had been writing throughout the tournament that the only fitting script for the Open was for me to meet Chris in the final, since Chris had won the tournament six times. I had kept insisting it didn't matter to me, but when Jane arrived on Saturday morning, I called over: "You got your wish." Then I paused and gave her the punch line: "So did I." I knew it was too late for Jane to turn my comment into a headline that Chris could see.

After the workout I changed and was sitting around with Mike in the lounge outside the locker room. It's pretty quiet the last two days because most of the players have already been eliminated and have moved on, somewhere cheaper than New York. The locker room is pretty generic, with no sense that you are at a Grand Slam event, the only personal effect being your name taped on your locker. But even in these sterile surroundings, I couldn't help thinking about the past champions of the U.S. Open: Maureen Connolly, Margaret Court, Billie Jean, Chris, Tracy. It seemed a little ludicrous that I had gotten to be twenty-six without putting my name on that list, but I was the only one who could do anything about that.

"I've waited two years and I'd better do it now," I said out loud.

I'll admit it, my knees started knocking as I told myself: The time is now. I had worked so hard to get here and I knew time was running out.

"God, I want to win so bad, I'll die if I don't," I said.

And Mike, who had never come close to a U.S. Open or any other major final, had all the poise in the world. In his raspy Texas voice, he said: "Relax, you've already won it in your mind. You just have to prove it to everybody else." That logic carried me through the quiet grounds and into the hot, sunny madness of the stadium, where 20,819 fans were waiting to see if I could finally win this big one.

From the start, everything went just as Mike had told me. I was charging Chris, forcing her to go for winners. Once in a while she would hit a super passing shot into the corner and the crowd would roar, thinking that Chris was finding her game. But I knew there was only a tiny patch on each side available to her, and if she could find it, more power to her.

When I won the first set, 6–1, in twenty-five minutes, with a forehand cross-court volley, I banged my racquet down hard on the surface, twice. One down, one to go.

I broke Chris in the first game of the second set with a hard forehand down the line, and then we both held serve to make it 2–1. I looked in the air and saw an airplane overhead and I remembered the plane at Wimbledon advertising the postal codes. I wondered what message was coming this time, and then I saw the little puffs of smoke coming out, spelling "Good Luck Chrissie—Lipton Tea." I'm no fool. I know Lipton uses Chris for endorsements, so I didn't bother keeping my eyes on the sky to see if they would add, "And Martina."

Chrissie didn't need luck from the sky. She had her lob and some great returns and my own dumb double fault to break me and make it 2–2. Then she won four straight points on her serve to go ahead, 3–2. But I held serve and then broke back with my own love game to take a 4–3 lead.

I understood why the crowd was pulling for Chris—they thought I was the favorite. They always want the favorite to sweat it out, no matter who it is. I started getting pumped up, hearing them root for Chris, and knew I had to hit better shots than what I had been hitting.

The big point came with me serving at 4–3 in the second set, when she pulled back to deuce by hitting a winner at the net. I knew if she broke me and made it 4–all, it would be a close one. But I went to advantage, and on game point I chased down a great get by Chris and managed to come around it on my forehand. Then I hit a winner down the line that handcuffed her. God, she was playing well. She had almost played herself right back into the match, but now I was only one game away.

Never believe it when athletes say they don't know what's happening in the stands. I always know what's going on, and so do most of the others. I could hear the applause from some fans who noticed the digital clock in the corner had inched its way from fifty-nine minutes to one hour. It was the first time in this tournament anybody had extended me that far.

Hearing the fans applaud a one-hour match was a moral victory for Chris, but it was also a compliment for me. People were shouting "We love you, Chris" while she was serving, but at the end some of the fans got excited for me because they knew I hadn't won it before. I heard their support, I felt I deserved it, and it was fun. How could you not hear people screaming "Go, Martina"?

I went ahead, 30-love, by flicking a winner at the net and then chasing down a lob and hitting a shot into the corner —two of the best back-to-back shots in my life. I was feeling so good, so confident. Then Chris served back to deuce, but I went to advantage with a long backhand lob.

On the fourth match point of the day, Chris hit a simple backhand past me, much like a million others she has hit by me in our lifetimes. I was standing near the net and I watched the ball float toward the baseline and I waited for it to come down, and it did—outside the line. I had won the U.S. Open. I had won my national championship.

I jumped into the air, but I quickly remembered the champion on the other side of the net, and how gracious she had always been to me. I had to show her the same respect. I rushed to the net, and Chris Evert Lloyd—my grandmother's favorite player—was there waiting. She put her arm around me and patted my head with her racquet. Then, arm in arm, we walked off the court.

The 6–1, 6–3 victory was my longest match of the tournament: sixty-three minutes. I had lost only nineteen games while winning eighty-four, and had averaged only fifty-two minutes per victory.

After I thanked the umpire, I rushed off to the corner of the stands where the dreaded Team Navratilova was lurking—Mike and Barbara Estep, Nancy, Pam, Lynn Conkwright, and a few other friends.

Some people had wondered how Nancy and I would greet each other after a victory. Would we hug, the way some friends do after a big victory? Nancy had had a dream a few weeks earlier about the two of us celebrating by giving high-fives, like basketball players, and that's just what we did.

I was shaking my fist and jumping up and down, shouting: "Off my back! Off my back!" because I had finally gotten rid of that monkey, that reputation for choking in the Open. I gave high-fives to the whole corner before I headed back to my bench.

Sitting there for a moment, drying off and fixing my hair, I was wondering whether my skirt was on right. After having my skirt almost fall off at Wimbledon, I didn't need it to happen again, not with all the photographers around.

Another crazy thought I had: I saw the champions' box in the corner of the stands and thought to myself: Now I get to sit there anytime I want to.

I knew I'd be interviewed live by CBS, with the sound piped into the stadium. So many thoughts go through your head at a moment like that. At some of the smaller tournaments, I have been known to sing a few bars of "Turn Out the Lights, the Party's Over," when I know I've got it won. Since this was the Big Apple, I got this crazy thought that when the CBS people came over to me I was going to start off by singing the opening line of *New York, New York:* "Start spreading the news, I'm leaving today . . ." But I didn't want to expose the national audience to my singing voice.

When they did come over with the camera, I had tears in my eyes and I thought to myself, All they have to do is play the national anthem and I'll break down for sure. I was so proud to have finally won my country's championship.

I made sure to praise Chris for being a great player, and to thank Mike Estep and Nancy Lieberman for all they had done for me, and, thank God, I remembered to praise Renee Richards, too. It's so hard to say the right thing at a time like that, but supposing I had forgotten her, just because of our disagreement? I wasn't happy about the way our working relationship ended, but she had helped me a lot, and she was still my friend, and later she sent me a telegram that said: WELL DONE. Well done both ways.

After the television interview, I was ushered into the press room, and one of the first people I saw was Frank Deford of *Sports Illustrated*. I had been teasing him for a long time because his magazine had never put me on the cover, and he knew I was pretty touchy about it because I had won Wimbledon four times and felt I had been snubbed. This seemed like the right time to ask him in something more than a whisper: "Do I make the cover now?"

Frank, who's a great writer and a lovely guy, mumbled something about hearing I might have to share it with Ivan Lendl if he won the men's division the next day. I would have bet one of my Porsches on the cover headline: "Czech and Double Czech." But Ivan lost to Connors, so I had it all to myself: "Martina Navratilova: U.S. Open Champion at Last."

When the questions started, one of the reporters noted that my $120,000 prize and $500,000 Playtex bonus gave me $6,089,756 for the year to date, the most ever in one year by any tennis player, male or female.

I said: "I know New York is an expensive city to live in. Maybe this can go toward a down payment somewhere."

Then I told the reporters about my real reward for winning the Open: "Wimbledon was worth three days' bingeing. This is worth a week."

Asked how long I could dominate women's tennis, I said: "Maybe you can compare me to *M*A*S*H.*"

Somebody raised the question about whether it was unfair to win so many tournaments by this big a margin. That raised my temperature a few degrees and I said: "They can do everything I do: all the line drills, the quarter-miles on the track, the full-court basketball games. . . . If they want to, they can do it. I know I'm blessed with talent and genes, but so are a lot of people. I've put in the work. I'm a size eight; the only thing big about me are my feet. How is it unfair?"

The tone of the interview, after I had thought I had gotten the monkey off my back, told me I might never totally get rid of it. If I lost, I was a choker. If I won big, I was unfair to women's tennis. How could I arrange to win by a narrow margin?

We celebrated my "unfair" victory at an Italian restaurant in Little Neck, with about thirty of my friends seated around one long table. They toasted me with champagne and I broke training with some garlic butter and a few other forbidden foods. I hoped Nancy was looking the other way.

When we got back to the house, all the tensions of the tournament seemed far behind. I felt total satisfaction. We had a little more champagne, but only a taste because I had a doubles match the next day, and then we sat back and watched television. This time Nancy let me watch the highlights.

Changes

My life did not stop evolving just because I had won the Open. A few months afterward, I realized that my relationship with Nancy had changed. I began to want more time by myself, even for things as simple as choosing what I watched on television, what I read, and when I practiced.

It was my career and my needs that had brought us together. When I first met Nancy, I was letting my tennis career get away from me. She was a great influence on me because of her attitude and also because we were on the same level athletically. I was not nearly the basketball player she was, but we could get a good workout together; and although she couldn't practice tennis with me, we could go to the gym together.

At first, we both had athletic careers of our own, and that made us equals in our own eyes and in other people's eyes. But after the women's league went down, Nancy needed an outlet, and she tried to take full control of my business— and my life. And, for a while, I let her.

No matter what has come between us, I will always say that Nancy Lieberman was one of the most important people in my life. When someone like Curry Kirkpatrick of *Sports Illustrated* calls her an "aide-de-gofer," he does both of us a disservice.

I've said it before, I'm a born procrastinator, and I let things go too long because I definitely need some shelter while I'm playing tennis. Nancy was worth every penny of salary she was being paid, but she continued fighting with Peter Johnson, my business manager, and discouraging some of my old friends from coming around. I'd start to read nicknames for her, like "Agent Orange," and I realized she was separating me from some of my friends.

Nancy felt I had to hate Chris in order to reach the top, but I knew Chris wasn't taking anything away from me. Nancy also told me not to talk to the players or show them what I was eating or how I was working out. I could never understand that. I felt I could beat them and still go out to dinner with them afterward.

After we decided to go our separate ways, Nancy contacted Chris to see if Chris was interested in helping her out, which Chris wasn't. That bothered me. Here was somebody she said she hated, yet she could just turn it on and off.

In other ways, Nancy tried to keep me to herself, to keep

the blinders on, and to not let me get interested in much else. That's fine, up to a point, but Nancy tended to control every part of my life.

When Nancy read a book, it would be an autobiography of Kareem Abdul-Jabbar or Bill Russell. I once got her to read a Sidney Sheldon book, *Master of the Game,* because there was a character in there I knew she could relate to, Kate Blackwell. That was the only novel I remember Nancy reading. If she read a book, it was always about sports. That was her horizon, and that's fine, but she'd get upset if I read novels or history books. She wanted me to read the same things she was reading.

At first I needed the outright bullying to get myself in shape, but after a while I learned what diet and workout I needed. I realized her methods worked sometimes, but other times they upset me. Sometimes I would say, "Just keep quiet." As I began getting tougher, I didn't need the prodding. For a long time I told myself that she was acting out of friendship and concern, but in the last year I got tired of being physically and emotionally controlled by her, and I began standing up to her.

At first I felt guilty because Nancy had put her public image on the line for me. In some ways I think she suffered guilt by association right after my Rita Mae Brown episode, but she knew what to expect when she invited me down to Texas. She had to know how Madison Avenue and a lot of other powerful groups don't like a certain image, and she probably was hurt a lot more than I was.

I could always go out and win a tournament—prove myself in competition and let people know what I was really like—but Nancy was competing off the basketball court, and the world is tougher away from the arena. She tried hard for some television jobs, but the big ones didn't come through. I'm sure she had to wonder if her association with me was the reason.

At the same time, Nancy was starting to get the itch to play basketball again. She was tired of being better known as Nancy Lieberman, Martina's helper-coach-friend, or whatever, than as an all-American basketball player. She wanted to stay in public life, to get her name in print, to compete as herself. There was talk of a new basketball league, and I was hoping she would get involved in that, put some distance between us.

I had learned to structure my own time better and really didn't need her on the road or while I was preparing for a tournament.

We had always argued, but now it seemed we were fighting over every detail of our life together.

When I was in the middle of a tournament, I needed to relax, not hunt around for a weight room so that Nancy could have her workout to prepare for the Superstars competition. I needed to eat and sleep when I felt like it. I began to realize that having Nancy around all the time had been good for a while, but now it was becoming too hectic. She was wheeling and dealing, and it was her life, but at times I could care less about it. I told her she should get on with her life. I started getting pretty tough about it.

There were times when I would go out on the track or play basketball by myself. I would never have done that on my own in the past. I would have found an excuse to avoid exercising. But now I like what exercise does for me, and I don't need to be pushed anymore. She knew it, and people around us knew it. Starting from Wimbledon in 1983, it was no secret that we were having some pretty nasty fights. Sometimes it seemed as if I cried every day.

One of the final straws came early in 1984 when Nancy wanted me to drop out of some tournaments to prepare for the annual Superstars competition in Florida. I had done pretty well there in the past, but now I was so involved in being the best tennis player possible that I just didn't care about the Superstars anymore. Nancy, with no basketball league, saw the Superstars as one of her few chances to compete. She wanted to practice all seven of the sports she would need in the Superstars, and she wanted me to work with her for a couple of weeks in Palm Springs.

I dropped out of one tournament in Washington, but I couldn't get out of my obligations to play in Oakland. I was going for Chris's record of fifty-six straight victories, and I was up to fifty at the end of 1983. Although I wanted to be at my sharpest for my next tournaments, I went to Oakland not totally prepared. I won my first four matches, but then Hana beat me, 7–6, 3–6, 6–4, to snap the streak at fifty-four.

Afterward, Nancy said: "I told you you shouldn't play." She was so obsessed with the Superstars, and she thought I should give something back to help her. I kept saying, "Who cares about the Superstars? It won't help you get a TV contract." But she blew it out of proportion, and I was upset. I began to realize that I had to take care of myself, to be the final judge on everything. Nancy had been great, but now it was time for me to take control.

The difference in me was quite obvious. In a little tournament in New Jersey, I had a bad match against Pam Casale. But even though I was playing terribly, I knew I would win it—and I did. Some friends of mine noticed that I never once looked over to Nancy or Mike for support during the match. I just got the job done. And that night I played doubles with Pam Shriver and we started kidding around on the court, and I just didn't care that Nancy was scowling at me.

I liked Mike to motion for me to relax or whatever, but it wasn't a need anymore. And I still liked playing in front of Nancy to show her what I could do thanks to the work we'd put in over the past few years, but it had become more of a performance level than a needs level, and she knew it.

305

The week before a tournament in Dallas in the spring of 1984, I was staying at Nancy's townhouse while she was in Virginia. I realized I was so relaxed, that I wanted to be alone, how easy it was to not have to perform. When Nancy was around, there was always a race to the weight room, a race to the track.

Nancy would do too much sometimes: if a doctor tells you not to do something, there's a reason. Nancy had a chronic knee injury because she came back too soon from an injury, and then she had a hairline fracture of the ankle, but again she started working out too soon. She thinks that if somebody says, "Do ten hundred-meter sprints," she should do twenty. She always thinks more is better, whereas I used to do less rather than more. Now I think somewhere in between is fine.

That same week in Dallas, I invited a friend of mine over for supper, and when I served pâté and French bread and beer, he looked at me and said, "What's happening here? This doesn't look like your usual training meal." How right he was.

I told Nancy on the phone how I was feeling. I said we just didn't help each other anymore, that I didn't think she should try to live through me.

Our relationship was like a drug, really, but it started wearing off. I think Nancy knows she tried to control me too much—even though I let her—but that it got counterproductive. She saved my career, helped me right to the top. She had been my best friend, but it was over.

She was hurt, but finally agreed to go her separate way. At first, the split was amicable, but later it became pretty unpleasant because she wanted to get paid for some of the business deals that had been made while we were together, things she had done as my friend, without any promise of compensation other than her salary. In the end, we dissolved the office in Dallas, and for a while we were uncomfortable being around each other, but I went to watch her play basketball for the Dallas Diamonds late in 1984, and lately we've been getting along much better.

Grand Slam

One of the hardest things for me to do was give up my house in Virginia Beach, but I didn't think I'd be going back there much while I was still playing. Mike Estep was getting tired of flying from Dallas–Fort Worth to Virginia, and Texas had really been home to me for years, so I put the waterfront house up for sale.

While I was looking for a house in the Dallas–Fort Worth area, I was living in a motel room, my possessions scattered between my old house in Virginia Beach and Nancy's townhouse in Dallas. I felt like a well-off nomad, but I knew eventually I'd be settled again.

I still had a lot to prove in 1984. I wanted to show I could stay on top of the tennis world without seeming to be controlled by another person. I also wanted to complete the sponsors' version of the Grand Slam—the four straight major championships: the French, Wimbledon, U.S., and Australian—and go after the traditional version of the Grand Slam, which is those four events in the same calendar year. I also was chasing Chris's record of fifty-six straight victories.

The Grand Slam was my primary goal after the breakup with Nancy in April. As usual, there was controversy about me as I prepared for the French Open at the end of May. Instead of being identified with an all-American basketball player, I was now identified with a mother of two children.

I had met Judy Nelson several years earlier at a tournament in Fort Worth. She likes to play tennis, and at the time she was running the ball boys and ball girls for that tournament. We ran into each other again in 1984, after my relationship with Nancy had reached its limits, and while Judy's marriage was nearing an end.

The newspapers would have a blast with the "Beauty Queen" angle, but although Judy—a former Maid of Cotton—is obviously beautiful, she's not your basic beauty queen. She had prepared for a television news career while she was in college, and later she operated several steak restaurants in Texas to help put her husband through medical school. She likes music, literature, and tennis, and is interested in about anything. When we met again in 1984, the last thing I wanted was to be identified with a married woman with children, but Judy said her marriage was already in trouble and that it was not my responsibility.

Although I've been accused of being naïve, I invited her to the French Open on the theory that I'm old enough to have my friends around when I want them. She got along well with my parents. In fact, my father was so taken with Judy that he invited her to visit them in Czechoslovakia.

The French did not make much of Judy joining my family and friends in the stands at Roland Garros, but after I beat Chris, 6–3, 6–1, in the finals for my fourth straight Grand Slam victory, Curry Kirkpatrick dumped all over us in *Sports Illustrated*. He referred to my parents as "Ozzie and Harriet" and got most of the facts wrong about my friends.

He confused Aja Zanova, the champion figure skater, who wasn't even there, with Svatka Hoschl from Chicago, who cooks dumplings for me because she's my friend, and Mumsey Nemiroff, an art expert from the University of California at Los Angeles. Kirkpatrick managed to make my friends sound unwholesome, even though these three women and their husbands have been part of my American "family" for more than a decade. It annoys me that you don't see the same level of snideness about male athletes, gay or straight.

The Curry Kirkpatrick article should have tipped me off about what to expect at Wimbledon. Until 1984 I'd never had much of a problem with the British press. I'd see the kind of gossip and innuendo they printed about royalty or rock stars or athletes and think to myself, How do they get away with it? But except for a few silly little things when Rita Mae and I were together one year, they had never gone over the line with me. In 1984, they did.

Judy arrived at Wimbledon during my second-round match with Amy Holton. The scandal-sheet photographers had been looking for her, and they started snapping away as soon as she appeared. To avoid making a scene during the match, she sat further back than the usual players' seats, and at first I didn't know where she was. But Peggy Gossett, the public-relations director of the W.T.A., was nice enough to send me a note during the second set, while I was behind, 2–3, to let me know where Judy was sitting.

I won the match, 6–2, 7–5, then went to the interview room under the stands. The British reporters didn't want to hear a thing about the young American player who had given me a good match. They just wanted to know who had sent me the note.

It sounded like a game of twenty questions. Who sent it?

None of your business. Did Mike Estep send it? No, that would be coaching. Was it a tennis note? None of your business. Any more clues? Draw your own conclusions; I'm sure you will. I couldn't believe they could go on like that. But everybody assumed Judy had sent me the note, and things got worse a few days later when Frank Deford wrote in *Sports Illustrated* that Judy had been the one to send me that note. Frank also wrote that Judy had been blowing kisses at me during a match. I respect Frank, and when I asked him about it, he insisted he had seen it—but she didn't. None of my friends or family would do anything like that.

Things got worse instead of better. The reporters from the British scandal sheets knocked on my door early in the morning and late at night. I told them I wouldn't comment on my private life, but they continued to try to get a photograph of us together. When we left the house, we wouldn't answer the questions they shouted at us. Then they also started camping out in Fort Worth, talking to Judy's neighbors and her kids and their friends.

I tried to distinguish between the tennis writers and the gossip writers, who descend on your doorsteps like locusts. Chris, who'd had a few problems with persistent reporters in the States and England, called the media frenzy "horrendous," and the All England Club said we didn't have to answer any press-conference questions that did not relate to tennis.

I don't know what the best remedy is for the British press. If you say anything, they'll use it in ways you never meant. If you don't say anything, they'll make something up. They were hard on everybody in 1984. There was one male and one female player who were never seen together, never practiced together, and didn't talk about each other —so that must prove they were an item. This kind of thing went on for two weeks.

It got so bad that I asked why I should subject myself

to this anymore. I suggested that I would not come back to England except to play at Wimbledon and, of course, Eastbourne leading up to it. Nothing can keep me from Wimbledon.

As it happened, I didn't play in England again that year, but I'll let the gossip sheets draw their own conclusions. I will say this: ninety-nine percent of my mail from England said, "Please come back, ignore these idiots." One day during Wimbledon I got 150 letters. That's another reason I'll never miss that great tournament. I've always loved Wimbledon and the British fans, and their papers can't keep me away.

It's hard not to love Wimbledon, after the success I've had there. The 1984 Wimbledon championship, my fifth, was one of the best because of the final match Chris played against me. After the hard three sets I won from her at the Virginia Slims in March, I doubted she could play me any better. But she played the first three games in the final flawlessly, placing every shot, coming to the net now and then, and taking me to a tiebreaker, before I escaped with a 7–6, 6–2 victory.

Then I got out of England and returned to Fort Worth, where I had found a three-bedroom house that was being built, so I had the option of choosing the fixtures and the colors. I loved the openness of the house, the two-story living room where I could put a huge Christmas tree, the bedroom with the doors opening onto the Jacuzzi and the pool. I immediately converted one bedroom into a weight room and began shopping for designer furniture. I had gorgeous marble floors put in one corner of the living room and was supposed to put a piano there, but later I decided I needed a dining room, so the designer came up with a custom three-corner marble dining room table. What a glorious Christmas: traditional Czech carp in a modernistic Fort Worth house.

My house is not too far from where Judy Nelson is living. Most of the controversy about her seems to have died down since the British press chewed it over in 1984.

Judy shares the boys with her husband, which means I've gotten to know them pretty well. Eddie is fourteen and Bales is eleven, and they love coming over to swim and shoot pool and throw a football with me. We all went skiing with Judy's parents in Aspen just before Christmas. The entire Virginia Slims management was worried that I'd break my bones skiing for the first time in years, but I didn't fall once. Then I got home and pulled a muscle on the tennis court. Dangerous place, the tennis court.

Being around Judy and the two boys has made me a little more realistic about being a mother. The responsibilities are enormous. Bales had a friend of his along on the ski trip, and sometimes Judy and I would be busy getting skis on one, boots on another, and gloves on a third. I'd be sweating bullets, and we hadn't even started skiing yet.

I look at Judy sometimes and think, "She had those children inside her, as tiny babies, and they get bigger and stay with you a long time." Judy's a great mother. I watch her taking care of the kids; she's got a trick knee that really needs treatment so she can continue to play tennis and ski, but she's so busy picking up their clothes and driving them around that she doesn't have time to ice the knee, so it keeps getting worse. I think that's what being a parent must be like: caring so much about other people that you don't have time for yourself.

But I can see the joy in raising kids. I love being around her two boys. If Eddie and Bales are fighting, I get angry with both of them, and they accept it. It must have been hard on my sister. When she was that age, I was already gone, and she needed me. I think about Jana a lot these days.

I drive the boys in the car pool sometimes, I visit Judy's

family, I've really settled down in Fort Worth again. I've got friends I can depend on there, people in all different circumstances. I go riding out in the country.

With some of the Grand Slam prize money, I began decorating my new apartment in one of Donald Trump's buildings in New York. I have always loved New York because you can do almost anything you want there at almost any hour of the day or night, because it's a worldly city, close to Europe, close to the rest of America. I enjoyed stopping off at my fourteenth-floor apartment, switching on the television or the stereo, and putting my feet up, being alone for a few minutes. I had been going hard ever since I left Czechoslovakia. Now I was ready to relax a bit.

The Future

I don't know if it's my national or family background or just my personal makeup, but until recently I've never felt the need to analyze my behavior. I was impulsive, and I acted on my feelings. I was always living with people, surrounded by close friends, and rarely took the time to think about what's really going on inside.

People say that sooner or later it's a good idea to talk things over, to find out more about yourself, but I just don't think about it. I've always felt able to take care of myself. Despite my real father's suicide, I'm a survivor. My grandmother's death was probably the worst thing that ever happened to me, but if you think about it, in terms of what many people have to endure, it's not that bad. I mean, she lived a long life and died happy, as far as I know.

There were a few times when my future might have been in jeopardy, and my feelings have been hurt, but it was nothing unbearable. A friend of yours gets in an accident, tragic things happen, a friend of yours gets cancer—I haven't been through a lot of that. I've never seen a dead body. I knew some people who died in a car accident, but I haven't been around death that much.

Nevertheless, the older I get, the more I think about it. I was watching a movie on cable TV the other day, Peter Sellers in *Being There,* and I suddenly thought, That man isn't alive. He won't make any more Pink Panther movies. There he was, making that movie, and now he no longer exists.

I guess it happens more the older you get. You think of all the people who aren't around anymore. I think about my grandmother, even dream about her, but I haven't been exposed to any traumatic experiences. I'm wondering what I'm going to do when I hit that low. I can't imagine being so low that you can't get up again, but some people don't see past tomorrow, so they commit suicide.

I can remember feeling so afraid of being alone that I slept with a pistol under my pillow in Dallas. Now I spend time alone in hotels or at my condo in Fort Lauderdale or my house in Texas or my apartment in New York, and I enjoy it. I hasten to add that I am still extremely well protected.

People ask me all the time what I'll do when my career is over. I used to worry about that when things were going badly, but now it doesn't bother me. I realize I won't be able to play forever, but I plan to keep playing for a while.

What amazes me is that I could make more with exhibitions, the way John McEnroe does fifty or sixty times a year, playing Guillermo Vilas and taking the money off the top. Last year I played only a few exhibitions, mostly because they were fun to do, between the major tournaments.

The people who run Wimbledon didn't like it when I complained about their prize money, but the truth is I'm not money hungry. When I first came here, one of the first people I met was a Czech guy who left in 1948 and was now a dentist. He was pulling in good money and I asked him why he only took one week of vacation. It turned out he was worried about making more money. People who are rich want to be richer, but what's the difference? You can't take it with you. The toys get different, that's all. The rich guys buy a football team, the poor guys buy a football. It's all relative.

A few years ago, I formed the Martina Youth Foundation, which helps underprivileged children, mainly from foster homes, broken homes, or poor families. In 1984, we held an auction during a tournament in Mahwah, New Jersey, selling off a lot of tennis items—a trip to Wimbledon, the racquet with which I won the Grand Slam in Paris, and a lesson with Mike Estep, which everyone knows is invaluable.

The big item was a 1984 BMW 528, which Pam Shriver got with a bid of $22,000. All the proceeds went straight to the foundation, to the kids—for clinics, tickets to tournaments, racquets, Christmas presents, and food.

Once I stop playing tennis for a living, I'll be able to devote a lot more time to my foundation as well as to other causes—working toward ending world hunger, helping preserve nature and wildlife, and cleaning up the environment that we have polluted so successfully.

When I die, I don't want a lot of money in the bank. I'll be happy spending my money, but not on tanks or B-52's. All that money wasted on warfare while millions of people starve to death. Something needs to be done here, and I can't think of a better way to spend the rest of my life, while I educate myself a little better. I plan to take some courses in English literature, American history, and perhaps architecture. But I don't want to take any more exams. I've had enough anxiety on the courts to last me a lifetime.

I don't know where I will live yet. Fort Worth is great right now, but I do love the mountains. Maybe I'll settle somewhere in Northern California or Colorado, where I can buy a lot of land and horses, including Grand Slam, an eleven-year-old grey mare quarter horse given to me by Judy Nelson for my birthday in 1984. Wherever I settle, I want it to be close to the slopes.

Retirement is still a ways off, however. People say I can play until I'm forty, and I don't see any reason why I can't. Besides, there is always something to prove. Even though I've won every tournament, I still hear the old "not mentally tough" rap used against me, as if I'm going to fold in the next big one. Before Chris and I played a best-of-five final at the 1984 Virginia Slims in New York, she told reporters that the longer the match went, the better chance she had. I understand her saying it, and in fact she played the best tennis anyone's ever played against me, but I won in straight sets, 6–3, 7–5, 6–1, and was going stronger at the end than at the beginning.

So as long as there are doubts, it's still fun to go out there and be overwhelming. And there was another challenge in 1984: the traditional Grand Slam. In 1982, the International Tennis Federation ruled that winning four straight Grand Slam tournaments was worth one million dollars in bonus money.

Some purists argued that a true Grand Slam meant winning the French, Wimbledon, U.S. Open, and Australian in the same calendar year. Only two women had ever done that: Maureen Connolly in 1953 and Margaret Smith Court in 1970, and both of them did it when the Australian tournament was held in January, at the beginning of the calendar.

In 1977, the Australians moved it to December—held it twice in one year, in fact—and that changed the emphasis somewhat. Now, for anybody with three straight Grand Slam victories, the Australian tournament was the finale of the season, a long December haul to Down Under for the traditional Grand Slam.

When I won four straight from Wimbledon of 1983 to the French of 1984, I earned the million-dollar Grand Slam bonus, but a lot of people insisted I still hadn't won the Grand Slam. That just gave me extra incentive at Wimbledon and the U.S. Open in 1984. When I beat Chris in the finals at Wimbledon for my fifth straight Grand Slam victory to balance our career series at thirty victories each, I told reporters that we should stop right there, as equals.

But time moves on, and two months later I had to deal with being the defending champion at the U.S. Open and a New Yorker of sorts, yet still hearing the fans root for Chris over me. I tried not to take it personally. I know New York fans like to cheer for the underdog, but when you go out for a match and you hear the great majority of the fans shouting "Let's go, Chris," you have to wonder.

Throughout the tournament, Chris kept saying that I wouldn't be able to maintain my mental toughness, that there would have to be a letdown. She was right. I didn't play consistently in the early rounds, and Chris was ready for me in the finals.

Before we could even go out on the court, we had to wait around until the men's semifinal between Ivan Lendl and Pat Cash was over. It's ridiculous to make two Grand Slam finalists wait for hours while a men's semifinal is being played. Cash and Lendl played five sets before Lendl won it in a tiebreaker, and Chris and I watched it on television in the women's locker room.

It's a good thing we're friends. Two opponents who didn't like each other would have been at each other's throat. I could only wonder what might have happened if Nancy had been around during the three-hour and thirty-nine-minute match. Left to our own devices, Chris and I enjoyed the match, and I even shared my supply of bagels with her.

Maybe I shouldn't have fed her. When we finally got out on the court, she played one of the best sets of her career, slashing passing shots off my serves to win the first set, 6–4. I finally figured out what the problem was on my serve. I was letting it drop too far before hitting it. Once I adjusted, I just did manage to pull out a 4–6, 6–4, 6–4 victory, one of the hardest matches I had ever played.

The New York fans cheered both of us when it was over, but I must say, I have never seen Chris so down after a match. She had played so well, and yet I still dug out a victory. At the moment, neither of us was interested in the statistics, but now I was ahead of her in our lifetime series, thirty-one to thirty. A few weeks later I passed Chris's record of fifty-five straight victories during a tournament at the Bonaventure resort in Fort Lauderdale, Florida, where I am the touring pro.

That left one major goal in 1984: the Australian Open, the fourth leg of the traditional Grand Slam. A victory there would have been my seventh straight Grand Slam event, the most any tennis player had ever won. Chris was down there, and I wouldn't have wanted it any other way.

But while I was looking ahead to another final against Chris, history caught up with me. Remember how proud my family was that my mother's mother had once beaten Vera Sukova's mother back home in Czechoslovakia? I had caused Vera some grief when I defected from her care in the States. Her daughter, Helena, the quiet little girl who used to work as a ball girl at some of my matches back in Prague was now six feet one and a half inches tall, and, at nineteen, was just beginning to appreciate the advantages of being so tall. Vera had been a master of the slow clay courts; Helena, with her big serve, whistling forehand, and lo-o-o-ng reach, is at her most dangerous on grass. And the Austrailian Open is played on grass.

I ran into Helena at Kooyong. She had beaten Pam Shriver in the quarters. I won the first set, 6–1, but felt lucky because I had won all the close games. In the second set, I played just as well as I had in the first, but Helena started winning close games and won the set, 6–3.

In the third set, I got nervous and soon was down, 0–3, with two service breaks. Somehow I managed to pull even at 4–4 and even went ahead, 5–4, but Helena played a great service game and followed it up by breaking my serve.

Soon I was down triple match point. I saved all three with perfect forehand winners and saved two more match points, but it was too late. I finally hit a backhand return wide and the match was over. My streaks were over: six straight Grand Slam events, seventy-four straight matches. But even while I felt the loss, I made sure to put my arm around Helena as we walked off the court. She was a better player than I was that day. Vera, who had died in 1982, would have been proud of her.

When I returned to the hotel, I had received more telegrams, calls, cards, and flowers than I do when I win. People were so solicitous. They called in a hushed, funereal voice: "How are you taking it?"

How was I taking it? I couldn't wait to get back home, get ready to ride my horse, go skiing, and do the remainder of my Christmas shopping—by catalogue, of course, (speaking of being Americanized; it's so much easier).

I was excited about going skiing again. Maybe some day I'll be able to ski in the Krkonose Mountains. My family wants me to visit Czechoslovakia in 1986 when the Federation Cup will be held in Prague. What a return that would be—playing for my new country against my native country.

Maybe I'll get to go home sooner if I can get a visa. I'd love to see my family's new home and my dog Babeta, who was just two years old when I left. I wonder if she'd remember me after ten years, but then again, Argos remembered Odysseus after twenty years. I'd love to see my old school and my tennis friends. I want to visit my grandmother's grave.

I don't quite know what to expect, how I'll react. Maybe it will be depressing because I'm so used to living in the States. I'm not blind. I see the problems and the injustices we have here, but I'm proud of America. That's where my life is.

Until I return to the Krkonose, I'll stick to skiing in Colorado. I made a decision in my teens to not risk my tennis career on the slopes, but in recent years I've wanted to feel the wind on my face again. Every winter my friends would always band together and talk me out of it skiing. After losing in Austrailia, I said to myself: "Enough is enough. I am going to ski this winter."

I wasn't willing to wait God-knows-how-many-years to stop playing and start living. Besides, with all the nuclear armament and wars everywhere, all in the name of peace and progress, what guarantees do we have that we'll be here. The time is now.

When I made my decision to go skiing, the tennis community went crazy: "What do you think you're doing? You'll hurt yourself." (Meaning: "You'll hurt us.") After losing Down Under, I couldn't think of a better way of getting away from it all. Nothing could be further from the ninety-five degree summer heat in Australia than the sub-zero temperatures in Aspen, Colorado.

So there I was, gliding down the mountain at my own pace (medium brisk), and all I could hear were the skis carving the snow and the wind blowing past my face, and all I knew was the feeling of being alive and free. I knew that losing the Australian Open was hardly the end of the road, that falling two matches short of my history-making goal could never be a failure.

Giving myself the freedom to ski down the mountain, taking responsibility for my own safety, was one more step toward being myself. I wasn't afraid to let myself go, to feel the exhilaration within me, and I was aware of the beauty of the world around me.

I didn't know how I was going to make the world better, but I knew I was going to try, and as my skis turned on the downhill slope, I said to myself, "You're just beginning."

ABOUT THE AUTHOR

Martina Navratilova has written her story with George Vecsey, sports columnist for THE NEW YORK TIMES and co-author with Loretta Lynn of her autobiography, COAL MINER'S DAUGHTER.